CLASSIC COUNTRY
Q·U·I·L·T·S

CLASSIC COUNTRY Q·U·I·L·T·S

Step-by-Step Directions for 25 All-Time Favorites

By Jane Townswick
and the Editors of *Quilter's Newsletter Magazine*
Introduction by Bonnie Leman

 Rodale Press, Emmaus, Pennsylvania

OUR PURPOSE

*"We inspire and enable people to improve
their lives and the world around them."*

Antique sewing props courtesy of:
Julie Powell, Kathy Sullivan, and
Helen Thompson
Vintage Textiles and Tools
Antique Quilts and Old Sewing Items
P.O. Box 265
Merion, PA 19066

If you make quilts from this collection, we would love to hear from you. Please send your comments, quilt stories, and photos of your projects to:
Jane Townswick, Senior Associate Editor
Rodale Press
33 East Minor Street
Emmaus, PA 18098

If you have any questions or comments concerning this book, please write:
Rodale Press
Book Readers' Service
33 East Minor Street
Emmaus, PA 18098

Executive Editor: *Margaret Lydic Balitas*

Editor: *Suzanne Nelson*

Senior Associate Editor: *Jane Townswick*

Copy Manager: *Dolores Plikaitis*

Copy Editor: *Sarah S. Dunn*

Editorial assistance: *Susan L. Nickol*

Office Manager: *Karen Earl-Braymer*

Art Director: *Anita G. Patterson*

Book and Cover Designer: *Lisa Palmer*

Photographer: *Mitch Mandel*

Photograph Stylist: *Marianne Grape Laubach*

Illustrator: *Sandy Freeman*

Library of Congress Cataloging-in-Publication Data

Townswick, Jane.
  Classic country quilts : step-by-step directions for 25 all-time favorites / by Jane Townswick and the editors of Quilter's newsletter magazine ; introduction by Bonnie Leman.
    p.   cm.
  ISBN 0-87596-573-3   hardcover
  1. Patchwork—Patterns.   2. Patchwork quilts.
I. Quilter's newsletter magazine.   II. Title.
TT835.T68 1993
746.9'7—dc20   92-29542
                                              CIP

Distributed in the book trade by St. Martin's Press

2   4   6   8   10   9   7   5   3   hardcover

◆ CONTENTS ◆

• *INTRODUCTION* •

What are "classic country quilts"? These three words fit together so naturally, the images they evoke seem so compatible, it is easy to accept them in combination without appreciating the full flavor of their individual meanings.

The whole body of quilt design could be defined as classic, in that the concept of the patchwork quilt has permanent value and enduring interest and appeal, forming part of the permanent cultural achievement of human imagination. But considering quilt designs individually, not all have had lasting impact. No one has yet tallied all the patterns from which quilts have been made, although speculation about the total number is often enjoyed by quiltmakers conversing with one another. It is safe to say there are several thousand different patterns that have been stitched in this century alone. Of these thousands, relatively few—perhaps fewer than 100—have earned the distinction of becoming recognized as truly "classic."

When you think of a patchwork quilt, what pattern pops immediately into your mind? Is it a basic nine-patch, a scrappy log cabin, or perhaps a six-pointed star? These are classic designs that have become virtually synonymous with the word "quilt" in most people's minds. There are other, less ubiquitous patterns that have endured just as lastingly, beautiful enough to be regarded with the highest respect, that are fitting to serve as models of good design. It is from this select group that we have chosen the quilts for this book. You will recognize them as traditional favorites, basic and simple designs that will always be loved, but complex enough to deserve your interest and give you creative enjoyment while you make them.

But what qualifies these particular quilts as "country"? This word is used so often today to describe such a variety of products and ideas that its meaning has become a little blurred.

The country look in decorating evokes the good things in life—the colors of blossoming plants and clear skies, natural materials, a kaleidoscope of changing patterns in the landscape, the pleasure and satisfaction that can be found in the symmetry and repetition of nature. In country decorating, fabrics are used to soften and to blend, to add to the feeling of relaxation with their yielding textures. Country decorating offers tranquillity, sparked with the energy of color; it makes you feel comfortable and in harmony with your surroundings. Country decorating implies ingenuity, a talent for making do and for making the most out of what is available.

These descriptions also apply exactly to the patchwork quilt. The simple, colorful shapes of patchwork, repeated over the surface of a softly but richly textured quilt, embody the spirit of country. Nothing offers warmth and welcome more surely, more dependably than a handmade quilt.

As to the definition of the word "quilt" itself, an often-seen, oversimplified one is that a quilt is a textile sandwich made of a back, a filler, and a top. While that is not inaccurate, it barely begins to describe what a quilt is. Sentiment is a basic ingredient in a quilt. Even if you make one simply because you want its look in your decorating plans, a bit of yourself will be added to it along with its patches and stitches. Your mind will clear and focus as you assemble it. Thoughts will come that tie you emotionally to the finished piece. If you give the quilt away, the person receiving it will feel a connection to you through it. The investment of self in the making of a quilt does not go unnoticed. Only by making one will you discover the true definition of a quilt, and even then your definition will be incomplete. As stitchers have discovered throughout the history of the art, there is a mystique about the making of a quilt that unfolds gradually and anew with each one. You will surely have a romance with every quilt you make, and each one will redefine for you the many facets of enjoyment these warm and wonderful objects can give you.

Another characteristic of decorative objects with a country feeling is that they are not difficult to make. That is true of these classic quilt designs as well. One reason they have been in favor for so many generations is that they can be made by ordinary folk unpossessed of above-average sewing skills. Be assured, this special group of patterns is stitcher-friendly. We know you will enjoy making them and having the quilts to add country comfort to your home.

Bonnie Leman

Bonnie Leman, Editor in Chief
Quilter's Newsletter Magazine

◆ HOW TO USE THIS BOOK ◆

This book has been written and designed with a quilter's needs in mind. Here is a summary of all the features that have been included for each of the 25 projects and how you can use them as you put your quilt together.

Color Photograph: Every quilt has been photographed flat, so you can see every inch of it (and nearly every quilting stitch!). This gives you the chance to study how all the blocks, borders, and other elements come together. Use this as a reference as you assemble the quilt. This photograph may also serve as inspiration for colors and fabrics to try in your own quilt.

Color Plan: Look for this drawing of the quilt at the beginning of the project directions. It looks like a "coloring book" version of the quilt design, with just outlines of the blocks, lattice strips, borders, and other elements. Make photocopies of this plan and use crayons or colored pencils to play around with different color schemes.

Materials List: All of the yardages are given for the fabrics shown in the quilt, but you should always feel free to make your own changes or substitutions. The yardages have been checked and double-checked and are based on fabric that is 42 inches wide.

Cutting Chart: With this chart you can see at a glance how many pattern pieces you will need to cut from various fabrics. The cutting information for borders, lattice strips, backing, binding, and batting appear immediately below the chart.

Numbered Step-by-Step Directions: These directions, accompanied by numbered diagrams, give you the most logical order of assembly for the quilt. When a more detailed discussion of a particular technique is needed, you will be referred to a specific page in the general techniques section, "Quiltmaking ABCs."

Full-Size Pattern Pieces: You will always find these at the end of the step-by-step directions for a project. Be careful about photocopying these—some photocopiers may slightly alter the dimensions of the pattern pieces. The best way to copy them is to trace them onto template plastic, as described in "Quiltmaking ABCs."

Quilting Designs: For the finishing touch, you will find instructions or full-size designs for all the quilting shown in every quilt. These quilting designs appear at the end of each project, near the pattern pieces.

An Extra Feature: As a special touch, we've included a little quilting history in this book. There are four groups of quilts in the book; each begins with a large color photograph featuring antique tools and accessories. These are identified and described in "Vintage Sewing Tools" on page 244. Take a moment to browse through the photos and learn a little about the favored tools of quilters in the nineteenth century.

TRIANGLES

· *AIR CASTLES* ·

*T*wo all-time favorite star patterns combine to create a lively and colorful quilt design. These two blocks, Air Castles and 54-40 or Fight, create a secondary contrasting star design wherever they meet. The small white triangles that interrupt the inner border form complete stars at the outer edges of the quilt top.

Skill Level: Intermediate

SIZE

Finished block is 12 inches square
Finished quilt is 80 × 92 inches
Quilt consists of 15 Y blocks, 15 Z blocks, pieced inner border, and outer border

FABRIC REQUIREMENTS AND SUPPLIES

❖ 3¾ yards dark purple print (blocks, outer border, and binding)
❖ 2⅞ yards large purple-and-tan print (blocks and pieced border)
❖ ½ yard medium purple print (blocks)
❖ 2½ yards light peach solid (blocks)
❖ ⅝ yard rose solid (blocks)
❖ ⅞ yard large rose print (blocks)
❖ 5½ yards for backing
❖ ¾ yard for binding (if other than dark purple print)
❖ Full-size batting (81 × 96 inches)

CUTTING CHART

Pattern pieces on pages 9–12

FABRIC	PATTERN PIECES												
	A	B	C	D	E	F	G	Gr	H	I	Ir	J	Jr
Dark purple print		60	60		4		60	60					
Large purple-and-tan print			60		15					11	11	11	11
Medium purple print				60									
Light peach solid			60	60		60							
Rose solid									120				
Large rose print	15								120				

✂ Cut 2 dark purple print border strips, each 6½ × 82½ inches
✂ Cut 2 dark purple print border strips, each 6½ × 94½ inches
✂ Cut 2 pieces of fabric for backing, each 44 × 92 inches

✂ Cut 9 dark purple print binding strips, each 3 × 44 inches
✂ Cut batting to 87½ × 92 inches

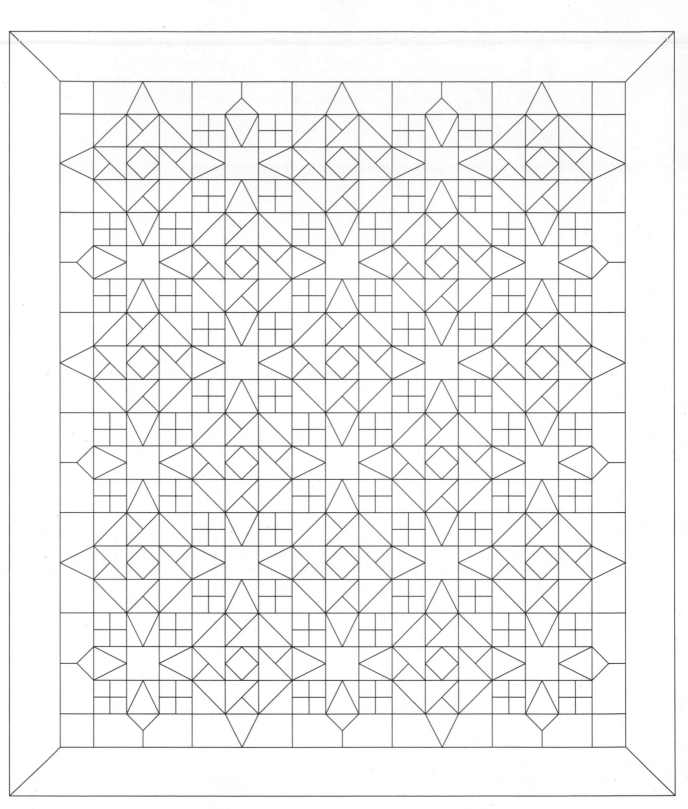

Air Castles Color Plan: You may photocopy this page
and use it to experiment with color schemes for your quilt.

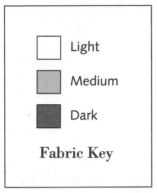

Fabric Key

- ☐ Light
- ▨ Medium
- ■ Dark

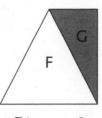

Diagram 3

4. Sew a dark purple G reverse (Gr) triangle to the other side of this F triangle, as shown in **Diagram 4.** Make a total of 4 of these GFGr units.

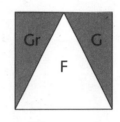

Diagram 4

Piecing Block Y (54-40 or Fight)

1. Sew a rose solid H square to a rose print H square, as shown in **Diagram 1.** Make a total of 8 of these HH units.

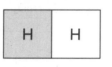

Diagram 1

2. Sew 2 HH units together, alternating the fabrics, as shown in **Diagram 2.** Make 4 of these HH/HH units.

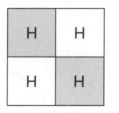

Diagram 2

3. Sew a dark purple G triangle to the right side of a light peach F triangle, as shown in **Diagram 3.**

5. Sew together an HH/HH unit, a GFGr unit, and another HH/HH unit, as shown in **Diagram 5.** Make 2 of these sections.

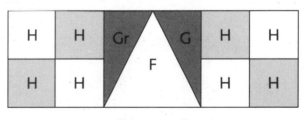

Diagram 5

6. Sew together a GFGr unit, a purple-and-tan print E square, and another GFGr unit, as shown in **Diagram 6.**

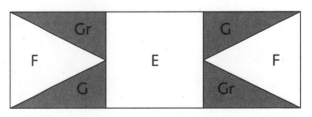

Diagram 6

7. Sew together the sections from Steps 5 and 6, as shown in **Diagram 7.**

Block Y

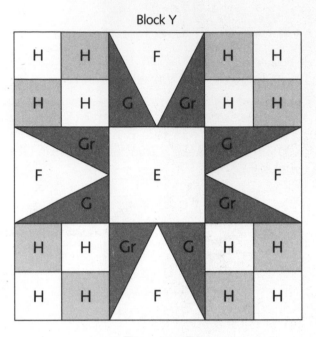
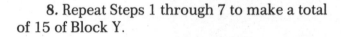

Diagram 7

8. Repeat Steps 1 through 7 to make a total of 15 of Block Y.

Piecing Block Z (Air Castles)

1. Sew a light peach C triangle to a dark purple C triangle, as shown in **Diagram 8.** Make a total of 4 of these CC units.

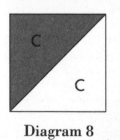

Diagram 8

2. Sew a light peach D triangle to a medium purple D triangle, making sure that the medium purple is on the *left,* as shown in **Diagram 9.** Make four of these DD units, each with the medium purple in the same position.

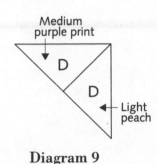

Medium purple print

Light peach

Diagram 9

3. Now sew a DD unit to a purple-and-tan print C triangle, as shown in **Diagram 10.** Make 4 of these CDD units, each with the purple-and-tan print and light peach triangles in the same positions.

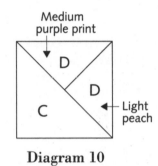

Medium purple print

Light peach

Diagram 10

4. Sew together a CC unit, a CDD unit, and a CC unit, as shown in **Diagram 11.** Make another section just like this one.

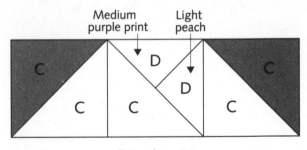

Medium purple print Light peach

Diagram 11

5. Referring to **Diagram 12,** sew a dark purple B triangle to each side of the rose print A square and add a CDD unit to each side.

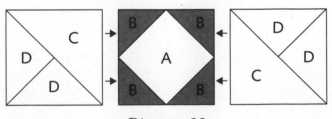

Diagram 12

6. Referring to **Diagram 13,** sew together the three sections from Steps 4 and 5 to make Block Z.

Block Z

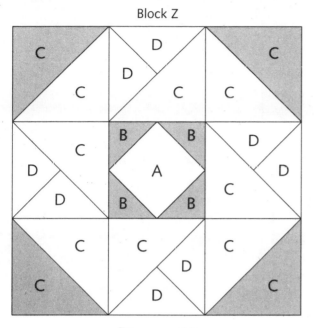

Diagram 13

7. Repeat Steps 1 through 6 to make a total of 15 of Block Z.

Piecing the Borders

1. Sew a purple-and-tan print I to the left side of a light peach F triangle, as shown in **Diagram 14.**

X Border Unit

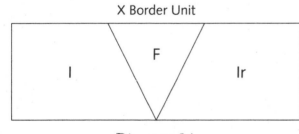

Diagram 14

2. Referring to **Diagram 14,** sew a purple-and-tan print I reverse (Ir) to the right side of the F triangle. Make a total of 11 of Border Unit X.

3. Sew a purple-and-tan print J to the left side of a light peach D triangle, as shown in **Diagram 15.**

W Border Unit

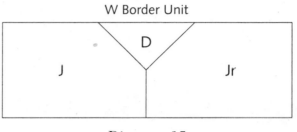

Diagram 15

4. Referring to **Diagram 15,** sew a purple-and-tan print J reverse (Jr) to the right side of the D triangle. Pivot the seam at the bottom of the D triangle, following the instructions on page 234 for setting pieces in at an angle. Make a total of 11 of Border Unit W.

5. To piece a border for the top of the quilt, sew a row of 5 border units in the following order: X, W, X, W, X. (Refer to the **Quilt Assembly Diagram on page 8.)**

6. To piece a border for the bottom of the quilt, sew a row of 5 border units in the following order: W, X, W, X, W. (Refer to the **Quilt Assembly Diagram.**)

7. To piece borders for the sides of the quilt, sew a row of 6 border units and 2 corner E squares in the following order: E, X, W, X, W, X, W, E. Repeat to make the second border. (Refer to the **Quilt Assembly Diagram.**)

Assembling the Quilt

1. Sew 6 horizontal rows, each containing 5 Y and Z blocks, alternating their placement, as shown in the **Quilt Assembly Diagram.**

2. Sew the pieced top and bottom borders to the quilt.

3. Sew the pieced side borders to the quilt.

4. Sew 2 dark purple 6½ × 82½-inch borders to the sides of the quilt, beginning and ending each seam ¼ inch in from the edge of the quilt.

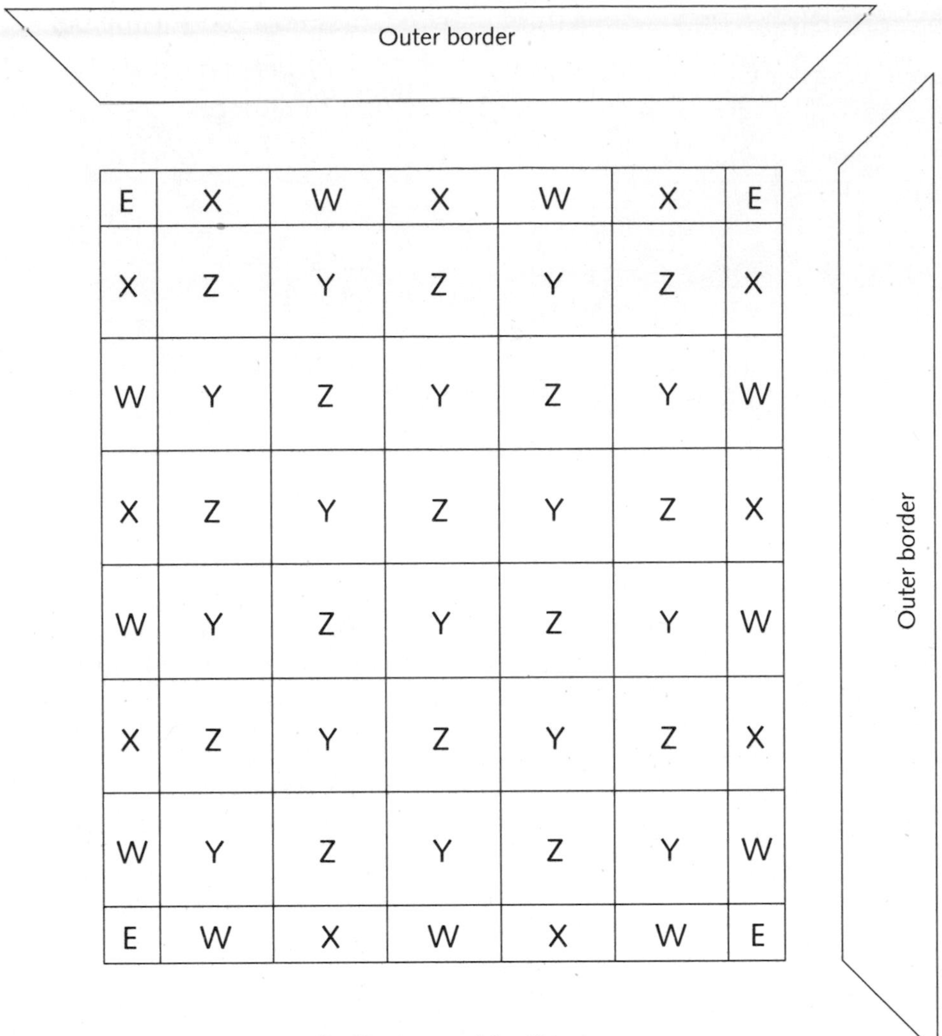

Outer border

E	X	W	X	W	X	E
X	Z	Y	Z	Y	Z	X
W	Y	Z	Y	Z	Y	W
X	Z	Y	Z	Y	Z	X
W	Y	Z	Y	Z	Y	W
X	Z	Y	Z	Y	Z	X
W	Y	Z	Y	Z	Y	W
E	W	X	W	X	W	E

Outer border

Quilt Assembly Diagram

5. Sew 2 dark purple 6½ × 94½-inch borders to the top and bottom of the quilt, beginning and ending each seam ¼ inch in from the edge of the quilt.

6. Miter the corner seams; trim the excess fabric to ¼ inch and press the seams open. For instructions on how to miter, see page 237.

S N I P P E T S

If you find that your pieced borders do not match the sides of your quilt exactly, don't panic! Always check the length of a pieced border before adding it to the quilt. If the pieced border is just a little bit too long, you can adjust it easily by increasing seam allowances in as many places as you need to to "eat up" the extra length. If the pieced border is too short, you can let out seam allowances in a few places to gain the length you need.

Quilting

1. Mark the outer border with the **Oval Quilting Design** on page 13.

2. Sew the 2 pieces of backing fabric together with a ¼-inch seam allowance. Press this seam open.

3. Layer the quilt top, batting, and backing and baste together. Refer to page 239 for pointers on how to layer and baste.

4. Quilt diagonally in both directions through each Block Y. Quilt ¼ inch away from each seam in each Block Z. Quilt the outer border design. (See page 239 for details on the quilting stitch.)

Finishing

1. To make the binding, sew the short ends of the 9 binding strips together with diagonal seams. Trim the excess fabric and press these seams open. (For more details on how to make and attach binding, see page 240.)

2. Fold the binding in half, wrong sides together, and press, creating a lengthwise fold.

3. Sew the binding to the quilt.

4. Sign and date your quilt.

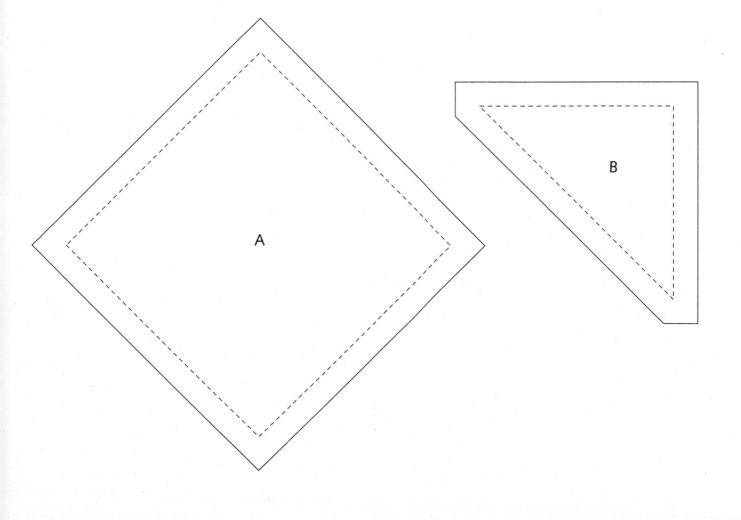

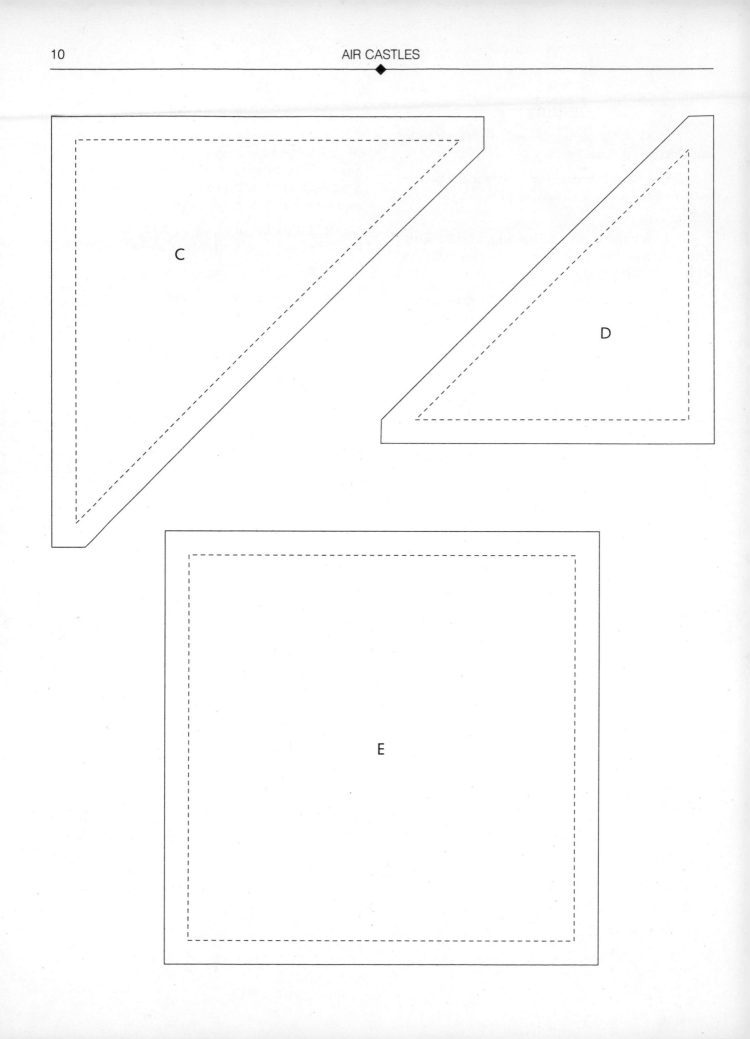

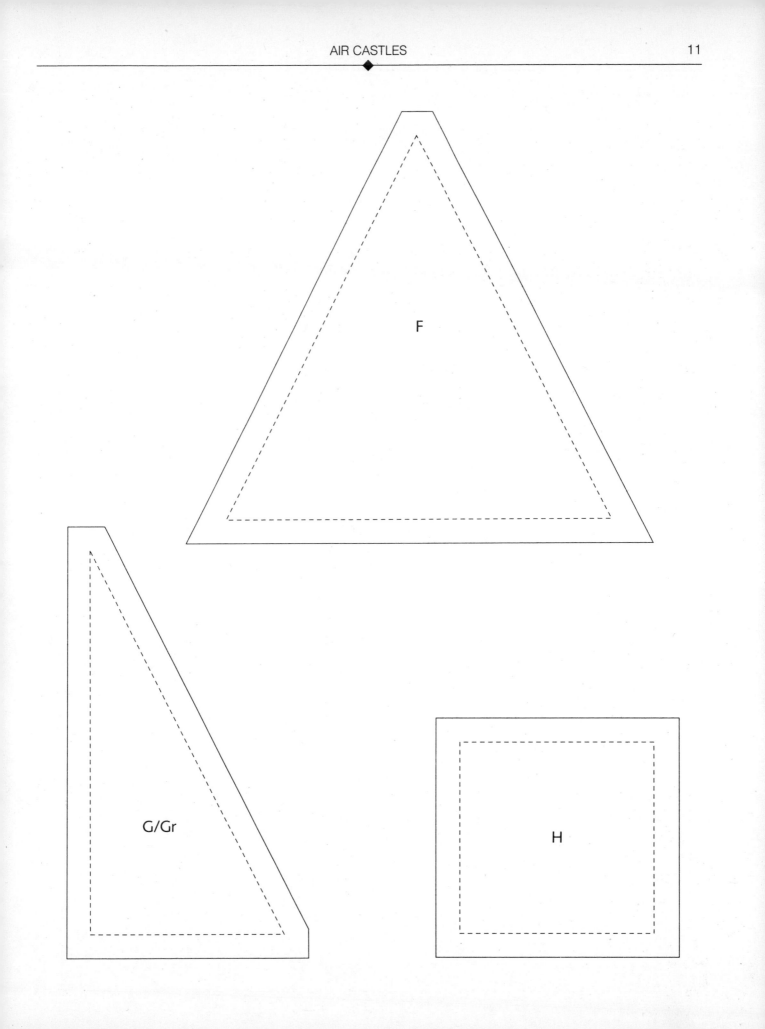

F

G/Gr

H

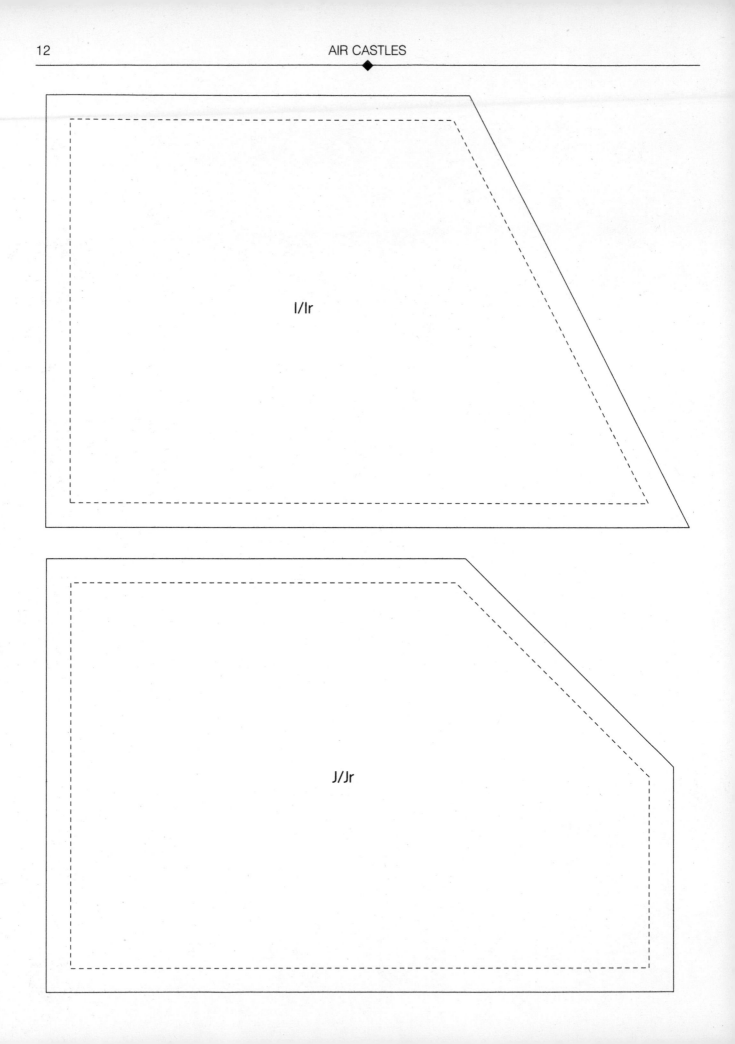

I/Ir

J/Jr

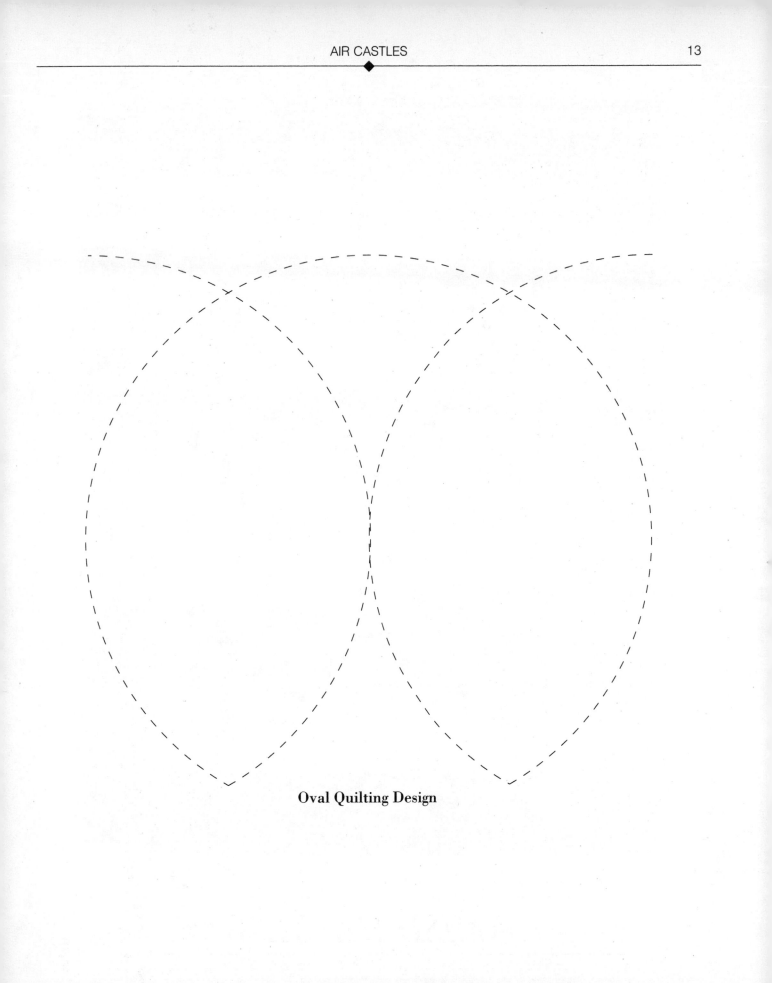

Oval Quilting Design

◆ AMISH BASKETS ◆

*W*hat could be more country than baskets? In this miniature Amish quilt, six pink baskets shimmer against a background of dark gray. How about creating one in varied blue tones on a black background, or delving into your scrap bag and making each of the six baskets in a different fabric? Have fun displaying your finished quilt on an antique doll bed, or hang it from a wall-mounted decorative wire quilt hanger.

Skill Level: Easy

SIZE

Finished block is 5 inches square
Finished quilt is 26 × 33 inches
Quilt consists of 6 pieced blocks, 2 alternating blocks, 6 side triangles, 4 corner triangles, and inner, middle, and outer borders

FABRIC REQUIREMENTS AND SUPPLIES

❖ ⅛ yard *each* of 7 different pink solids (baskets and middle border)
❖ ¾ yard dark gray solid (pieced blocks and inner and outer borders)
❖ ¼ yard light gray solid (alternating blocks and side and corner triangles)
❖ ⅞ yard for backing
❖ ¼ yard dark rose solid for binding
❖ Crib-size batting (45 × 60 inches)

CUTTING CHART

Pattern pieces on pages 21 and 22

FABRIC	PATTERN PIECES						
	A	B	C	D	E	F	G
Pink 1	9	1					
Pink 2	9	1					
Pink 3	9	1					
Pink 4	9	1					
Pink 5	9	1					
Pink 6	9	1					
Dark gray	42	6	12	6			
Light gray					2	6	4

(continued)

15

Amish Baskets Color Plan: You may photocopy this page
and use it to experiment with color schemes for your quilt.

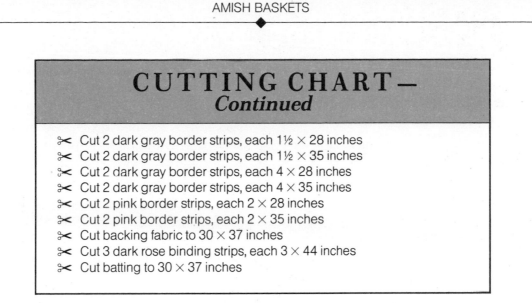

CUTTING CHART— *Continued*

✂ Cut 2 dark gray border strips, each 1½ × 28 inches
✂ Cut 2 dark gray border strips, each 1½ × 35 inches
✂ Cut 2 dark gray border strips, each 4 × 28 inches
✂ Cut 2 dark gray border strips, each 4 × 35 inches
✂ Cut 2 pink border strips, each 2 × 28 inches
✂ Cut 2 pink border strips, each 2 × 35 inches
✂ Cut backing fabric to 30 × 37 inches
✂ Cut 3 dark rose binding strips, each 3 × 44 inches
✂ Cut batting to 30 × 37 inches

Fabric Key

3. Sew a dark gray B triangle to a pink B triangle, as shown in **Diagram 3.**

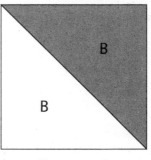

Diagram 3

Piecing the Block

1. To make a basket block, sew a dark gray A triangle to a pink A triangle, as shown in **Diagram 1.** Make 7 of these AA units. (Use the same color pink in a single basket block.)

Diagram 1

4. Sew a pink A triangle to the right side of a dark gray C rectangle, as shown in **Diagram 4.**

Diagram 4

2. Sew together 1 row of 4 AA units and 1 row of 3 AA units, as shown in **Diagram 2.**

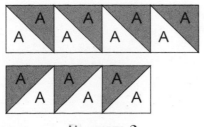

Diagram 2

5. Sew a pink A triangle to the left side of a dark gray C rectangle, as shown in **Diagram 5.**

Diagram 5

6. For Steps 6 through 9, refer to the **Block Piecing Diagram.** Sew the AA unit with 3 pieces to the side of the BB unit, placing the pink A triangles next to the dark gray B triangle.

7. Sew the AA unit with 4 pieces to the side of the BB unit, again placing the pink A triangles next to the dark gray B triangle.

8. Sew AC units to two opposite sides of the BB unit, making sure the A pieces are positioned as shown in the **Block Piecing Diagram.**

9. Finish the basket block by sewing a dark gray D triangle to the 2 pink A pieces.

10. Repeat Steps 1 through 9 to make a total of 6 basket blocks, each with a different shade of pink.

Piecing the Borders

1. Sew together a 1½ × 28-inch dark gray border strip, a 2 × 28-inch pink border strip, and a 4 × 28-inch dark gray border strip, as shown in **Diagram 6.** Repeat this step with the same size border strips that remain to make another border unit like this one.

2. Sew together a 1½ × 35-inch dark gray border strip, a 2 × 35-inch pink border strip, and a 4 × 35-inch dark gray border strip, as shown in **Diagram 7.** Repeat this piecing with the same size border strips that remain to make another border unit like this one.

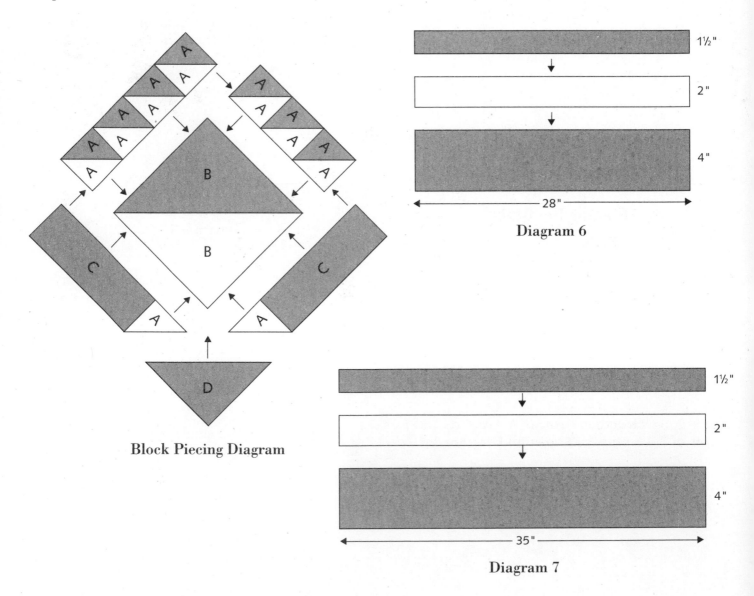

Block Piecing Diagram

Diagram 6

Diagram 7

Assembling the Quilt

1. For the steps in this section, refer to the **Quilt Assembly Diagram.** Begin by sewing light gray F triangles to opposite sides of each of two basket blocks.

2. Sew basket blocks to opposite sides of a light gray E square, making sure the tops of the baskets point in the same direction. Sew a light gray G corner triangle to the left end and a light gray F triangle to the right end of the row.

3. Sew basket blocks to opposite sides of a light gray E square, making sure the basket tops point in the same direction. Sew a light gray F triangle to the left end of the row and a light gray G corner triangle to the right end of the row.

4. Assemble these rows, as shown in the **Quilt Assembly Diagram.** Sew light gray G triangles to the upper right and lower left corners of the quilt top.

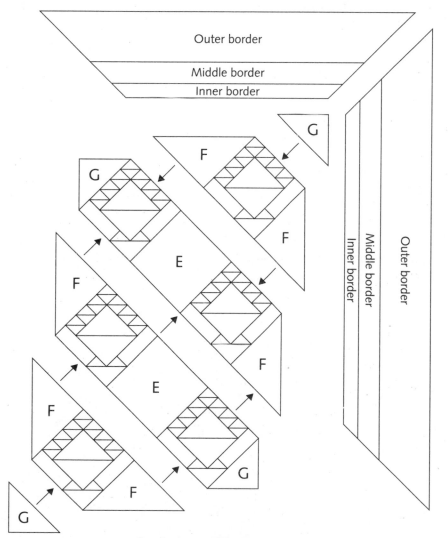

Quilt Assembly Diagram

5. Sew the 28-inch-long border units to the top and bottom edges of the quilt, beginning and ending the stitching ¼ inch from the ends.

6. Sew the 35-inch-long border units to the sides of the quilt, beginning and ending the stitching ¼ inch from the ends.

7. Miter the corner seams, trim the excess fabric to ¼ inch, and press the seams open. For instructions on how to miter, see page 237.

Quilting

1. Mark the two E blocks with the **Floral Quilting Design** on page 23.

2. Mark each F triangle with *one-half* of the **Floral Quilting Design.**

3. Mark each G triangle with *one-quarter* of the **Floral Quilting Design.**

4. In each basket block, mark a grid of diagonal lines at 1-inch intervals in both directions.

5. Mark the pink middle border with the **Scroll Quilting Design** on page 23.

6. Mark the corners of the pink middle border with the **Leaf Quilting Design** on page 23.

7. Mark a grid of diagonal lines at 3/4-inch intervals in both directions in the dark gray outer border.

8. Mark the corners of the dark gray outer border with the **Small Floral Quilting Design** shown on page 23. Mark straight lines to enclose the corner design, as shown in the photo on page 14.

SNIPPETS

To pull a quilting needle through several stitches at one time, why not borrow a tool from the medical field? Try wearing a surgical finger cot on the index finger of the hand you use to quilt. These little "finger gloves" are lightweight, comfortable, durable, and effective. They'll enable you to pull up to 5 stitches at a time through the quilt sandwich without a struggle—possibly even more!

9. Layer the quilt top, batting, and backing and baste together. Refer to page 239 for pointers on how to layer and baste.

10. Quilt all marked designs. See page 239 for details on the quilting stitch.

Finishing

1. To make the binding, sew the short ends of the three binding strips together with diagonal seams. Trim the excess fabric and press these seams open. (For more details on how to make and attach binding, see page 240.)

2. Fold the strip in half lengthwise, wrong sides together, and press.

3. Sew the binding to the quilt.

4. Sign and date your quilt.

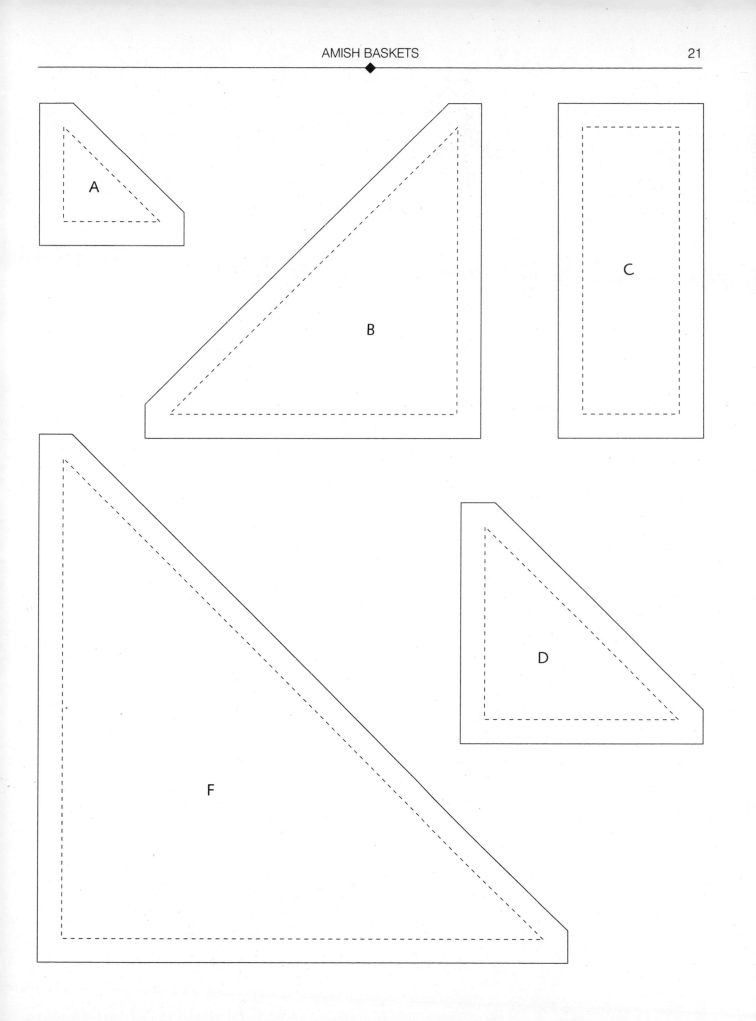

A

B

C

D

F

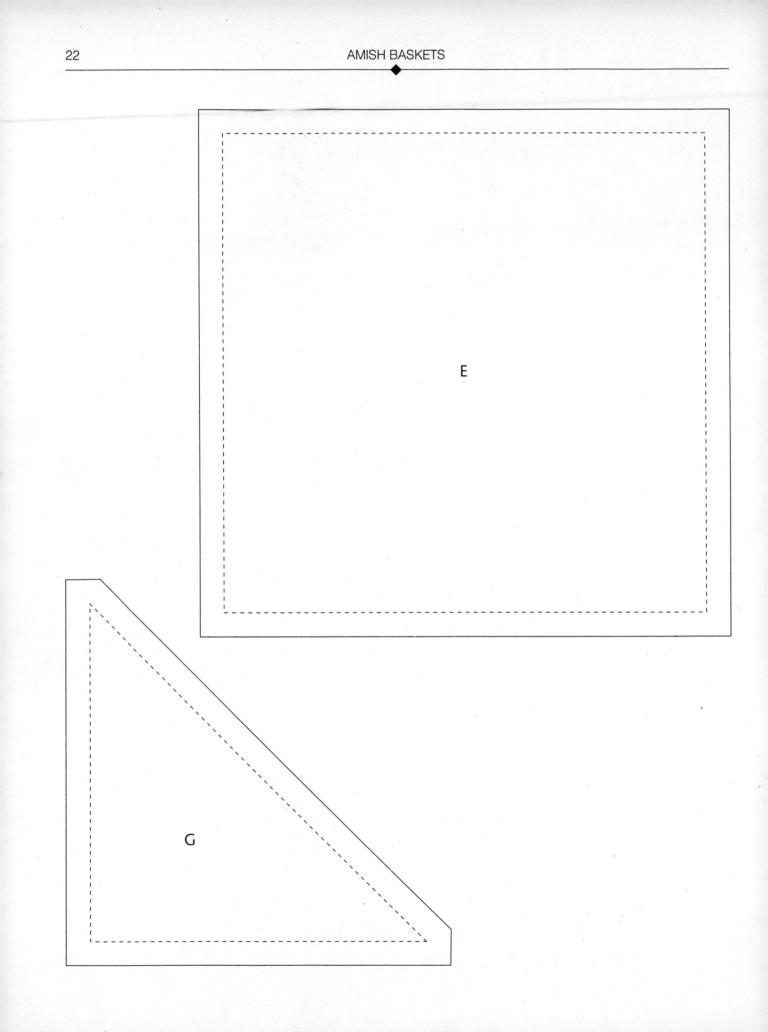

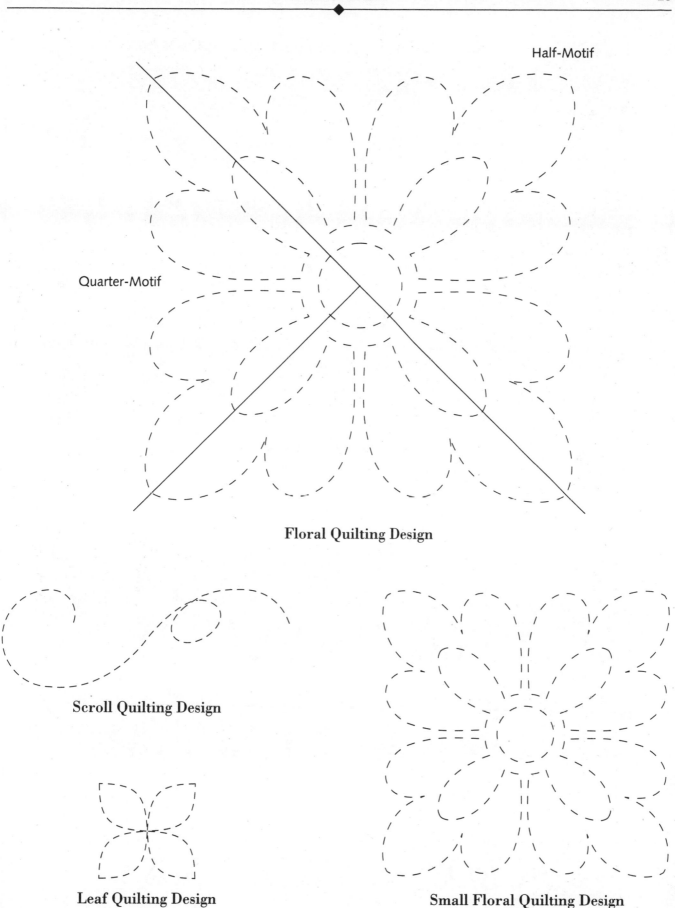

Half-Motif

Quarter-Motif

Floral Quilting Design

Scroll Quilting Design

Leaf Quilting Design

Small Floral Quilting Design

• CROSSES AND LOSSES •

*T*his classic pattern could be made as a delicate crib quilt, a comfortable lap quilt, or an elegant wall quilt. The colors and quilting motifs resemble those in traditional Amish quilts, but this design looks just as lovely in country calicos and contemporary marbleized fabrics.

◆◆◆◆◆◆◆◆◆◆◆◆◆◆◆◆◆◆◆◆◆◆◆◆◆

Skill Level: Easy

SIZE

Finished block is 5 inches square
Finished quilt is 40 × 47 inches
Quilt consists of 20 pieced blocks, 12 alternating blocks, 14 side triangles, 4 corner triangles, and inner and outer borders

FABRIC REQUIREMENTS AND SUPPLIES

- ❖ 1 yard medium blue (alternating blocks, side and corner triangles)
- ❖ 1⅞ yards dark blue (outer border and binding)
- ❖ ⅓ yard peach (inner border)
- ❖ ¼ yard *each* of 5 pastels: yellow, mauve, lilac, blue, and rose (pieced blocks)
- ❖ 1½ yards backing fabric
- ❖ ½ yard for binding (if other than dark blue)
- ❖ Crib-size batting (45 × 60 inches)

CUTTING CHART

Pattern pieces on pages 30 and 31

FABRIC	PATTERN PIECES					
	A	B	C	D	E	F
Medium blue	12	14	4			
Dark blue				80	200	
Pastel yellow					24	8
Pastel mauve					24	8
Pastel lilac					24	8
Pastel blue					24	8
Pastel rose					24	8

- ✄ Cut 4 peach inner border strips, each 2½ × 44 inches
- ✄ Cut 4 dark blue outer border strips, each 4½ × 44 inches
- ✄ Cut 5 dark blue binding strips, each 3 × 44 inches
- ✄ Cut batting to 44 × 53 inches

Crosses and Losses Color Plan: You may photocopy this page
and use it to experiment with color schemes for your quilt.

Fabric Key

Pastel

Dark

Piecing the Block

Note: You will need to make 4 pieced blocks from each of the 5 pastel fabrics. The directions that follow are for making a single block with a single pastel fabric.

1. Sew a pastel E triangle to a dark blue E triangle, as shown in **Diagram 1**. Make 2 of these EE units. Press the seams toward the darker fabric (this holds true for all of the following steps, unless otherwise indicated).

Diagram 1

2. Sew a dark blue D square to the short side of a pastel E triangle on each of these EE units, as shown in **Diagram 2**.

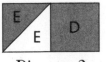

Diagram 2

3. Sew these 2 pieced ED units together, alternating the position of the D squares, as shown in **Diagram 3**.

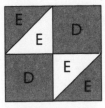

Diagram 3

4. Repeat Steps 1 through 3 to create another pieced unit like the one in **Diagram 3.**

5. Sew a dark blue E triangle to a pastel E triangle along their long sides, as shown in the left corner of **Diagram 4.** Sew a dark blue E triangle to the two remaining sides of the pastel E triangle.

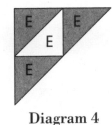

Diagram 4

6. Sew the E triangle unit from Step 5 to a pastel F triangle along the long edges, as shown in **Diagram 5.**

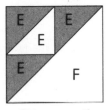

Diagram 5

7. Repeat Steps 5 and 6 to create another EF unit like the one in **Diagram 5.**

8. To assemble the block, sew an EF unit to a ED unit, joining a short side of triangle F to the ED unit. Refer to the **Block Assembly Diagram** on page 28 to be sure you are positioning the ED unit correctly. Repeat to sew the remaining EF and ED units together, using the diagram for reference.

9. Join the two EF/ED sections together to complete the block, referring to the **Block Assembly Diagram** for positioning.

10. Repeat Steps 1 through 9 to make a total of 20 blocks. Make 4 blocks out of each pastel fabric.

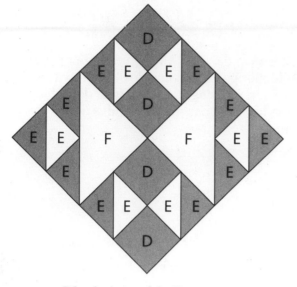

Block Assembly Diagram

Assembling the Quilt

1. Referring to the **Quilt Assembly Diagram,** arrange the 20 pieced blocks into 8 diagonal rows, alternating them with A blocks. Add B triangles at the ends of each row and C triangles at each of the corners.

2. When you are satisfied with the color arrangement of the pieced blocks, sew the blocks in each row together.

3. Sew the diagonal rows together to complete the center portion of the quilt top.

4. Sew a 2½ × 44-inch peach inner border strip to each side of the quilt. Trim the excess fabric so that the borders are even with the top and bottom edges of the quilt. Sew the 2 remain-

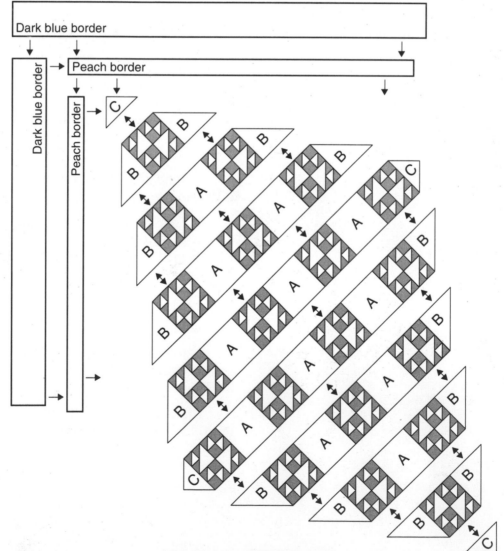

Quilt Assembly Diagram

ing peach inner border strips to the top and bottom of the quilt. Trim even with the outer edges of the side borders.

5. Sew a 4½ × 44-inch dark blue outer border strip to each side of the quilt. Trim the excess fabric. Attach the 2 remaining dark blue outer border strips to the top and bottom of the quilt and trim as you did for the peach border.

Quilting

1. Mark each solid A block with the **Floral Quilting Design** on page 31.

2. In each corner of the peach border, mark a single leaf from the pair of leaves in the **Leaf Quilting Design** on page 31. Refer to the photograph on page 24 for positioning. Then mark 9 pairs of leaves on the top and bottom peach border strip and 11 pairs of leaves along the side peach borders.

3. Mark diagonal quilting lines at 1-inch intervals along the outer borders and add a second quilting line ¼ inch away from the first. Refer to the photograph to see the angle at which these lines are drawn in each border. The lines should form a chevron at the corners where the borders meet.

4. Layer the quilt top, batting, and backing and baste together. Refer to page 239 for pointers on how to layer and baste.

5. Quilt along the marked lines. (See page 239 for details on the quilting stitch.)

S N I P P E T S

Marking diagonal quilting lines and having them meet exactly at the corners can be tricky. You'll have best results if you begin by marking the quilting lines in each corner, then work toward the center of the border. The diagonal lines will form perfect chevrons at the corners and you can compensate in the center of the border, if necessary, by marking the lines a little closer together or a little farther apart.

Finishing

1. To make the binding, sew the short ends of the 5 binding strips together with diagonal seams. Trim the excess fabric and press these seams open. (For more details on how to make and attach binding, see page 240.)

2. Fold this strip in half, wrong sides together, and press, creating a lengthwise fold.

3. Sew the binding to the quilt.

4. Sign and date your quilt.

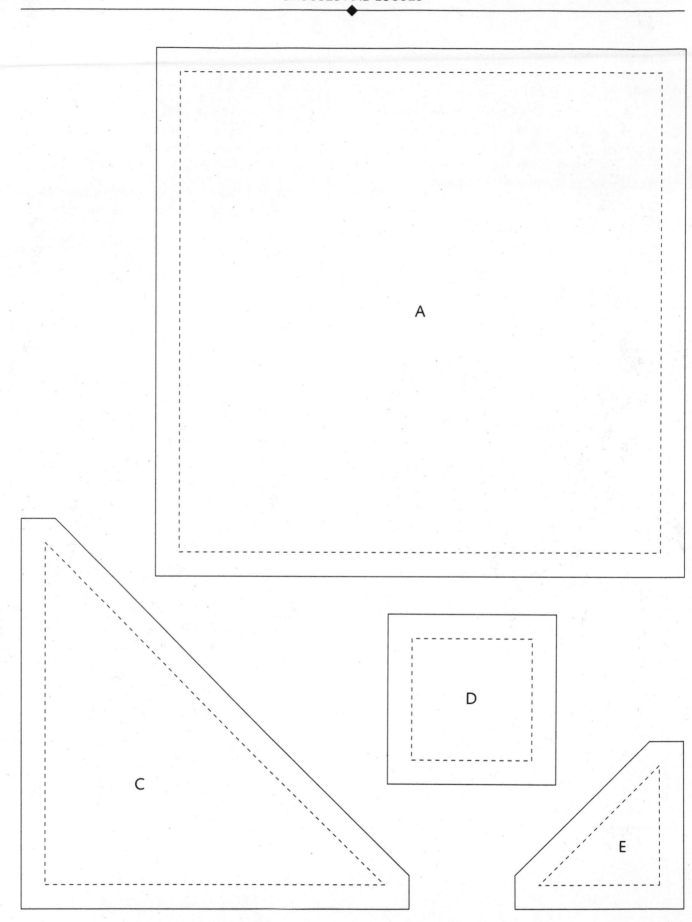

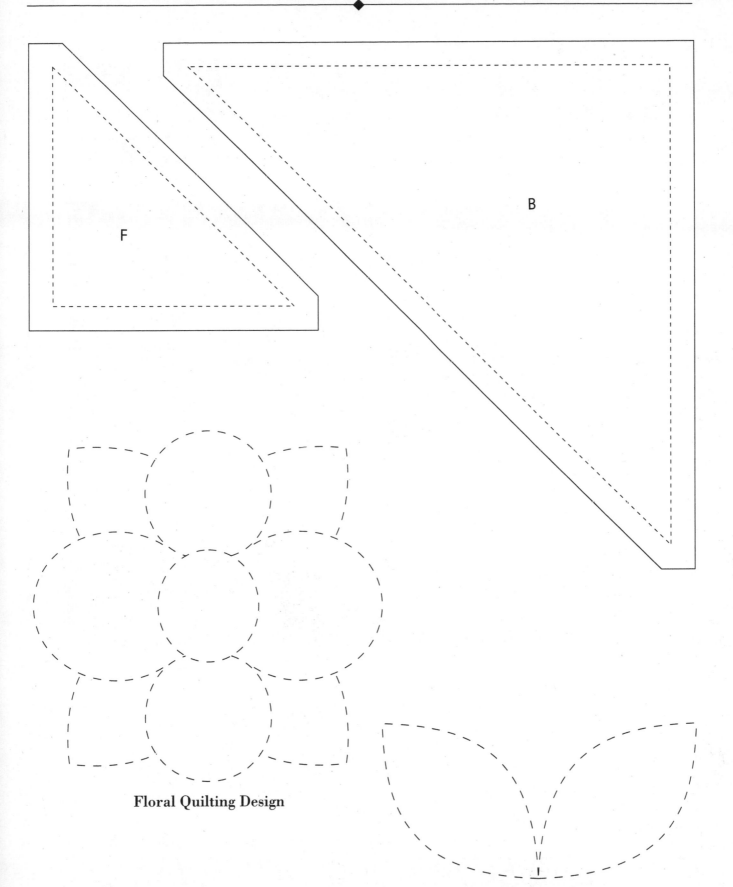

Floral Quilting Design

Leaf Quilting Design

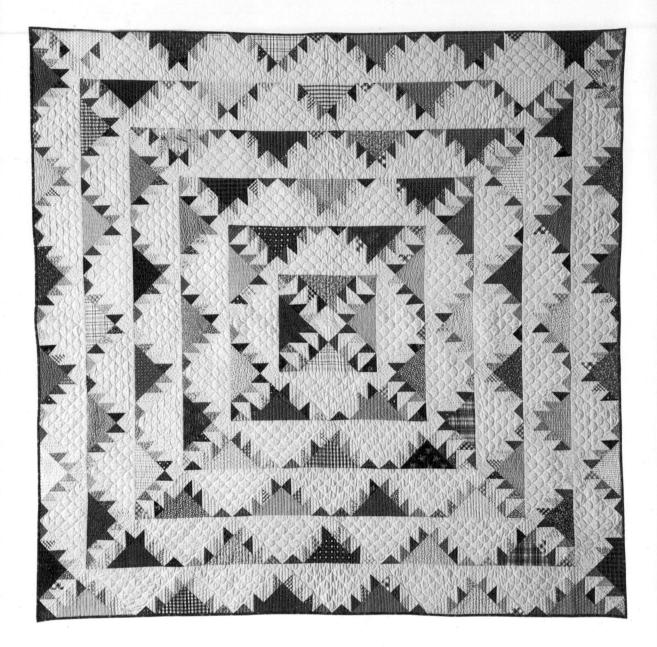

◆ DELECTABLE MOUNTAINS ◆

*T*he name for this popular scrap quilt came from the mountains in the seventeenth-century book by John Bunyan, Pilgrim's Progress. *In each of the four sections of this quilt, colorful triangles face toward the center, creating a subtle row of white flying geese that seem to soar across the surface of the quilt. A very folksy country look is created when you use an assortment of fabrics from your scrap bag, as in the quilt shown. You can also try for a more formal-looking quilt by planning a coordinated color scheme.*

Skill Level: Easy

SIZE

Finished block is 10⅝ inches square
Finished quilt is 90 inches square
Quilt consists of 60 pieced blocks and 24 pieced side triangles

FABRIC REQUIREMENTS AND SUPPLIES

- ❖ 5⅜ yards white solid (C triangles, D squares, A triangles)
- ❖ 4¼ yards assorted bright scraps (C and B triangles)
- ❖ 8 yards for backing
- ❖ ¾ yard dark print for binding
- ❖ King-size batting (120 inches square)

CUTTING CHART

Pattern pieces on pages 38 and 39
Instructions for cutting pattern piece A below

FABRIC	PATTERN PIECES			
	A	B	C	D
White	60		504	84
Assorted bright scraps		84	672	

- ✄ For pattern piece A, cut 30 white 11¼-inch squares. Cut each square in half diagonally to make 2 A triangles, for a total of 60 A triangles
- ✄ Cut 3 pieces of fabric for backing, each 32 × 94 inches
- ✄ Cut 9 dark print strips for binding, each 3 × 44 inches
- ✄ Cut batting to 94 inches square

Delectable Mountains Color Plan: You may photocopy this page and use it to experiment with color schemes for your quilt.

White solid

Bright

Fabric Key

Piecing the Block

1. Sew a bright C triangle to a white C triangle, as shown in **Diagram 1.** Make a total of 6 of these CC units.

Diagram 1

2. Sew a row of 3 CC units, as shown in **Diagram 2.** Repeat to make a second row.

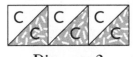

Diagram 2

3. Sew a bright C triangle to the left end of one row of CC units, as shown in **Diagram 3.** Sew a bright C triangle to the right end of the other CC row, referring to the diagram.

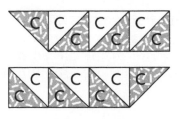

Diagram 3

4. Sew a D triangle to the CC row with the bright C triangle on the right end, as shown in **Diagram 4.**

Diagram 4

5. Sew the CC row without the D triangle to one side of a B triangle, as shown in **Diagram 5.**

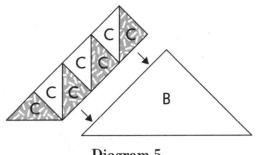

Diagram 5

6. Sew the row of CC units with the D square to the other side of this B triangle, as shown in **Diagram 6.**

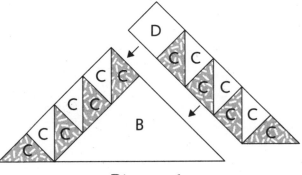

Diagram 6

7. Repeat Steps 1 through 6 to make a total of 84 pieced triangles. Note that 24 of these pieced triangles will be placed at the side edges of the quilt. The remaining 60 pieced triangles will be used to make the pieced blocks in the body of the quilt.

8. Sew a white A triangle to a pieced triangle from Step 7, referring to **Diagram 7.** Make a total of 60 of these pieced blocks.

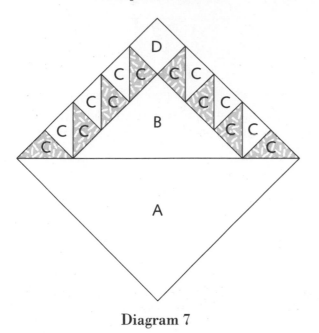

Diagram 7

S N I P P E T S

Looking at your quilt blocks on a vertical surface can be a great way to see how the design and color placement are coming together. Changing your perspective is easy with the help of a design wall you can make yourself. Purchase a large sheet of Celotex (or other similar lightweight construction sheet material) at any lumber store, cover it with flannel, and thumbtack the flannel in place on the back. The flannel will hold the quilt blocks in place without the need for any pins or tape. Have fun viewing your quilts from a new angle!

Assembling the Quilt

1. The easiest way to lay out the quilt top is to organize the 60 pieced blocks according to quarter sections, as shown in the **Quilt Assembly Diagram.** Arrange the blocks so that the pieced triangles face toward the center. Fill in the edges with the 24 side triangles made in Step 7.

2. Sew the blocks and side triangles in each quarter together in diagonal rows.

3. Sew the diagonal rows in each quarter together, creating four pieced quarter sections.

4. Sew Section 1 and Section 2 together along their short sides. Repeat, sewing Section 3 and Section 4 together.

5. Sew the two halves of the quilt together.

Quilting

1. Beginning at the base of the triangle, mark a row of clamshells in each of the white A triangles. Use the **Clamshell Quilting Design** on page 39. The clamshell motifs should overlap in rows to fill the entire triangle.

2. Sew the 3 pieces of backing fabric together with ¼-inch seam allowances. Press these seams open.

3. Layer the quilt top, batting, and backing and baste together. Refer to page 239 for pointers on how to layer and baste.

4. Quilt the clamshell designs marked in the white A triangles and quilt ¼ inch away from each seam in the pieced triangles. (See page 239 for details on the quilting stitch.)

Finishing

1. To make the binding, sew the short ends of the 9 binding strips together with diagonal seams. Trim the excess fabric and press these seams open. (For more details on how to make and attach binding, see page 240.)

2. Fold the binding strip in half lengthwise, wrong sides together, and press.

3. Sew the binding to the quilt.

4. Sign and date your quilt.

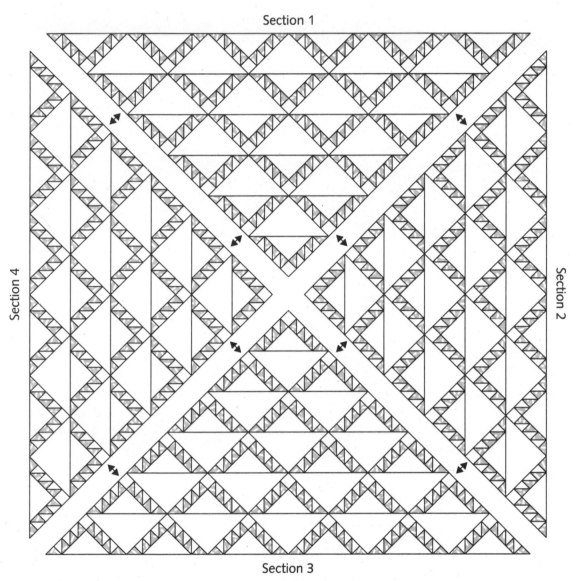

Quilt Assembly Diagram

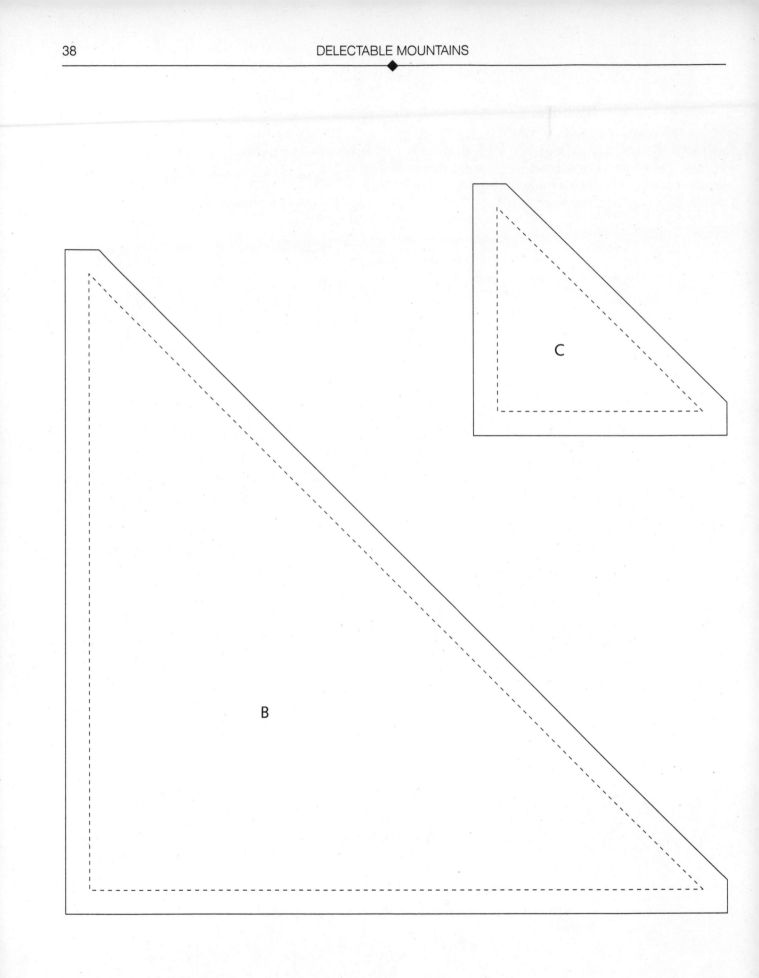

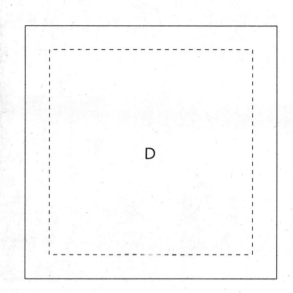

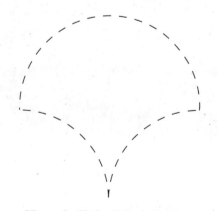

Clamshell Quilting Design

· FLYING GEESE ·

*S*imple, yet dramatically beautiful, this quilt looks like wild geese flying across a midnight sky. The familiar Flying Geese pattern takes on a decidedly different feel with the distinctive and bold colors in this quilt. For a softer, yet just as elegant, color combination, you could use Wedgwood blues and mauves, or create a more classic look in red, white, and blue.

Skill Level: Easy

SIZE

Finished block is 3 × 6 inches
Finished quilt is 85 × 106 inches
Quilt consists of 6 flying geese panels, 7 paisley
    stripe panels, border, and 4 corner squares

FABRIC REQUIREMENTS AND SUPPLIES

❖ 3 yards dusty rose solid (large triangles,
   corner squares, binding)
❖ 2⅛ yards paisley stripe (lattice panels)
❖ 5¾ yards black solid (small triangles, borders)
❖ 9¼ yards black solid for backing
❖ ⅞ yard for binding (if other than rose solid)
❖ King-size batting (120 inches square)

CUTTING CHART

Pattern pieces on page 45

FABRIC	PATTERN PIECES	
	A	B
Dusty rose solid	144	
Black solid		288

✂ Cut 4 dusty rose corner squares,
    each 14½ inches square
✂ Cut 7 paisley stripe panels,
    each 3½ × 72½ inches
✂ Cut 2 paisley stripe panels,
    each 3½ × 57½ inches
✂ Cut 2 black solid border strips,
    each 14½ × 57½ inches
✂ Cut 2 black solid border strips,
    each 14½ × 78½ inches
✂ Cut 3 pieces of fabric for backing,
    each 30 × 110 inches
✂ Cut 10 dusty rose binding strips,
    each 3 × 44 inches
✂ Cut batting to 89 × 110 inches

Flying Geese Color Plan: You may photocopy this page
and use it to experiment with color schemes for your quilt.

Fabric Key

Dusty rose

Black

Piecing the Block

1. Sew a black B triangle to a dusty rose A triangle, as shown in **Diagram 1.**

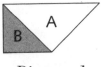

Diagram 1

2. Sew a black B triangle to this BA unit, as shown in **Diagram 2.** Make a total of 144 of these BAB units.

3. Sew a vertical row of 24 BAB units, as shown in **Diagram 3.** Make 6 of these vertical rows of flying geese.

Diagram 2

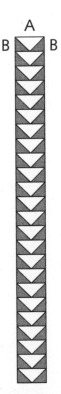

Diagram 3

Assembling the Quilt

1. Referring to the **Quilt Assembly Diagram,** sew the 6 vertical rows of flying geese between the 3½ × 78½-inch paisley stripe panels.

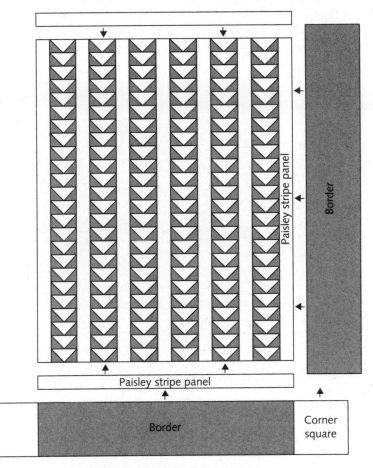

Quilt Assembly Diagram

2. Sew 3½ × 57½-inch paisley stripe panels to the top and bottom of the section from Step 1.

3. Sew a black 14½ × 78½-inch border to each side of the quilt.

4. Sew a dusty rose corner square to each side of a black 14½ × 57½-inch border, referring to the **Quilt Assembly Diagram.** Make 2 of these border rows.

5. Sew the top and bottom border rows from Step 4 to the quilt.

Quilting

1. Mark the paisley stripe panels with the **Cable Quilting Design.**

2. Referring to the photograph on page 40, mark diagonal lines at 2-inch intervals in each of the black borders.

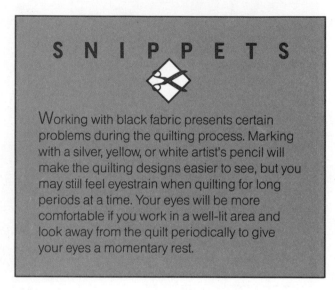

S N I P P E T S

Working with black fabric presents certain problems during the quilting process. Marking with a silver, yellow, or white artist's pencil will make the quilting designs easier to see, but you may still feel eyestrain when quilting for long periods at a time. Your eyes will be more comfortable if you work in a well-lit area and look away from the quilt periodically to give your eyes a momentary rest.

3. Mark concentric squares at 2-inch intervals in each of the 4 corner squares and mark diagonal lines through the center square.

4. Sew the 3 pieces of backing fabric together with ¼-inch seam allowances. Press these seams open.

5. Layer the quilt top, batting, and backing and baste together. Refer to page 239 for pointers on how to layer and baste.

6. Quilt the marked designs and in the ditch of each seam of the flying geese panels. See page 239 for details on the quilting stitch.

Finishing

1. To make the binding, sew the short ends of the 10 dusty rose binding strips together with diagonal seams. Trim the excess fabric and press these seams open. (For more details on how to make and attach binding, see page 240.)

2. Fold the binding in half lengthwise, wrong sides together, and press.

3. Sew the binding to the quilt.

4. Sign and date your quilt.

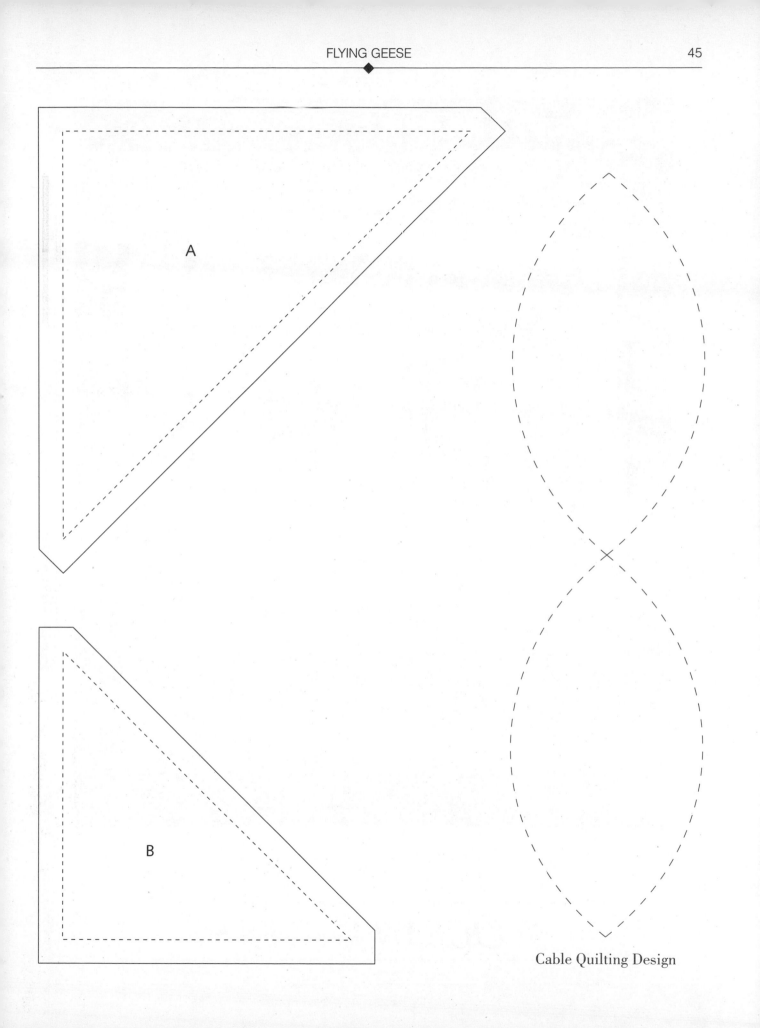

A

B

Cable Quilting Design

• *OCEAN WAVES* •

*A*n easy block made from a single shape like a triangle can create many delightful visual effects. This Ocean Waves quilt seems to be alive and bursting with energy and movement because each four-block unit in it is placed with the darker halves at the center, producing a pattern of light and dark squares on point.

Skill Level: Easy

SIZE

Finished block is 7½ inches square
Finished quilt is 73 × 88 inches
Quilt consists of 80 pieced blocks and inner
　　and outer borders

FABRIC REQUIREMENTS AND SUPPLIES

- ❖ 2 yards assorted light scraps (blocks)
- ❖ 1 yard assorted medium scraps (blocks)
- ❖ 3 yards assorted dark scraps (blocks)
- ❖ 2⅜ yards black print or solid (inner border)
- ❖ 3⅜ yards dark print (outer border and binding)
- ❖ 5¼ yards muslin for backing
- ❖ ¾ yard for binding (if other than dark print)
- ❖ Full-size batting (81 × 96 inches)

CUTTING CHART

Pattern piece on page 51

FABRIC	PATTERN PIECES
	A
Assorted light scraps	480
Assorted medium scraps	240
Assorted dark scraps	720

- ✂ Cut 2 black print or solid inner border strips, each 2 × 65½ inches
- ✂ Cut 2 black print or solid inner border strips, each 2 × 80½ inches
- ✂ Cut 2 dark print outer border strips, each 5½ × 75½ inches
- ✂ Cut 2 dark print outer border strips, each 5½ × 90½ inches
- ✂ Cut 2 pieces of fabric for backing, each 39 × 92 inches
- ✂ Cut 8 dark print binding strips, each 3 × 44 inches
- ✂ Cut batting to 77 × 92 inches

Ocean Waves Color Plan: You may photocopy this page
and use it to experiment with color schemes for your quilt.

Fabric Key

- Light
- Medium
- Dark

Piecing the Block

1. Sew together a row of 3 light and 2 medium A triangles, as shown in **Diagram 1.**

Diagram 1

2. Sew together a row of 2 light and 1 medium A triangles, as shown in **Diagram 2.**

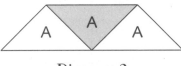

Diagram 2

S N I P P E T S

If you use a planned color scheme for this quilt rather than working with scraps, you can rotary cut the triangles quickly and easily. Cut several 3 × 44-inch cross-grain strips of light, medium, and dark fabrics and stack them in layers of 4 to 6 strips. Cut these strips into 3-inch squares. Cut the 3-inch squares in half diagonally into triangles. These triangles will be slightly smaller than 2¼ inches when finished, which means that a quilt made using this cutting method will be a tiny bit smaller than a quilt made using templates.

3. Sew together the 2 rows of light and medium A triangles, adding 1 light A triangle at the top, as shown in **Diagram 3.** This completes the light half of the block. Make a total of 80 of these light half-units.

Light Half-Unit

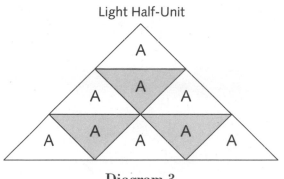

Diagram 3

4. Sew together a row of 5 dark A triangles, as shown in **Diagram 4.**

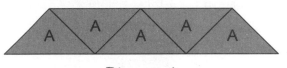

Diagram 4

5. Sew together a row of 3 dark A triangles, as shown in **Diagram 5.**

Diagram 5

6. Sew together the 2 rows of dark A triangles, adding 1 dark A triangle at the top, as shown in **Diagram 6.** This completes the dark half of the block. Make a total of 80 of these dark half-units.

Dark Half-Unit

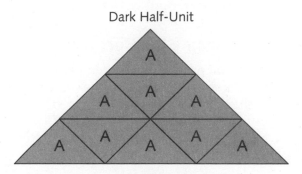

Diagram 6

7. Sew together a light and a dark half-unit, as shown in **Diagram 7.** Make a total of 80 of these pieced sections.

Pieced section

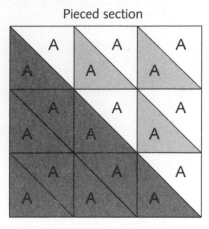

Diagram 7

8. Sew together 4 pieced sections from Step 7, as shown in the **Block Assembly Diagram.**

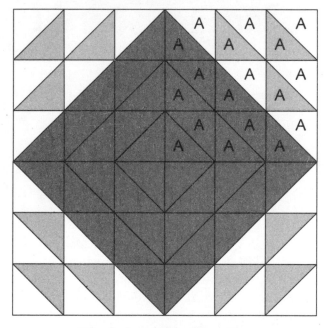

Block Assembly Diagram

Piecing the Borders

1. Fold and press each border strip in half to mark the center point. Matching the center points, sew together a black print or solid 2 × 65½-inch inner border and a dark print 5½ × 75½-inch outer border, as shown in **Diagram 8.** Repeat this step to make the second short border.

Center point

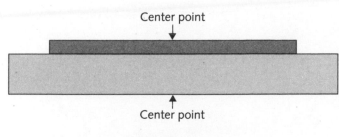

Center point

Diagram 8

2. Referring to **Diagram 8,** sew together a black print or solid 2 × 80½-inch inner border and a dark print 5½ × 90½-inch outer border. Repeat to make the second long border.

Assembling the Quilt

1. Referring to the **Quilt Assembly Diagram,** sew 5 horizontal rows of 4 blocks each.

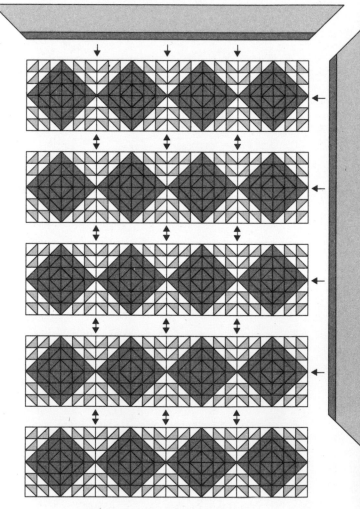

Quilt Assembly Diagram

2. Sew together the 5 rows of blocks.

3. Sew the border units to the quilt, with the black print or solid inner borders next to the center of the quilt. Begin and end each seam ¼ inch from each corner.

4. Miter the corner seams; trim the excess fabric to ¼ inch and press open. For instructions on how to miter, see page 237.

Quilting

1. In the dark half of each block, mark diagonal lines ½ inch in from the diagonal seams, as shown in **Diagram 9.**

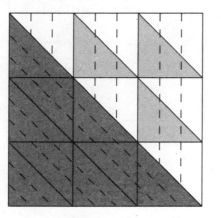

Diagram 9

2. In the light half of each block, mark vertical lines ¾ inch in from the vertical seams, as shown in **Diagram 9.**

3. Mark diagonal lines at 2-inch intervals in the outer borders.

4. Sew the 2 pieces of backing fabric together with a ¼-inch seam allowance. Press this seam open.

5. Layer the quilt top, batting, and backing and baste together. Refer to page 239 for pointers on how to layer and baste.

6. Quilt all marked lines. (See page 239 for details on the quilting stitch.)

Finishing

1. To make the binding, sew the short ends of the 8 dark print binding strips together with diagonal seams. Trim these seams to ¼ inch and press open. (For more details on how to make and attach binding, see page 240.)

2. Fold the binding lengthwise, wrong sides together, and press.

3. Sew the binding to the quilt.

4. Sign and date your quilt.

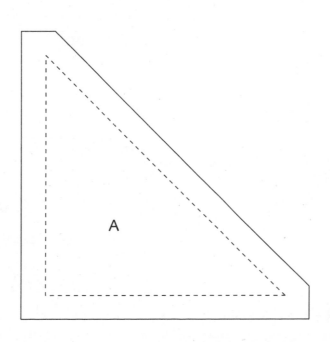

A

SQUARES
AND
RECTANGLES

· BEAR'S PAW ·

*T*his time-honored favorite has gone by many names in the past. Some featured imaginative images based on animals, such as Duck's Foot in the Mud, Cat's Paw, and Illinois Turkey Track. Other names evoked a more human touch, like Best Friend and Hand of Friendship, while others were more tied to nature, like Leaf Design. Today this quilt is most often known as Bear's Paw. Whether done in stripes and plaids or the contemporary prints used in this quilt, Bear's Paw makes a beautiful country accent for any room.

Skill Level: Intermediate

SIZE

Finished block is 14 inches square
Finished quilt is 93 × 110 inches
Quilt consists of 20 pieced blocks, 30 cornerstones, 49 lattice strips, and inner, middle, and outer borders

FABRIC REQUIREMENTS AND SUPPLIES

❖ 3½ yards dark teal print (pieced blocks and middle border)

❖ 3¾ yards beige print (pieced blocks and inner border)
❖ 3⅛ yards small rose-and-teal stripe (lattice strips and binding)
❖ ⅜ yard dusty rose solid (cornerstones)
❖ 3⅛ yards large rose-and-teal stripe (outer border)
❖ 9½ yards for backing
❖ ⅞ yard for binding (if other than small rose-and-teal stripe)
❖ King-size batting (120 inches square)

CUTTING CHART

Pattern pieces on pages 61–63

FABRIC	A	B	C	D	E	F
Dark teal print	80	320	20			
Beige print		320	80	80		
Small rose-and-teal stripe					49	
Dusty rose solid						30

(continued)

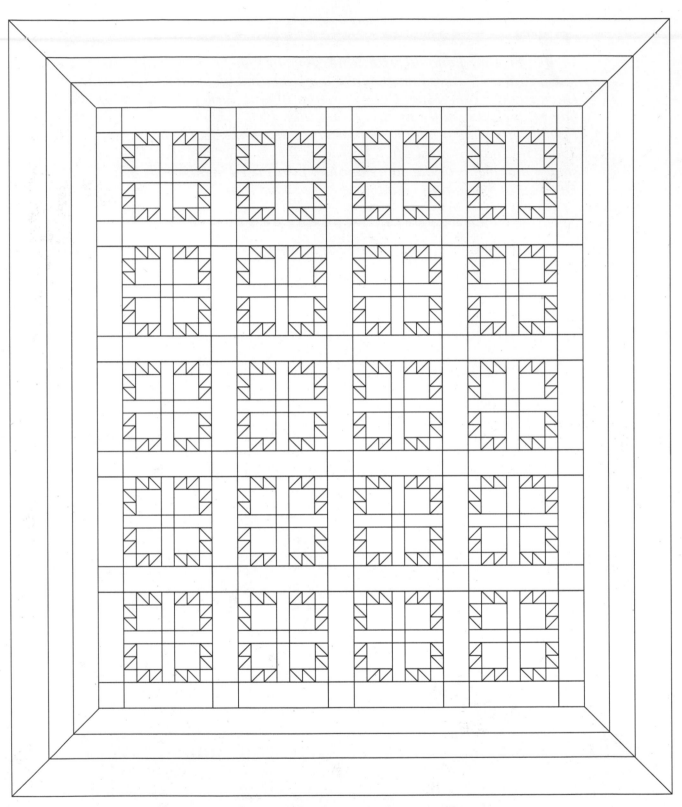

Bear's Paw Color Plan: You may photocopy this page
and use it to experiment with color schemes for your quilt.

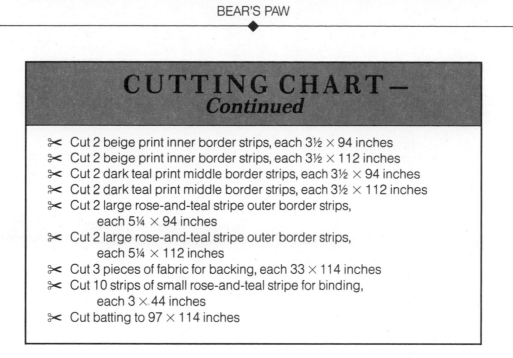

CUTTING CHART—
Continued

✂ Cut 2 beige print inner border strips, each 3½ × 94 inches
✂ Cut 2 beige print inner border strips, each 3½ × 112 inches
✂ Cut 2 dark teal print middle border strips, each 3½ × 94 inches
✂ Cut 2 dark teal print middle border strips, each 3½ × 112 inches
✂ Cut 2 large rose-and-teal stripe outer border strips,
    each 5¼ × 94 inches
✂ Cut 2 large rose-and-teal stripe outer border strips,
    each 5¼ × 112 inches
✂ Cut 3 pieces of fabric for backing, each 33 × 114 inches
✂ Cut 10 strips of small rose-and-teal stripe for binding,
    each 3 × 44 inches
✂ Cut batting to 97 × 114 inches

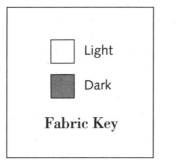

Light

Dark

Fabric Key

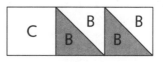

Diagram 2

3. Sew a beige C square to the left end of this BB unit, as shown in **Diagram 3**.

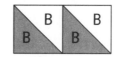

Diagram 3

Piecing the Block

1. Sew a dark teal B triangle to a beige B triangle, as shown in **Diagram 1**. Make 4 of these BB units.

Diagram 1

2. Sew two BB units together, positioning the dark teal triangles at the lower left, as shown in **Diagram 2**.

4. Sew 2 BB units together, positioning the dark teal triangles at the lower right, as shown in **Diagram 4**.

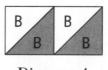

Diagram 4

5. Sew a dark teal A square to the right of the BB unit, as shown in **Diagram 5** on page 58.

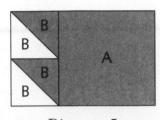

Diagram 5

6. Sew the CBB unit from Step 3 to the top of this ABB unit, as shown in **Diagram 6.** Repeat Steps 1 through 6 to make a total of 4 of these "paw" sections.

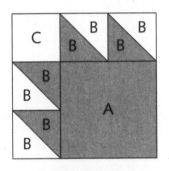

Diagram 6

7. Sew a dark teal C square between 2 beige D rectangles, as shown in **Diagram 7.**

Diagram 7

8. Sew a D rectangle between 2 "paw" sections, as shown in **Diagram 8.** Make 2 of these rows.

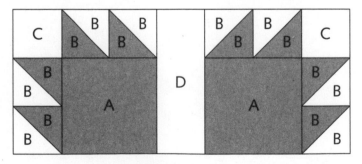

Diagram 8

9. Referring to the **Block Assembly Diagram,** sew together the 3 rows of the block, making sure to align the seams.

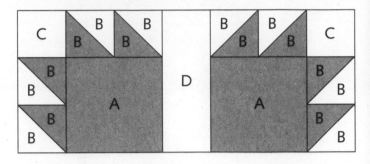

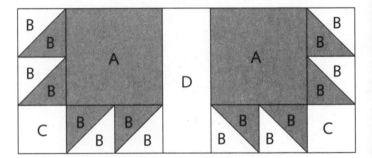

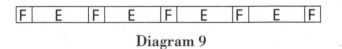

Block Assembly Diagram

10. Repeat Steps 1 through 9 to make a total of 20 pieced blocks.

Assembling the Quilt

1. Sew a row of 4 E lattice strips and 5 F cornerstones together, alternating their placement, as shown in **Diagram 9.** Make 6 of these rows.

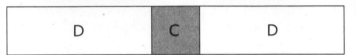

Diagram 9

2. Sew an E lattice strip to one side of each of the 20 pieced blocks, as shown in **Diagram 10.**

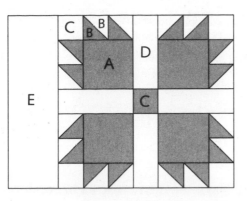

Diagram 10

6. Sew the quilt together, being sure to align all the seams of the blocks, lattice strips, and cornerstones.

3. Sew E lattice strips to the opposite sides of 5 of the pieced blocks, as shown in **Diagram 11.**

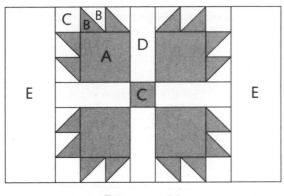

Diagram 11

4. Referring to **Diagram 12,** sew a row of 4 pieced blocks with lattice strips on each side. Use 3 blocks with only 1 E lattice strip; the fourth block on the right end of the row should have 2 E lattice strips. Make a total of 5 of these rows.

5. Following the **Quilt Assembly Diagram,** lay out the 5 rows of blocks from Step 4 and the 6 rows of lattice strips and cornerstones from Step 1. Begin and end with a lattice strip/cornerstone row.

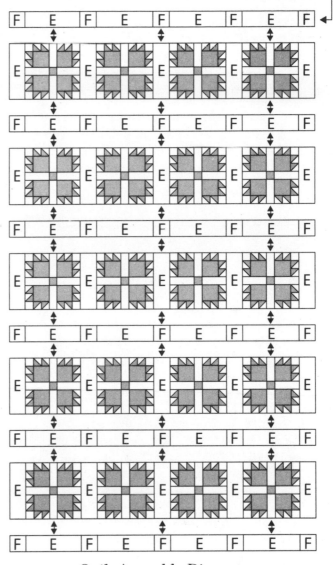

Quilt Assembly Diagram

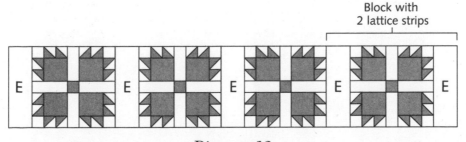

Diagram 12

7. The top and bottom borders are each made of three 94-inch border strips sewn together. Join the border strips in this order: beige inner border, dark teal middle border, and large rose-and-teal stripe outer border. Press the seams outward, toward the edges of the quilt.

8. In the same way, the side borders are each made of three 112-inch border strips sewn together. Join the border strips in the same order and press the seams outward, toward the edges of the quilt.

9. Sew the top and bottom borders to the quilt, beginning and ending each seam ¼ inch in from the edge. Then sew the side borders to the quilt, beginning and ending these seams at the same points.

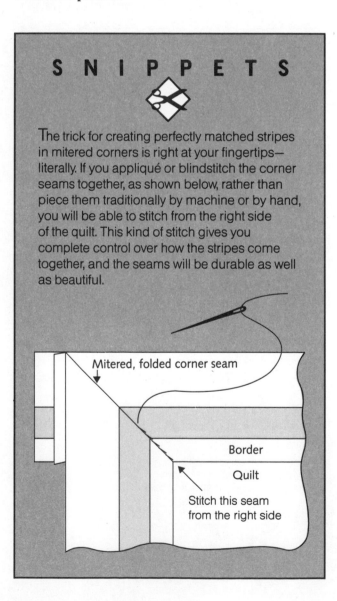

S N I P P E T S

The trick for creating perfectly matched stripes in mitered corners is right at your fingertips—literally. If you appliqué or blindstitch the corner seams together, as shown below, rather than piece them traditionally by machine or by hand, you will be able to stitch from the right side of the quilt. This kind of stitch gives you complete control over how the stripes come together, and the seams will be durable as well as beautiful.

Mitered, folded corner seam

Border

Quilt

Stitch this seam from the right side

10. Miter the corner seams, matching the border stripes. Trim the excess fabric to ¼ inch and press the seams open. For instructions on how to miter, see page 237.

Quilting

1. Mark the dark teal A squares with the **Tulip Quilting Design** on page 63.

2. Mark the dusty rose F cornerstones with the **Leaf Quilting Design** on page 65.

3. Mark the beige inner border with the **Shamrock Quilting Design** on page 64.

4. Mark the dark teal middle border with the **Diamond Quilting Design** on page 65.

5. Mark the striped outer border with the **Cable Quilting Design** on page 65.

6. Sew the 3 pieces of backing fabric together along their long sides, using a ¼-inch seam allowance. Press these seams open.

7. Layer the quilt top, batting, and backing and baste together. Refer to page 239 for pointers on how to layer and baste.

8. Quilt all marked designs, as well as ¼ inch away from each seam in the pieced blocks. (See page 239 for details on the quilting stitch.)

Finishing

1. To make the binding, sew the short ends of the 10 binding strips together with diagonal seams. Trim the excess fabric and press these seams open. (For more details on how to make and attach binding, see page 240.)

2. Fold the binding in half lengthwise, wrong sides together, and press.

3. Sew the binding to the quilt.

4. Sign and date your quilt.

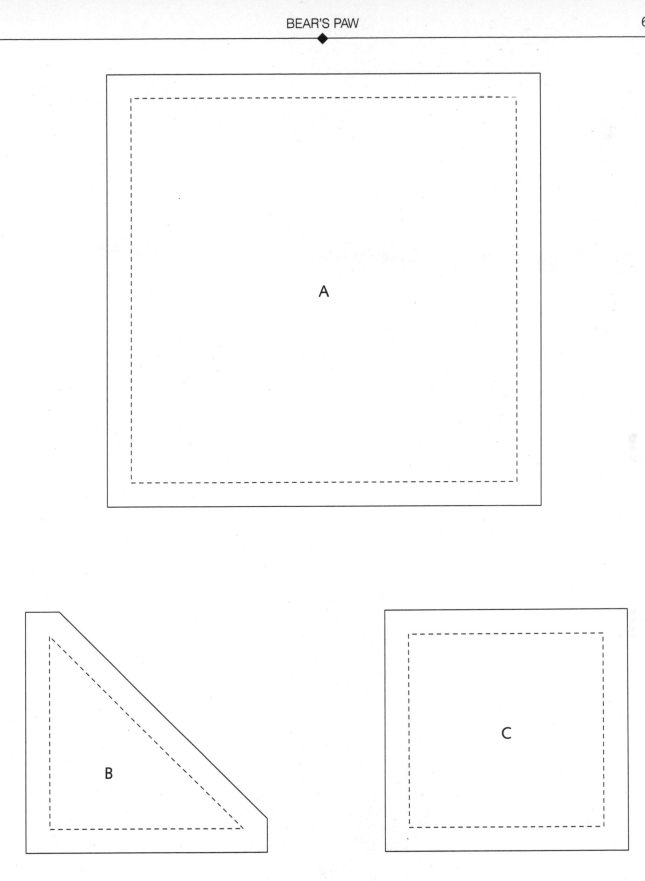

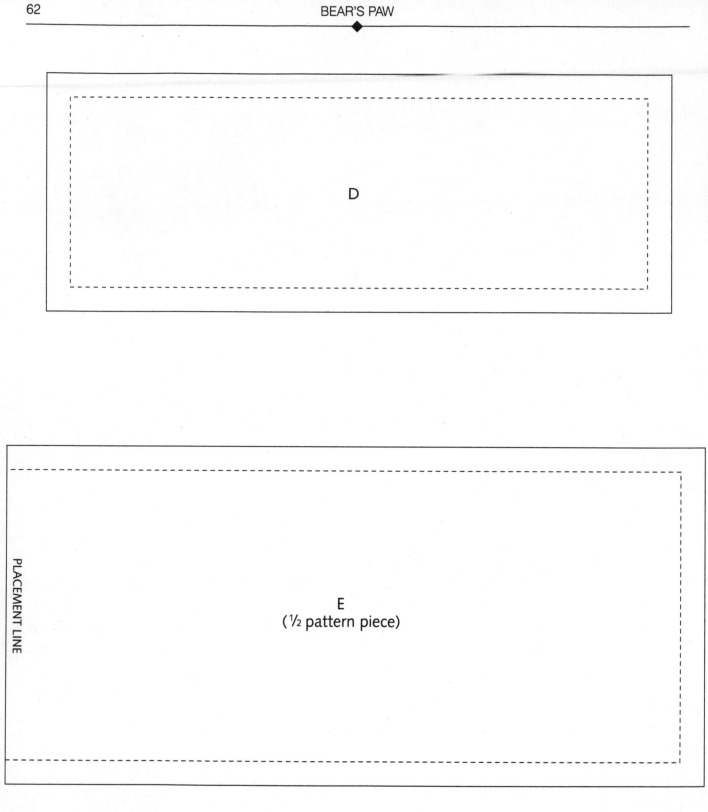

D

E
(½ pattern piece)

PLACEMENT LINE

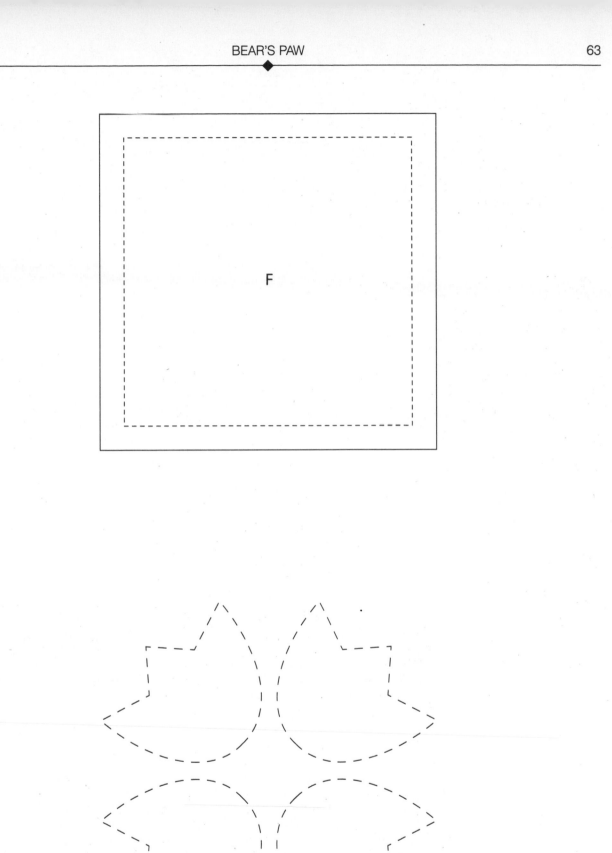

F

Tulip Quilting Design

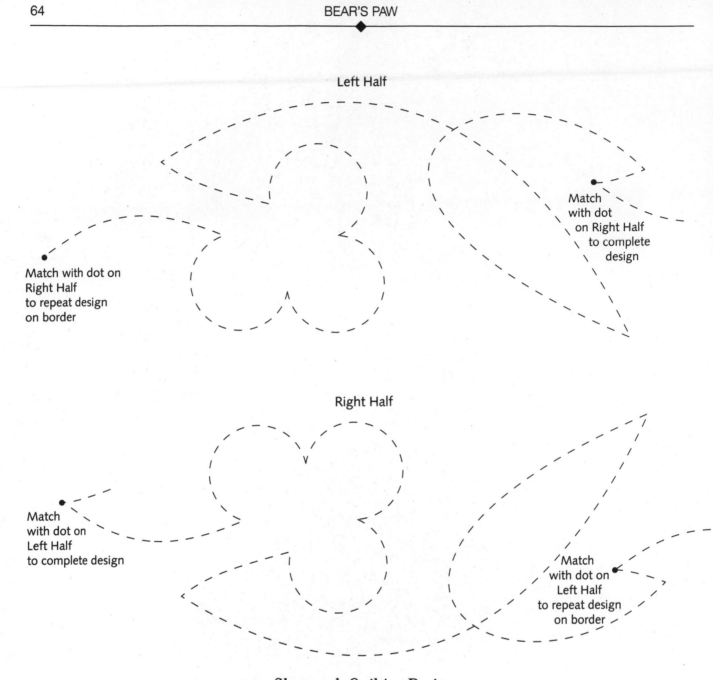

Left Half

Match
with dot
on Right Half
to complete
design

Match with dot on
Right Half
to repeat design
on border

Right Half

Match
with dot on
Left Half
to complete design

Match
with dot on
Left Half
to repeat design
on border

Shamrock Quilting Design

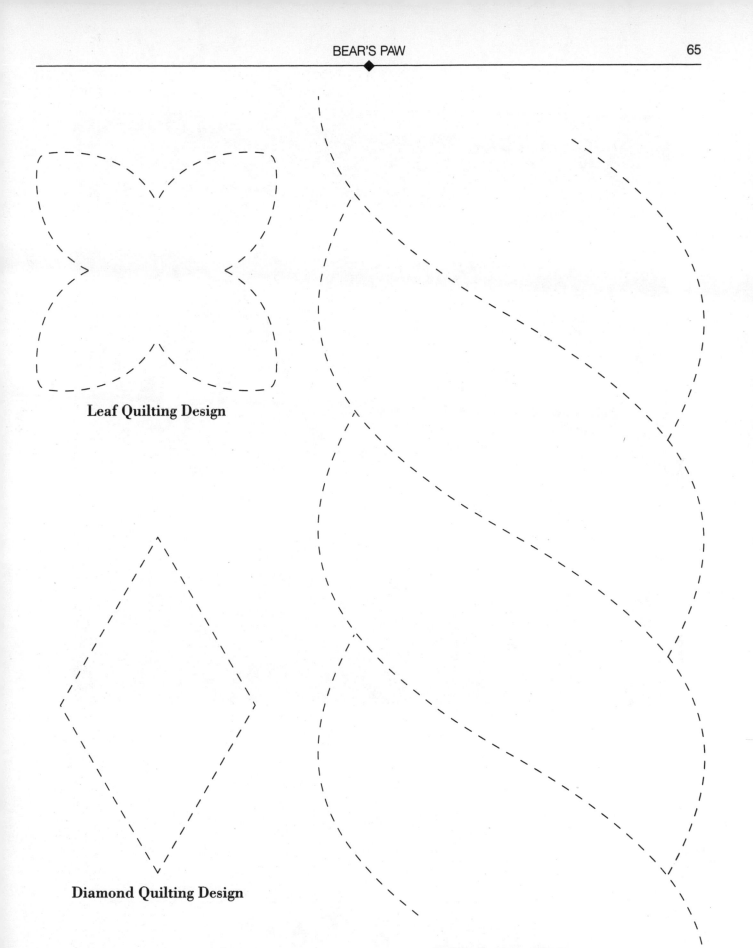

Leaf Quilting Design

Diamond Quilting Design

Cable Quilting Design

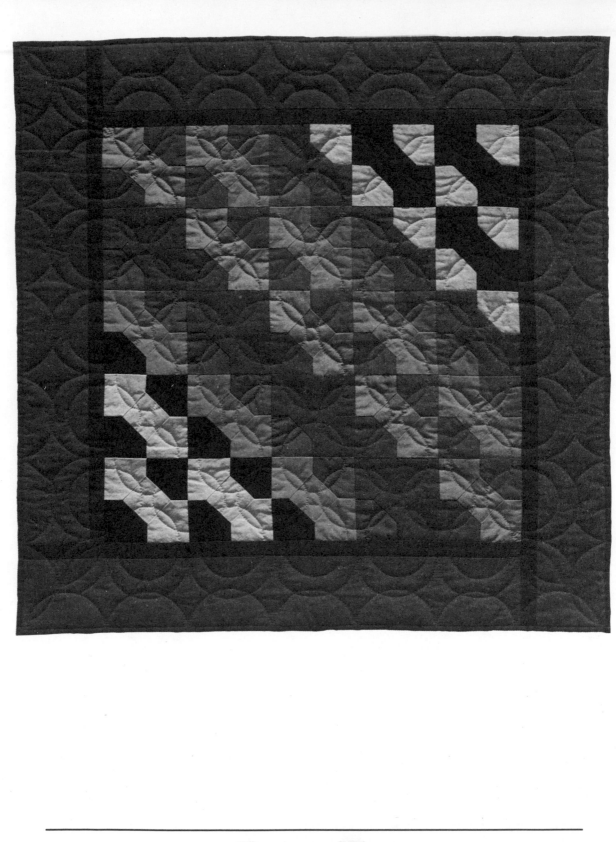

• BOW TIE •

*T*he Bow Tie pattern is a great chance to use up some of your remnants and scrap basket treasures. This colorful Amish version makes use of only solid fabrics, but plaids and stripes could produce an old-time scrap look that almost seems to glow with the patina of age. Or you could use a planned color scheme, with each Bow Tie and center square in repeated colors against a single background, for a more contemporary look.

Skill Level: Challenging

SIZE

Finished block is 5 inches square
Finished quilt is 35 inches square
Quilt consists of 25 pieced blocks and inner
    and outer borders

FABRIC REQUIREMENTS AND SUPPLIES

Note: *All fabrics are solids*

❖ ⅛ yard pale peach (blocks)
❖ ⅛ yard carnation pink (blocks)
❖ ⅛ yard blue-violet (blocks)
❖ ⅛ yard burgundy (blocks)
❖ ⅛ yard brick (blocks)
❖ ⅛ yard turquoise (blocks)
❖ ⅛ yard dusty red (blocks)
❖ ⅛ yard dusty rose (blocks)
❖ ⅛ yard mauve (blocks)
❖ ⅛ yard grape (blocks)
❖ ⅛ yard pale pink (blocks)
❖ ¼ yard black (blocks)
❖ ⅝ yard wine (narrow border, binding)
❖ 1 yard deep rose (wide border)
❖ 1⅛ yard for backing
❖ ⅜ yard for binding (if other than wine)
❖ Crib-size batting (45 × 60 inches)

CUTTING CHART

Note: The pieces for this quilt are cut from strips using a rotary cutter. Use the Quick-Cutting Directions on page 69 and refer to the numbers in the Cutting Chart to prepare the correct number of pieces for the quilt. (If you'd like to try hand piecing, pattern pieces appear on page 73 and directions are given in "Snippets" on page 70.)

FABRIC	PATTERN PIECES		
	A	B	C
Pale peach	3	6	
Carnation pink	3	6	
Blue-violet			7
Burgundy	4	8	
Brick			9
Turquoise	5	10	
Dusty red			9
Dusty rose	4	8	
Mauve			7
Grape	3	6	
Pale pink			9
Black	3	6	9

✂ Cut 4 wine inner border strips,
     each 1½ × 31 inches
✂ Cut 4 deep rose outer border strips,
     each 4½ × 31 inches
✂ Cut backing fabric to 39 inches square
✂ Cut 4 wine binding strips,
     each 3 × 44 inches
✂ Cut batting to 39 inches square

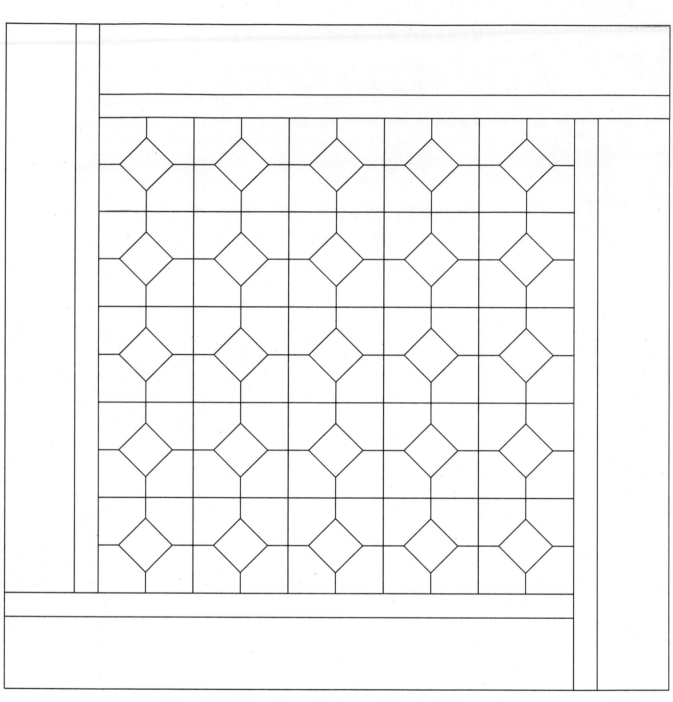

Bow Tie Color Plan: You may photocopy this page
and use it to experiment with color schemes for your quilt.

Quick-Cutting Directions

Note: All of the B and C pieces are the same size. The B pieces will combine with the center A square to form the bow ties, and the C pieces will form the background.

1. To rotary cut pattern pieces B and C, start by cutting a 3 × 44-inch strip from each fabric. Refer to the Cutting Chart and cut the designated number of 3-inch squares from each strip. Place several 3-inch squares into a stack, with cut edges even, and place a see-through ruler on top diagonally so that the 1-inch line touches two opposite corners, as shown in **Diagram 1.** With a rotary cutter, cut next to the ruler, creating a B or C pattern piece. Discard the small piece you cut off. Repeat this process for all B and C pieces.

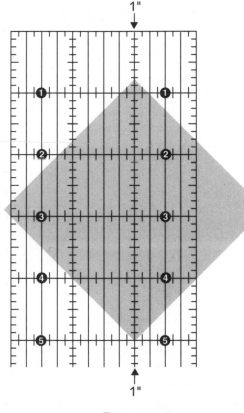

Diagram 1

2. To rotary cut the A squares, start by trimming ½ inch from the strips of fabric that remain after you have cut pieces B and C, making these strips now measure 2½ inches wide. Referring

to the Cutting Chart, cut the designated number of 2½-inch A squares from these strips.

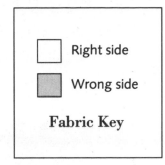

Fabric Key

Piecing the Block

1. Mark sewing lines on the wrong side of a pale peach A square, ¼ inch from each edge, as shown in **Diagram 2.** The points at which these sewing lines cross indicate where to begin and end each seam.

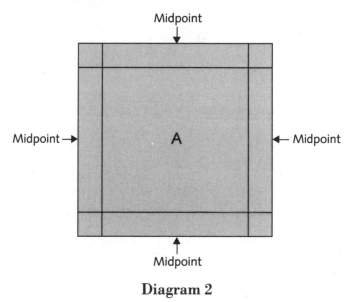

Diagram 2

2. Referring to **Diagram 2,** find the midpoint on each side of the pale peach A square by folding it in half, both horizontally and vertically, and finger-pressing a crease on each side.

3. In the same manner, find the midpoint on the trimmed edge of a pale peach B piece, as shown in **Diagram 3** on page 70. Do the same for 2 black C pieces and 1 more pale peach B piece.

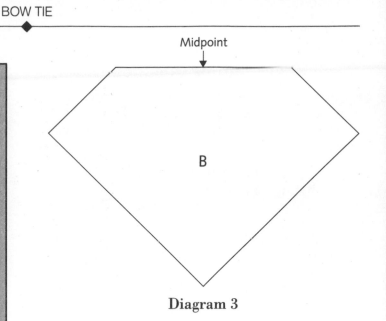

Diagram 3

SNIPPETS

If you'd like to explore the fine art of hand piecing, the Bow Tie is a nice pattern to use. (Pattern pieces A and B/C appear on page 73; the yardages given apply to both rotary-cut and scissor-cut pattern pieces.) Hand-pieced seams are stitched from point to point, ¼ inch in from each cut edge, which leaves the seam allowances free at these points. This allows you to set pieces in at an angle very easily, and it gives you complete control over which way the seams will lie after they are pressed. To hand piece, begin the seam with a knotted thread, ¼ inch in from the cut edge. Take 3 or 4 small running stitches and then 1 backstitch, as shown below. Repeat this stitching pattern for the length of the seam and end the seam with a knot ¼ inch in from the opposite cut edge.

For hand piecing, ¼-inch seam allowances are *not included* in pattern pieces. This means that you will be marking the actual seamlines of pattern pieces A and B/C onto the right side of your fabric. Working with marked seamlines is essential for stitching accurate seams.

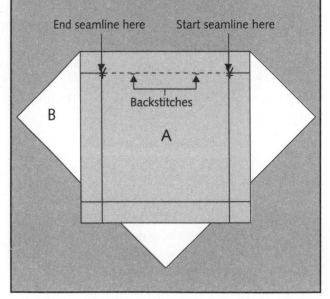

4. Place the pale peach A square and a pale peach B piece right sides together, matching midpoints. With the A square on top, sew from the exact beginning point to the exact ending point of the marked seamline, as shown in **Diagram 4.**

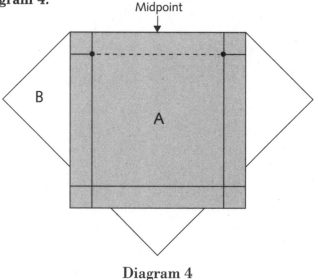

Diagram 4

5. In the same manner, place the other pale peach B piece right sides together with the opposite side of the same pale peach A square. This completes one of the pale peach Bow Ties, with a center A square and two B pieces on either side of it.

6. Working with the pale peach Bow Tie you just completed, sew a black C piece to the center A square. As you sew this seam, keep the C piece on top, as shown in **Diagram 5.** Check to be sure that the seam begins and ends exactly at the points marked on the A square.

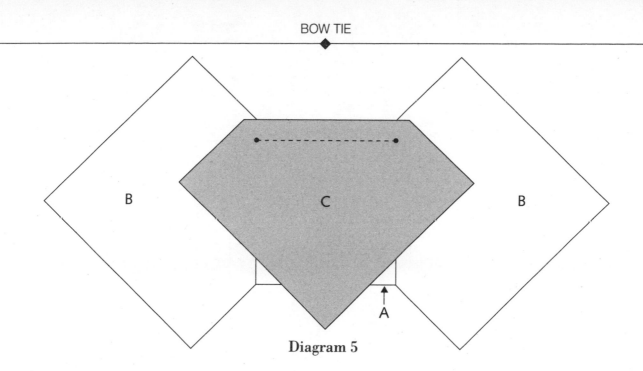

Diagram 5

7. In the same manner, sew a second black C piece to the opposite side of the center A square. Each B and C piece should be sewn to the center A square and all seam allowances should be free at the beginning and end of each seam.

8. To sew the seams that go from each corner of the center A square out to the edge of the Bow Tie, place one of the pale peach B pieces right sides together with the black C piece. Sew from the exact corner point of the center A square to the outer edge of the Bow Tie, as indicated by the arrows in **Diagram 6.** Repeat

Sew in direction of arrows

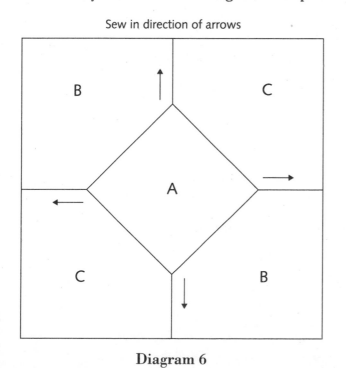

Diagram 6

this process for each of the other 3 seams, completing the Bow Tie block. Press the seams toward the center of the block.

9. Sew the remaining 24 Bow Tie blocks in the same manner, referring to the photo on page 66 for accurate placement of color in each block.

Piecing the Border

Sew a 1½ × 31-inch wine inner border strip to a 4½ × 31-inch deep rose outer border strip. Repeat to make a total of 4 wine-and-rose border strips.

Assembling the Quilt

1. Referring to the photo on page 66 for color placement, lay out the 25 Bow Tie blocks in 5 rows of 5 blocks each. When you are satisfied with the arrangement, sew the blocks together to form horizontal rows, then sew the rows together to form the center of the quilt.

2. Referring to the **Quilt Assembly Diagram** on page 72, sew a wine-and-rose border (labeled 1 on the diagram) to the top of the quilt, matching the left edges. Begin sewing at the left top edge and leave the right side free. This segment will be stitched after the remaining three borders have been added.

3. Sew a border (labeled 2 on the diagram) to the left side of the quilt. Align this border strip with the bottom edge of the quilt.

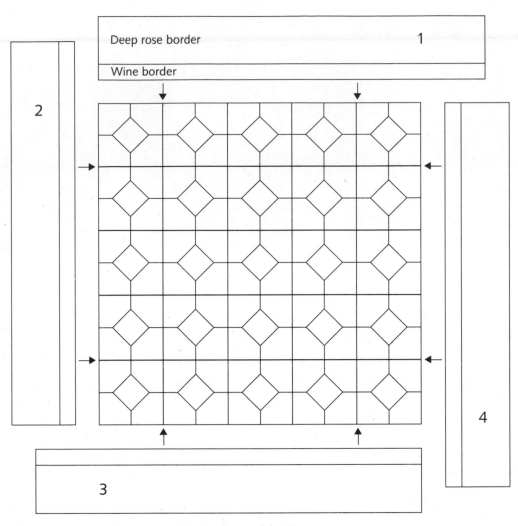

Quilt Assembly Diagram

4. Sew the borders labeled 3 and 4 to the remaining two edges of the quilt in the same way, referring to the **Quilt Assembly Diagram** for placement.

5. Sew the free end of border 1 to the end of border 4, beginning this seam at the inner corner, where the borders meet the quilt top, and sewing out to the edge of border 4. Trim the excess fabric from each border.

Quilting

1. In each Bow Tie block, mark around the outer curve of a protractor, creating a design of interlocked curves, as shown in **Diagram 7**.

2. Extend these curves into the borders and along the edges of the quilt, as shown in **Diagram 8.**

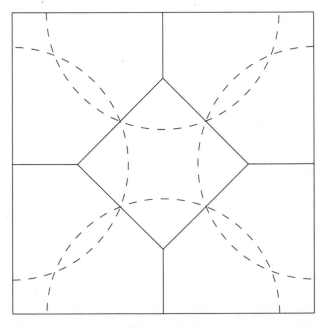

Diagram 7

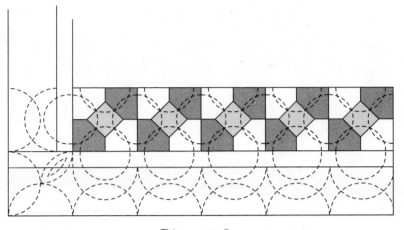

Diagram 8

3. Referring to **Diagram 8,** mark intersecting curved lines in the corners. Also add a melon-shaped quilting design to extend into the corners of the bow tie portion of the quilt.

4. Layer the quilt top, batting, and backing and baste together. Refer to page 239 for pointers on how to layer and baste.

5. Quilt all marked designs. (See page 239 for details on the quilting stitch.)

Finishing

1. To make the binding, sew the short ends of the 4 binding strips together with diagonal seams. Trim the excess fabric and press these seams open. (For more details on how to make and attach binding, see page 240.)

2. Fold the binding in half lengthwise, wrong sides together, and press.

3. Sew the binding to the quilt.

4. Sign and date your quilt.

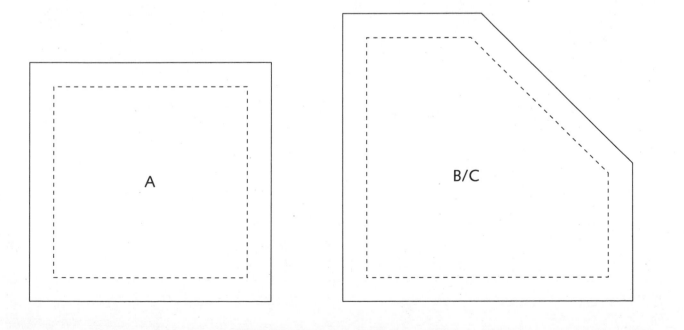

A

B/C

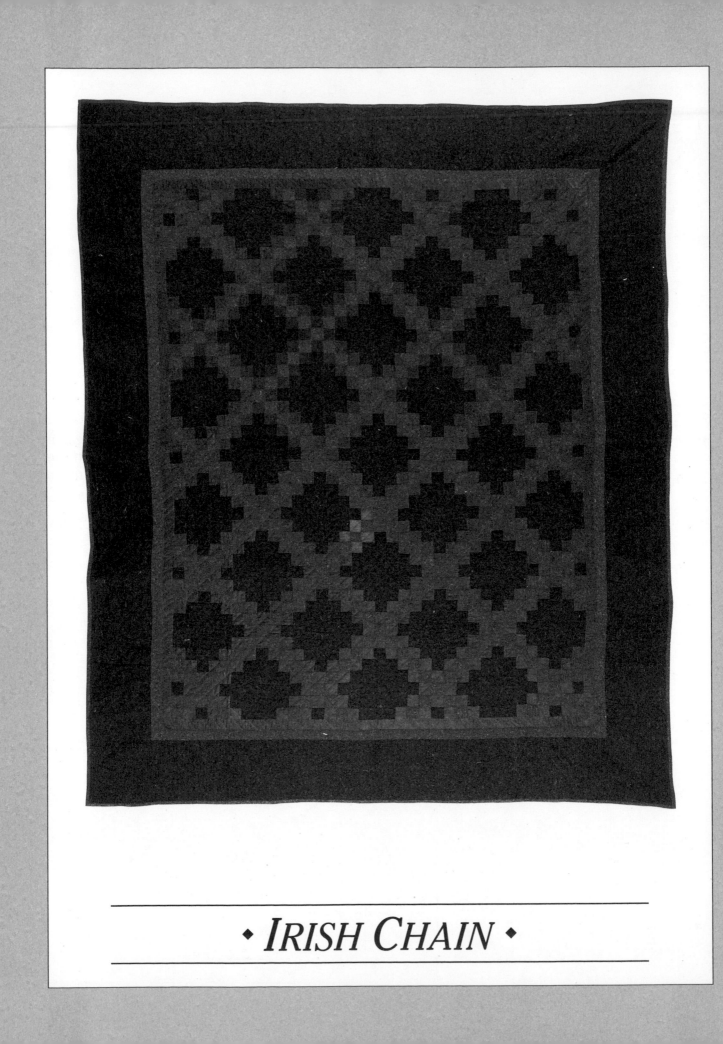

• *IRISH CHAIN* •

*T*here is almost no more universally known quilt pattern than the Irish Chain. It is one of the few designs that have never been known by another name. A popular design with Amish quilters in the 1800s, it has remained popular through today's generation of quiltmakers. This Double Irish Chain, constructed of five-patch blocks, is a common variation that is updated to include the best of modern-day quiltmaking methods—strip piecing and rotary cutting.

Skill Level: Easy

SIZE

Finished block is 7½ inches square
Finished quilt is 73½ × 88½ inches
Quilt consists of 63 pieced blocks and inner, middle, and outer borders

FABRIC REQUIREMENTS AND SUPPLIES

- ❖ 2¼ yards red solid (blocks, middle border, binding)
- ❖ 2⅛ yards khaki solid (blocks, inner border)
- ❖ 4½ yards navy solid (blocks, outer border)
- ❖ 5¼ yards for backing
- ❖ ¾ yard for binding (if other than red)
- ❖ Full-size batting (81 × 96 inches)

Note: The borders in this quilt are pieced. If you prefer to make seamless borders, add the following yardages to those already listed above.

- ❖ 2 yards red solid
- ❖ 2⅛ yards khaki solid
- ❖ ½ yard navy solid

CUTTING CHART

FIRST BLOCK
- ✂ Cut 14 red strips, each 2 × 44 inches
- ✂ Cut 19 khaki strips, each 2 × 44 inches
- ✂ Cut 7 navy strips, each 2 × 44 inches

SECOND BLOCK
- ✂ Cut 6 khaki strips, each 2 × 44 inches
- ✂ Cut 10 navy strips, each 5 × 44 inches

BORDERS
- ✂ Cut 8 red strips, each 2 × 44 inches
- ✂ Cut 8 khaki strips, each 2 × 44 inches
- ✂ Cut 10 navy strips, each 8 × 44 inches

SEAMLESS BORDERS (OPTIONAL)
- ✂ Cut 2 red strips, each 2 × 64½ inches
- ✂ Cut 2 red strips, each 2 × 79½ inches
- ✂ Cut 2 khaki strips, each 2 × 60½ inches
- ✂ Cut 2 khaki strips, each 2 × 75½ inches
- ✂ Cut 2 navy strips, each 8 × 77½ inches
- ✂ Cut 2 navy strips, each 8 × 92½ inches

BACKING AND BINDING
- ✂ Cut 2 pieces of fabric for backing, each 39 × 93 inches
- ✂ Cut 8 binding strips, each 3 × 44 inches
- ✂ Cut batting to 77 × 93 inches

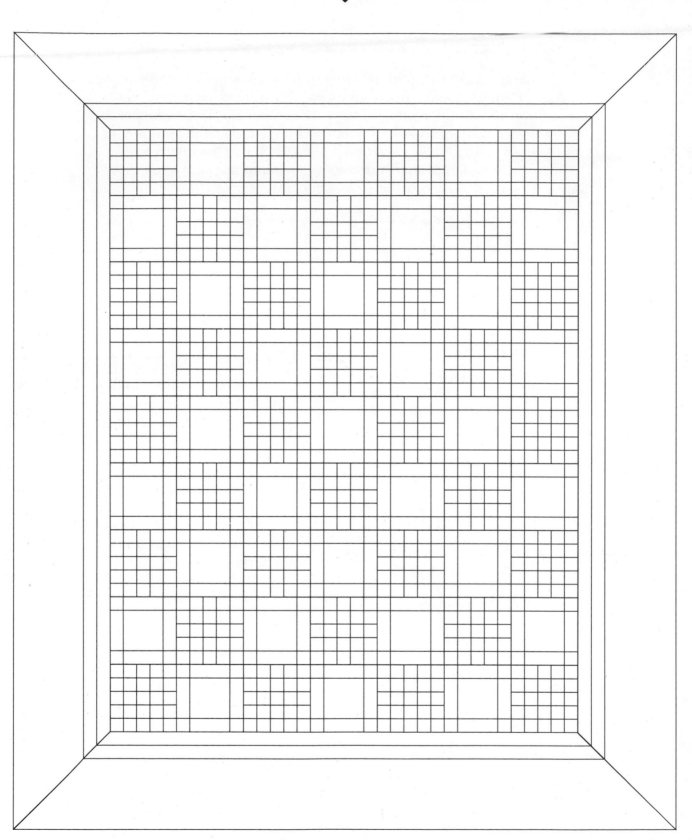

Irish Chain Color Plan: You may photocopy this page
and use it to experiment with color schemes for your quilt.

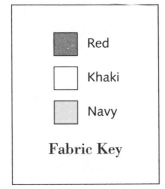

Red

Khaki

Navy

Fabric Key

Piecing the First Block

1. Sew together 1 navy, 2 khaki, and 2 red 2 × 44-inch strips, as shown in **Diagram 1**. Make 3 of these strip units. For this step and the rest that follow in this section, press each seam toward the darker fabric immediately after sewing.

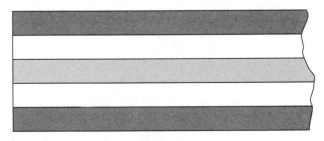

Diagram 1

2. Cut the strip units from Step 1 apart at 2-inch intervals, creating Row A, as shown in **Diagram 2**. Cut 64 of Row A.

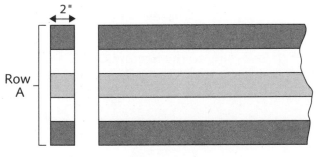

Diagram 2

3. Sew together 3 khaki and 2 red 2 × 44-inch strips, as shown in **Diagram 3**. Make 3 of these strip units.

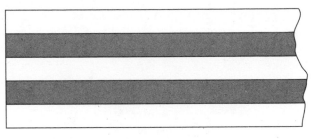

Diagram 3

4. Cut the strip units from Step 3 apart at 2-inch intervals, creating Row B, as shown in **Diagram 4**. Cut 64 of Row B.

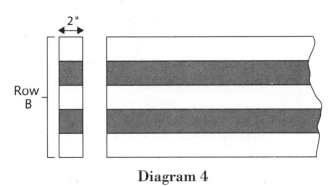

Diagram 4

5. Sew together 2 navy, 1 red, and 2 khaki 2 × 44-inch strips, as shown in **Diagram 5**. Make 2 of these strip units.

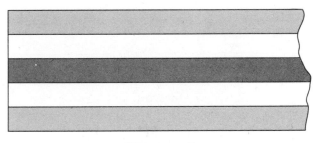

Diagram 5

6. Cut the strip units from Step 5 apart at 2-inch intervals, creating row C, as shown in **Diagram 6**. Cut 32 of Row C.

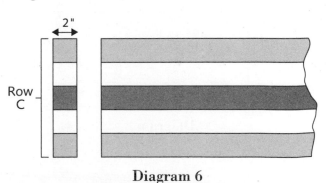

Diagram 6

7. Sew together 2 A rows, 2 B rows, and 1 C row in the order shown in the **First Block Assembly Diagram.** Make a total of 32 of these First Blocks.

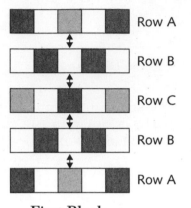

Row A

Row B

Row C

Row B

Row A

**First Block
Assembly Diagram**

Piecing the Second Block

1. Sew together 1 navy 5 × 44-inch strip and 2 khaki 2 × 44-inch strips, as shown in **Diagram 7.** Make 3 of these strip units.

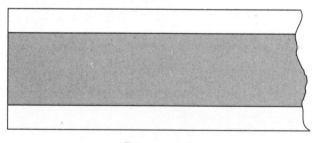

Diagram 7

2. Cut the strip units from Step 1 apart at 2-inch intervals, creating Row D, as shown in **Diagram 8.** Cut 62 of Row D.

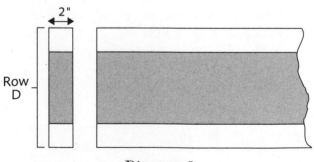

Row D

Diagram 8

3. Cut 4 navy 5 × 44-inch strips into 5-inch squares, creating the center of the second block, as shown in **Diagram 9.** Make a total of 31 squares.

5"

5"

Diagram 9

4. Cut 3 navy 5 × 44-inch strips apart at 2-inch intervals, creating rectangles that are 2 × 5 inches, as shown in **Diagram 10.** Make a total of 62 rectangles.

2"

5"

Diagram 10

5. Sew 2 navy 2 × 5-inch rectangles to 1 navy 5-inch square to create the block center, as shown in **Diagram 11.** Make a total of 31 block centers.

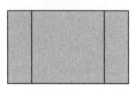

Diagram 11

6. Referring to the **Second Block Assembly Diagram,** sew a Row D to each side of each block center. Make a total of 31 Second Blocks.

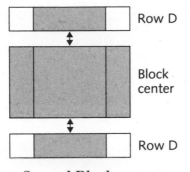

**Second Block
Assembly Diagram**

Piecing the Borders

Note: If you are making seamless borders, skip to Step 5.

1. Sew together 2 khaki 2 × 44-inch border strips, as shown in **Diagram 12,** creating an inner border that is 2 × 87½ inches. Repeat to make 3 more inner borders.

2. Sew together 2 red 2 × 44-inch border strips, as shown in **Diagram 12,** creating a middle border that is 2 × 87½ inches. Repeat to make 3 more middle borders.

3. Sew together 2 navy 8 × 44-inch border strips, as shown in **Diagram 13,** creating a *short* outer border that is 8 × 87½ inches. Make 1 more *short* outer border.

4. Sew together 3 navy 8 × 44-inch border strips, as shown in **Diagram 13,** creating a *long* outer border. Trim 19 inches of fabric from each end, leaving a long outer border measuring 8 × 93 inches. Make 1 more *long* outer border.

5. Sew together 1 khaki inner border, 1 red middle border, and 1 navy *short* outer border, as shown in **Diagram 14** on page 80. Repeat to make another short border like this one.

6. Sew together 1 khaki inner border, 1 red middle border, and 1 navy *long* outer border, as shown in **Diagram 15** on page 80. Repeat to make another long border like this one.

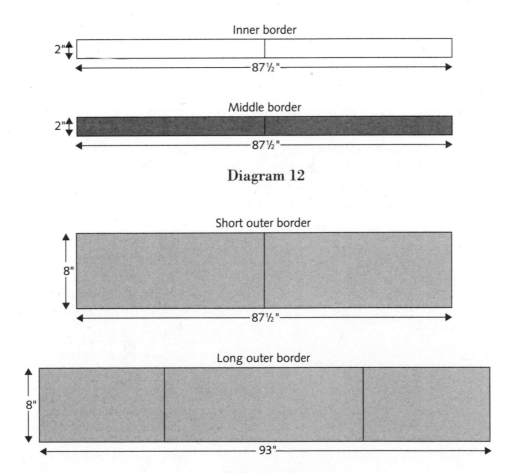

Diagram 12

Diagram 13

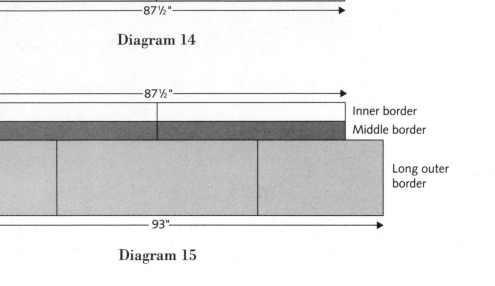

Diagram 14

Diagram 15

Assembling the Quilt

1. Referring to the **Quilt Assembly Diagram** for block placement, sew the blocks into 9 horizontal rows of 7 blocks each. Alternate the placement of First and Second Blocks from row to row.

2. Referring to the **Quilt Assembly Diagram,** find the midpoint of each border by folding it in half and pressing a light crease. Match the center of each border to the middle of the center block on each side of the quilt. Sew the border seams, beginning and ending each seam ¼ inch from the edge.

3. Miter the corner seams, trim the excess fabric to ¼ inch, and press the seams open. For instructions on how to miter, see page 237.

Quilting

1. Mark diagonal lines in both directions through the red and khaki squares. Continue quilting diagonal lines at the same intervals in both directions in each of the plain navy areas.

2. Mark a pair of diagonal lines ½ inch apart in the khaki inner border. Mark another pair of diagonal lines 1 inch away from the first pair. Continue marking diagonal lines in this manner, as shown in **Diagram 16.**

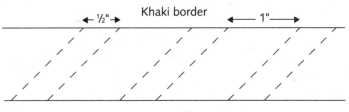

Diagram 16

3. Mark each corner of the outer border with the **Corner Cable Quilting Design** on page 82. Mark the borders with the **Cable Quilting Design** on page 83, making slight adjustments in the cables to fit the borders, if necessary.

4. Sew the 2 pieces of backing fabric together with a ¼-inch seam allowance and press this seam open.

5. Layer the quilt top, batting, and backing and baste together. Refer to page 239 for pointers on how to layer and baste.

6. Quilt all marked designs. See page 239 for details on the quilting stitch.

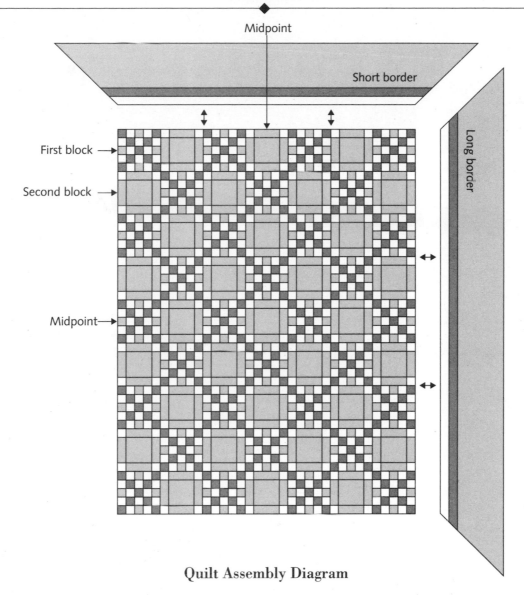

Midpoint

Short border

Long border

First block →

Second block →

Midpoint→

Quilt Assembly Diagram

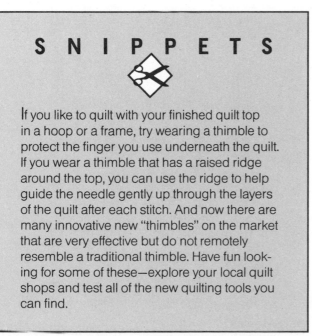

S N I P P E T S

If you like to quilt with your finished quilt top in a hoop or a frame, try wearing a thimble to protect the finger you use underneath the quilt. If you wear a thimble that has a raised ridge around the top, you can use the ridge to help guide the needle gently up through the layers of the quilt after each stitch. And now there are many innovative new "thimbles" on the market that are very effective but do not remotely resemble a traditional thimble. Have fun looking for some of these—explore your local quilt shops and test all of the new quilting tools you can find.

Finishing

1. To make the binding, sew the short ends of the 8 binding strips together with diagonal seams. Trim the excess fabric and press these seams open. (For more details on how to make and attach binding, see page 240.)

2. Fold the binding in half lengthwise, wrong sides together, and press.

3. Sew the binding to the quilt.

4. Sign and date your quilt.

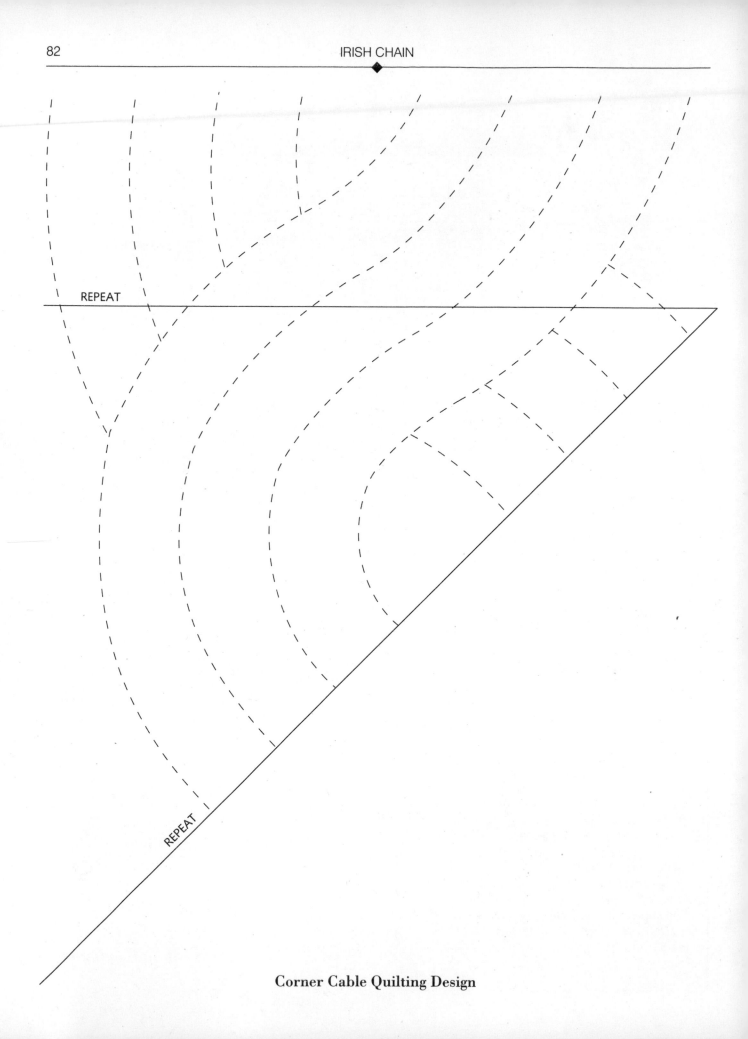

REPEAT

REPEAT

Corner Cable Quilting Design

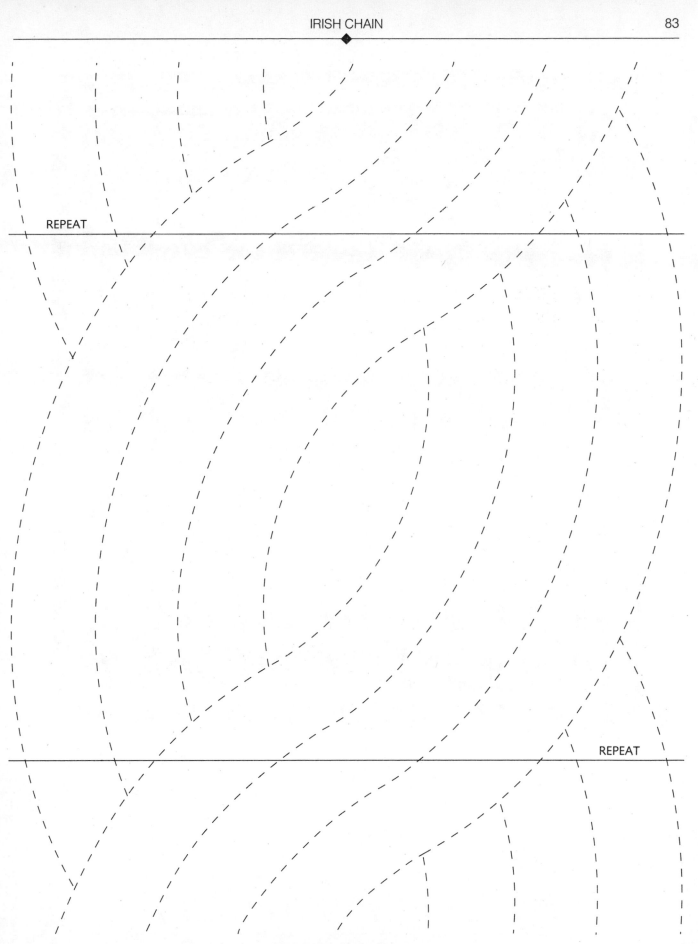

REPEAT

REPEAT

Cable Quilting Design

◆ PINEAPPLE LOG CABIN ◆

A close relative of the classic Log Cabin, the Pineapple pattern has been a perennial favorite of quilters in every generation for the last 100 years. This spectacular blue and white version was probably one of the "best" quilts in a nineteenth-century quiltmaker's collection. The combination of clear blue and crisp white is just as beautiful today as it was then.

◆◆◆◆◆◆◆◆◆◆◆◆◆◆◆◆◆◆◆◆◆◆◆◆◆

Skill Level: Intermediate

SIZE

Finished block is $10^{13/16}$ inches square
Finished quilt is $74\frac{3}{8} \times 85\frac{1}{4}$ inches
Quilt consists of 42 pieced blocks and inner, middle, and outer borders

FABRIC REQUIREMENTS AND SUPPLIES

❖ 4 yards assorted blue scraps (pieced blocks)
❖ 4⅞ yards white solid (pieced blocks, middle border)
❖ 3¼ yards blue dot (inner and outer borders)
❖ 5⅛ yards for backing
❖ ¾ yard for binding (if other than blue dot)
❖ Full-size batting (81 × 96 inches)

CUTTING CHART

Pattern pieces on pages 90 and 91

FABRIC				PATTERN PIECES				
	A	B	C	D	E	F	G	H
Assorted blue scraps	42		168	168	168	168	168	
White solid		168		168	168	168	168	168

✂ Cut 2 blue dot inner border strips, each 1¾ × 70 inches
✂ Cut 2 blue dot inner border strips, each 1¾ × 81 inches
✂ Cut 2 white solid middle border strips, each 2 × 73 inches
✂ Cut 2 white solid middle border strips, each 2 × 84 inches
✂ Cut 2 blue dot outer border strips, each 2½ × 77 inches

✂ Cut 2 blue dot outer border strips, each 2½ × 88 inches
✂ Cut 2 strips of fabric for backing, each 39 × 90 inches
✂ Cut 8 blue dot binding strips, each 3 × 44 inches
✂ Cut batting to 79 × 90 inches

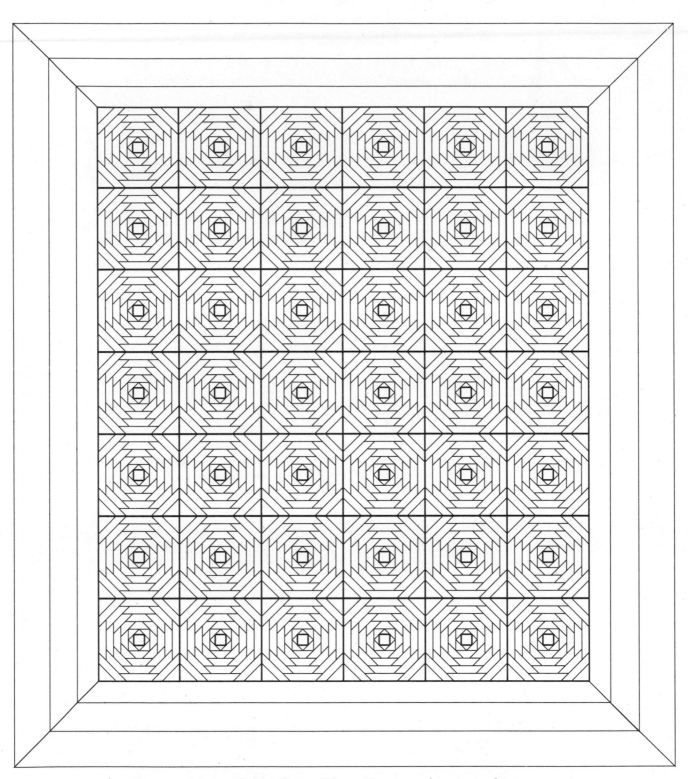

Pineapple Log Cabin Color Plan: You may photocopy this page
and use it to experiment with color schemes for your quilt.

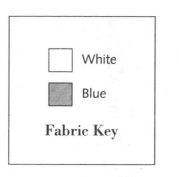

Fabric Key

Piecing the Block

Note: The center section of this block is shown in **Diagrams 1, 2,** and **3.** From that step on, refer to the **Block Piecing Diagram** on page **88** and sew each round of pattern pieces in the same manner.

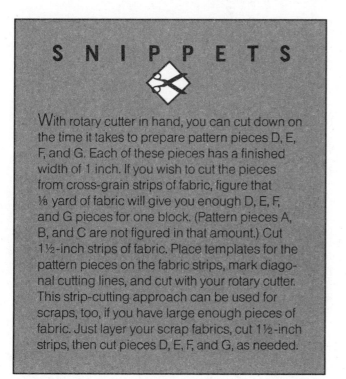

S N I P P E T S

With rotary cutter in hand, you can cut down on the time it takes to prepare pattern pieces D, E, F, and G. Each of these pieces has a finished width of 1 inch. If you wish to cut the pieces from cross-grain strips of fabric, figure that ⅛ yard of fabric will give you enough D, E, F, and G pieces for one block. (Pattern pieces A, B, and C are not figured in that amount.) Cut 1½-inch strips of fabric. Place templates for the pattern pieces on the fabric strips, mark diagonal cutting lines, and cut with your rotary cutter. This strip-cutting approach can be used for scraps, too, if you have large enough pieces of fabric. Just layer your scrap fabrics, cut 1½-inch strips, then cut pieces D, E, F, and G, as needed.

1. Sew 4 white B triangles to a blue A square, as shown in **Diagram 1.**

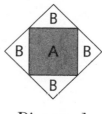

Diagram 1

2. Sew 4 blue C triangles to the AB unit, as shown in **Diagram 2.**

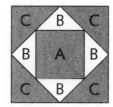

Diagram 2

3. Sew 4 white D pieces to the ABC unit, as shown in **Diagram 3.**

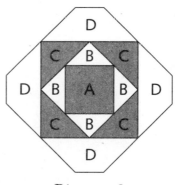

Diagram 3

4. Sew 4 blue D pieces to the center unit.

5. Sew 4 white E pieces to the center portion of the block.

6. Sew 4 blue E pieces to the center portion of the block.

7. Sew 4 white F pieces to the center portion of the block.

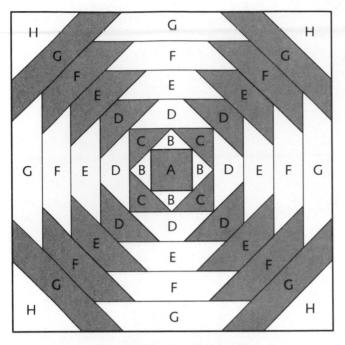

Block Piecing Diagram

8. Sew 4 blue F pieces to the center portion of the block.

9. Sew 4 white G pieces to the center portion of the block.

10. Sew 4 blue G pieces to the center portion of the block.

11. Sew 4 white H triangles to the center portion of the block, completing the Pineapple block.

12. Repeat Steps 1 through 11 to complete a total of 42 blocks.

Piecing the Borders

1. Fold each border strip in half and press lightly to mark the center point. Sew a blue dot 1¾ × 70-inch inner border strip to a white 2 × 73-inch middle border strip, centering them, as shown in **Diagram 4.**

2. Referring to **Diagram 5,** sew a blue dot 2½ × 77-inch outer border strip to these two borders, centering it as described in Step 1.

3. Repeat Steps 1 and 2 to make a second set of short borders.

4. Sew a blue dot 1¾ × 81-inch inner border strip to a white 2 × 84-inch middle border strip, centering them as for the short borders.

5. Sew a blue dot 2½ × 88-inch outer border strip to these two borders, centering it as before.

6. Repeat Steps 4 and 5 to make a second set of long borders.

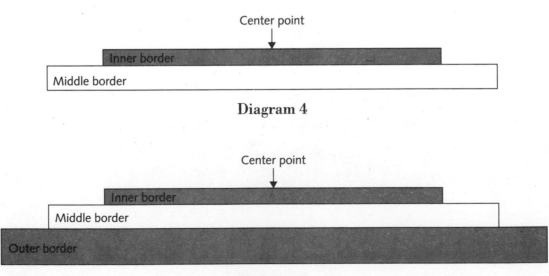

Diagram 4

Diagram 5

Assembling the Quilt

1. Refer to the **Quilt Assembly Diagram** for all the steps in this section. Sew the Pineapple blocks into 7 rows of 6 blocks.

2. Sew the 7 rows of blocks together.

3. Beginning and ending ¼ inch in from the cut edges of the quilt, sew the short borders to the top and bottom of the quilt.

4. Beginning exactly at the points where the previous seams stop, sew the long borders to the sides of the quilt.

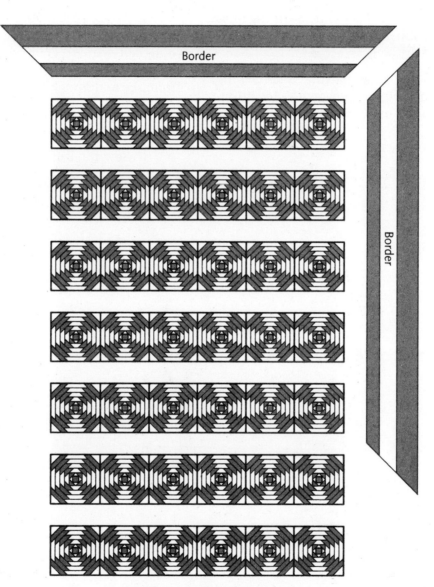

Border

Border

Quilt Assembly Diagram

5. Miter the corner seams; trim the excess fabric to ¼ inch and press the seams open. For instructions on how to miter, see page 237.

Quilting

1. Mark the white middle borders with the **Leaf Quilting Design.**

2. Sew the 2 pieces of backing fabric together with a ¼-inch seam allowance. Press this seam open.

3. Layer the quilt top, batting, and backing and baste together. Refer to page 239 for pointers on how to layer and baste.

4. Quilt in the ditch of each seam in the pieced blocks and each border seam. (See page 239 for details on the quilting stitch.)

5. Quilt the marked designs in the white borders.

Finishing

1. To make the binding, sew the short ends of the 8 blue dot binding strips together with diagonal seams. Trim these seams to ¼ inch and press them open. (For more details on how to make and attach binding, see page 240.)

2. Fold the binding lengthwise, wrong sides together, and press.

3. Sew the binding to the quilt.

4. Sign and date your quilt.

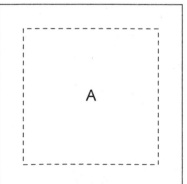
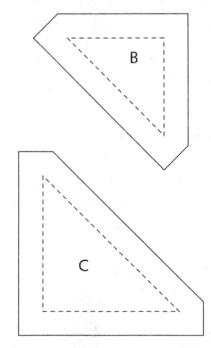
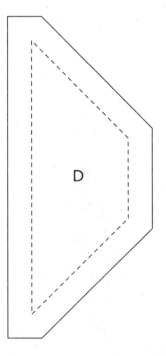

Leaf Quilting Design

• ROLLING STONE •

*B*lue and white quilts were often among nineteenth-century quilt-makers' masterpieces, with intricate piecing, skillful appliqué, elaborate quilting, and stuffed work. This striking example, Rolling Stone, was made sometime between 1840 and 1870. In your own version of this classic, you may want to try red and white or a combination of any two highly contrasting hues.

Skill Level: Easy

SIZE

Finished block is 12 inches square
Finished quilt is 110 inches square
Quilt consists of 36 pieced blocks, 25 alternating blocks, 20 setting triangles, 4 corner triangles, inner border, pieced middle border, and outer border

FABRIC REQUIREMENTS AND SUPPLIES

- ❖ 5¼ yards dark blue print (pieced blocks, inner border, pieced middle border, binding)
- ❖ 9 yards white solid (pieced blocks, alternating blocks, pieced middle border, outer border)
- ❖ 9¾ yards for backing
- ❖ 1 yard for binding (if other than dark blue print)
- ❖ King-size batting (120 inches square)

CUTTING CHART

| Pattern pieces on pages 98–100 | | | | | | Instructions for cutting pattern piece F below | | |

FABRIC				PATTERN PIECES					
	A	B	C	D	E	F	G	H	I
Dark blue print	36	144		144				186	
White solid		144	576		25	20	4	186	2

- ✂ For pattern piece F, cut 10 white solid 12⅞-inch squares. Cut each square in half diagonally to make 2 F triangles, for a total of 20 F triangles
- ✂ Cut 12 dark blue inner border strips, each 1¼ × 35 inches
- ✂ Cut 12 white outer border strips, each 1½ × 37 inches

- ✂ Cut 3 pieces of fabric for backing, each 38½ × 114 inches
- ✂ Cut 11 binding strips, each 3 × 44 inches
- ✂ Cut batting to 114 inches square

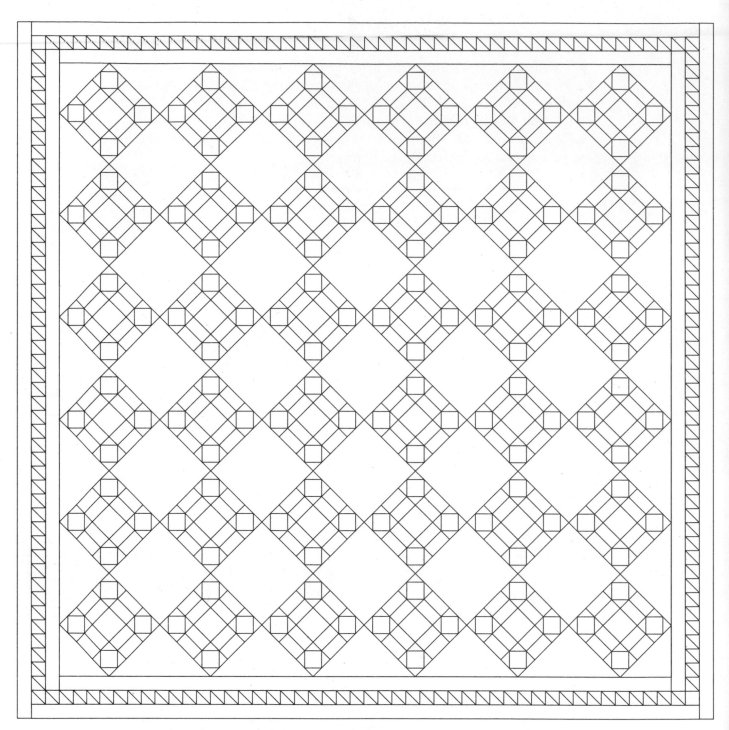

Rolling Stone Color Plan: You may photocopy this page
and use it to experiment with color schemes for your quilt.

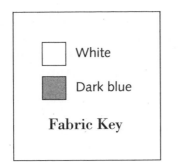

Fabric Key

- White
- Dark blue

Piecing the Block

1. Sew a blue B rectangle to a white B rectangle, as shown in **Diagram 1.** Make a total of 4 of these BB units.

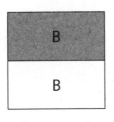

Diagram 1

2. Sew a white C triangle to each side of a blue D square, as shown in **Diagram 2.** Make a total of 4 of these CD units.

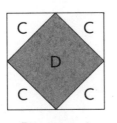

Diagram 2

3. Sew a CD unit to each side of a BB unit, as shown in **Diagram 3.** Make 2 of these sections.

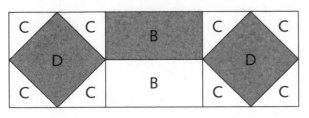

Diagram 3

4. Sew a BB unit to each side of a blue A square, as shown in **Diagram 4.**

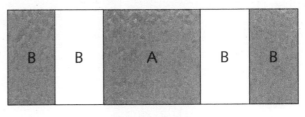

Diagram 4

5. Sew the 3 rows of the block together, referring to the **Block Piecing Diagram.**

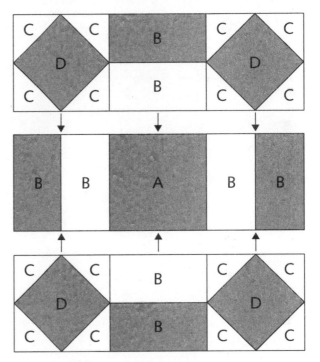

Block Piecing Diagram

6. Repeat Steps 1 through 5 to make a total of 36 pieced blocks.

Making the Borders

1. Sew the short ends of 3 blue 1¼ × 35-inch border strips together. Make a total of 4 of these blue inner border strips.

2. Sew the short ends of 3 white 1½ × 37-inch border strips together. Make a total of 4 of these white outer border strips.

3. Sew a blue H triangle to a white H triangle, as shown in **Diagram 5.** Make a total of 186 of these HH units.

Diagram 5

4. Referring to the **Quilt Assembly Diagram,** sew together two rows of 46 HH units each. These will form the pieced middle border strips for the top and bottom of the quilt.

5. Sew together two rows of 47 HH units each. Sew a white I square to opposite ends of these two rows, referring to **Quilt Assembly Diagram.** These will form the pieced middle border strips for the sides of the quilt.

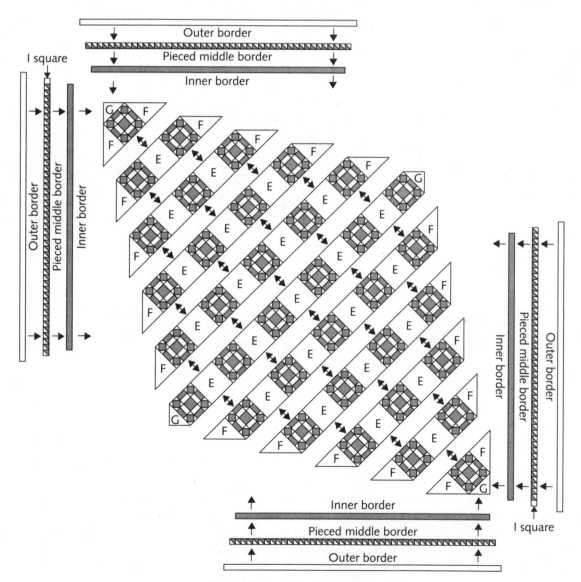

Quilt Assembly Diagram

Assembling the Quilt

1. Referring to the **Quilt Assembly Diagram,** sew the pieced and alternating blocks of the quilt into diagonal rows. Begin and end each row with an F triangle, except for the longest row containing 11 blocks; this row has G triangles at each end.

2. Sew the diagonal rows together, placing a G triangle at each of the two remaining corners.

3. Sew a blue inner border to the top and bottom of the quilt, trimming any extra length from each border.

4. Referring to the photograph on page 92 for color placement, sew a pieced middle border of 46 HH units to the top and bottom edges of the quilt.

5. Sew the remaining pieced middle borders of 47 HH units to the sides of the quilt, referring again to the photograph for color placement. Check to see that the white I squares fall at opposite ends of these two borders.

6. Sew a white outer border to the top and bottom of the quilt, trimming any extra length from each seam. Then sew a white outer border to the sides of the quilt, trimming excess fabric from each seam.

Quilting

1. Mark each alternating block with the **Feathered Circle Quilting Design** on page 101.

2. Mark the side triangles with *one-half* of the **Feathered Circle Quilting Design.**

3. Mark the corner triangles with *one-quarter* of the **Feathered Circle Quilting Design.**

4. Stitch the 3 pieces of backing fabric together with ¼-inch seam allowances. Press these seams open.

5. Layer the quilt top, batting, and backing and baste together. Refer to page 239 for pointers on how to layer and baste.

S N I P P E T S

Try this "knotless" start to your next line of quilting stitches. Begin by cutting a strand of thread that is twice as long as you would normally use (for example, 36 inches instead of 18 inches). Thread a needle and make your first quilting stitch, bringing the thread only halfway out of the quilt sandwich and leaving the other half of the thread free. Continue quilting with the threaded needle and end as usual by knotting and popping the end of this thread through to the layer of batting. Then go back and thread the first half of the thread and continue quilting, knotting and popping this thread through to the batting layer, as usual.

---

6. Quilt the designs marked in the alternating, side, and corner blocks; quilt ¼ inch on either side of each seam in the pieced blocks and borders. (See page 239 for details on the quilting stitch.)

Finishing

1. To make the binding, sew the short ends of the eleven 3-inch binding strips together with diagonal seams. Trim the excess fabric and press these seams open. (For more details on how to make and attach binding, see page 240.)

2. Fold the binding strip in half lengthwise, wrong sides together, and press.

3. Sew the binding to the quilt.

4. Sign and date your quilt.

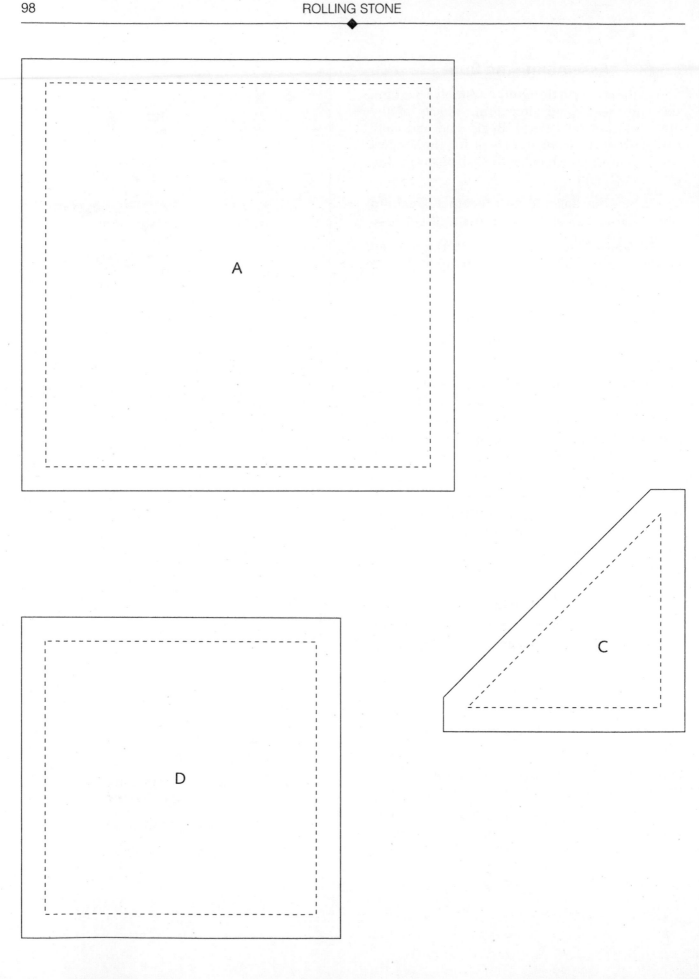

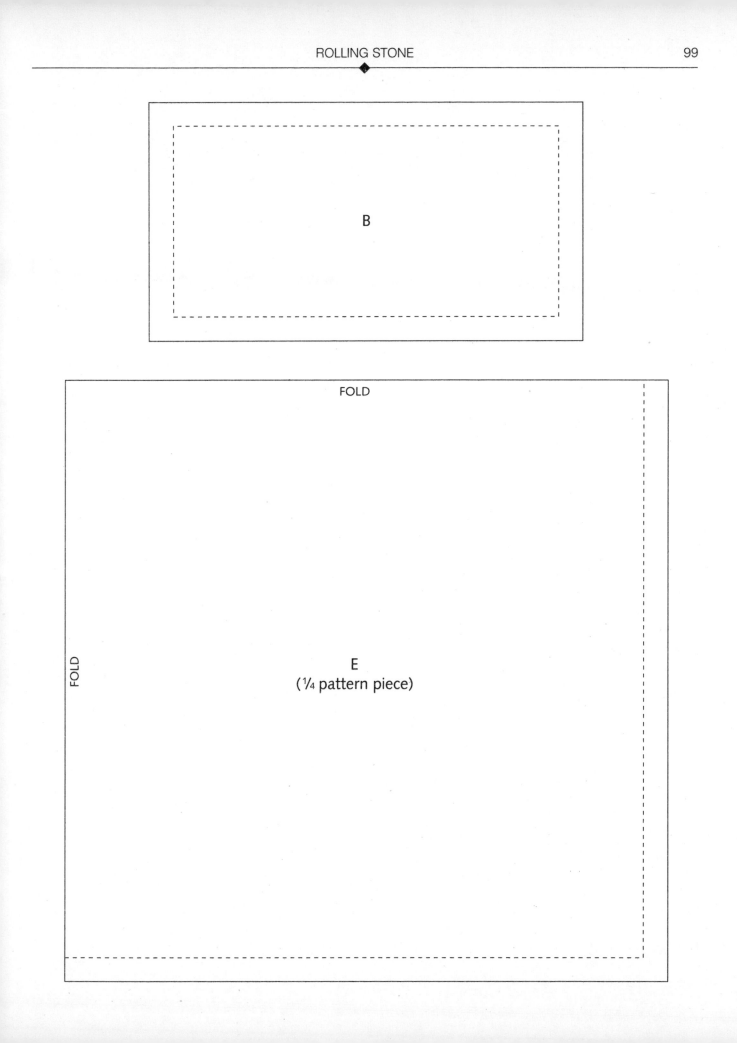

B

FOLD

FOLD

E
(¼ pattern piece)

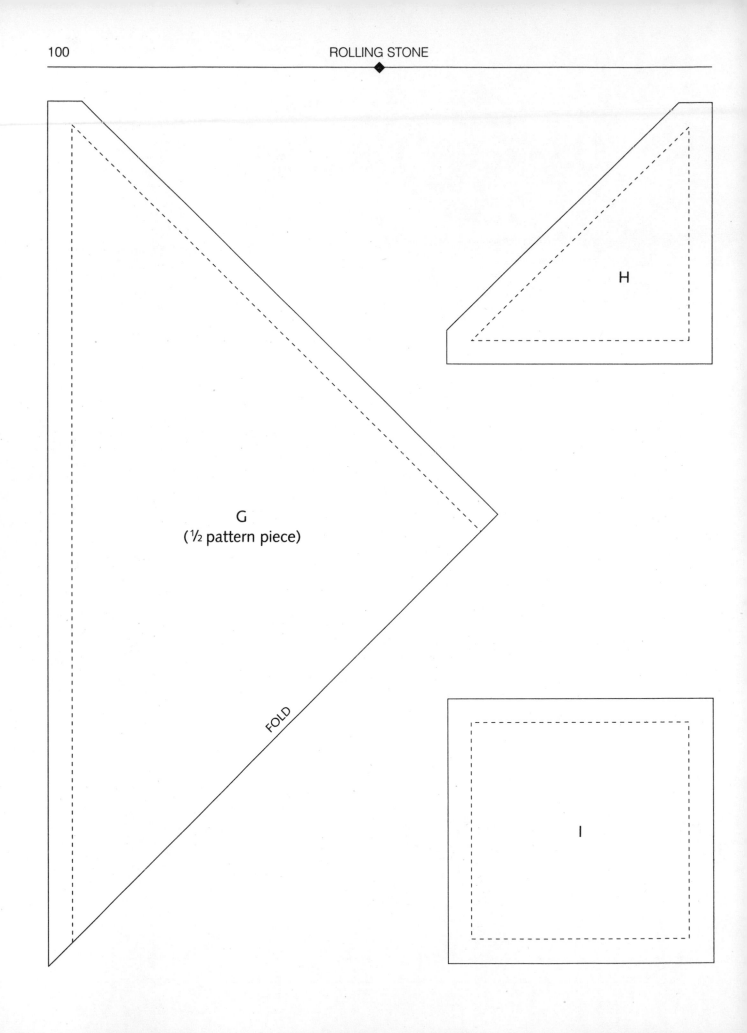

G
(½ pattern piece)

FOLD

H

I

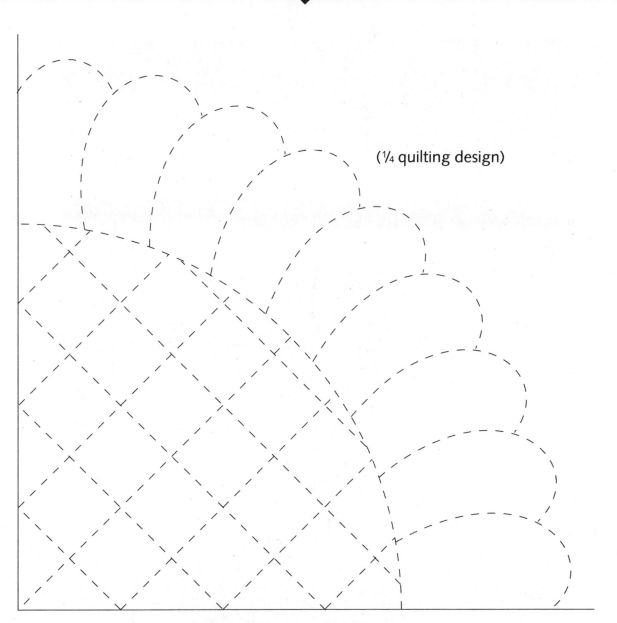

(¼ quilting design)

Feathered Circle Quilting Design

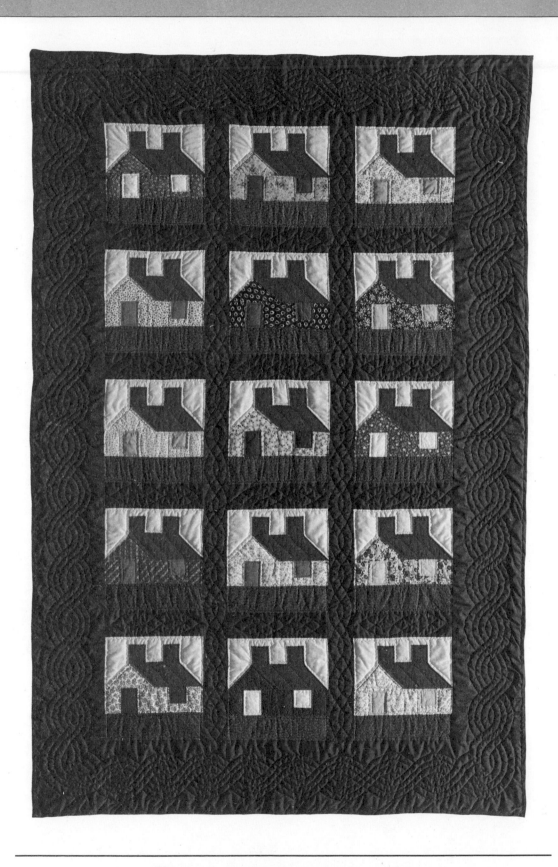

• SCHOOLHOUSE •

*T*his vibrant Schoolhouse quilt would brighten a child's bedroom wall or add a spark of color to any family room, living room, or den. Its bold primary colors make it look like folk art, which blends easily and comfortably with classic country decor.

Skill Level: Intermediate

SIZE

Finished block is 12 inches square
Finished quilt is 59 × 89 inches
Quilt consists of 15 pieced blocks, 2 lattice strips, and border

FABRIC REQUIREMENTS AND SUPPLIES

- ❖ ¾ yard light blue solid (sky)
- ❖ ¾ yard red solid (roof, chimneys)
- ❖ 1½ yards assorted prints (sides of houses)
- ❖ ¼ yard assorted bright solids (windows and doors)
- ❖ ¾ yard green print (grass)
- ❖ 3½ yards navy solid (lattice strips, borders, binding)
- ❖ 5¼ yards for backing
- ❖ ¾ yard for binding (if other than navy solid)
- ❖ Full-size batting (81 × 96 inches)

CUTTING CHART

Pattern pieces on pages 108–110

FABRIC				PATTERN PIECES					
	A	B	C	D	E	F	G	Gr	H
Light blue solid	15		30				15	15	
Red solid		30				15			
Assorted prints	30		15	15	15				
Assorted bright solids	15	15							
Green print									15
Navy solid									12

✂ Cut 2 navy solid lattice strips, each 3½ × 72½ inches
✂ Cut 2 navy solid borders, each 9 × 65½ inches
✂ Cut 2 navy solid borders, each 9 × 72½ inches

✂ Cut 8 navy solid binding strips, each 3 × 44 inches
✂ Cut 2 pieces of fabric for backing, each 32 × 93 inches
✂ Cut batting to 63 × 93 inches

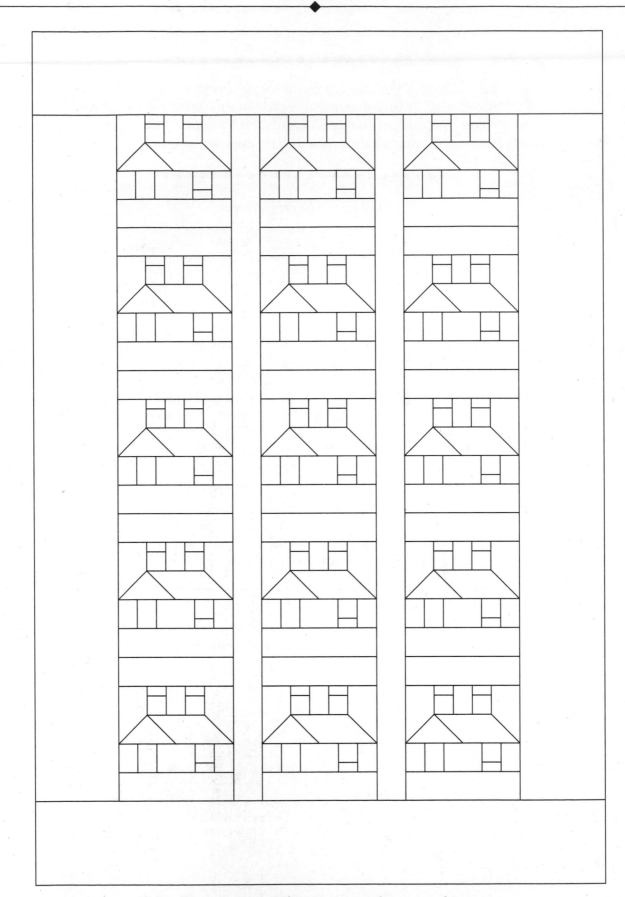

Schoolhouse Color Plan: You may photocopy this page
and use it to experiment with color schemes for your quilt.

"House" prints

Other fabrics

Fabric Key

Piecing the Block

1. Sew a print A rectangle to the left side of a bright solid A rectangle, as shown in **Diagram 1.**

Diagram 1

2. Sew a print D rectangle to this AA unit, as shown in **Diagram 2.**

Diagram 2

3. Sew a bright solid B square to a print C rectangle, as shown in **Diagram 3.**

Diagram 3

4. Sew this BC unit to the AAD unit from Step 2, as shown in **Diagram 4.**

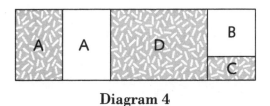

Diagram 4

5. Sew a print A rectangle to the right side of the unit from Step 4, as shown in **Diagram 5.** Set this piece aside. This will form the bottom portion of the Schoolhouse block and will be joined to the roof portion of the block.

Diagram 5

6. Sew a print E triangle to a red F parallelogram, as shown in **Diagram 6.**

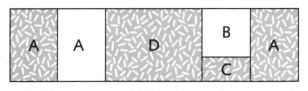

Diagram 6

7. Sew a light blue C rectangle to a red B square, as shown in **Diagram 7.** Make two of these CB units.

Diagram 7

8. Sew a CB unit to each side of a light blue A rectangle, as shown in **Diagram 8.**

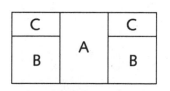

Diagram 8

9. Sew the CBA unit from Step 8 to the top of the EF unit from Step 6, as shown in **Diagram 9.**

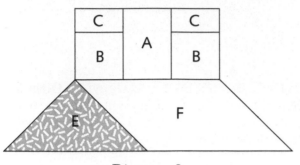

Diagram 9

10. Sew a light blue G reverse (Gr) piece to the left side of the CBA unit, as shown in **Diagram 10,** pivoting the seam at the inner angle. Refer to page 234 for more on setting pieces in at an angle.

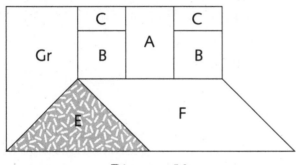

Diagram 10

11. Sew a light blue G piece to the right side of the unit from Step 10, as shown in **Diagram 11.** Pivot the seam at the inner angle. This completes the rooftop and sky portion of the Schoolhouse block.

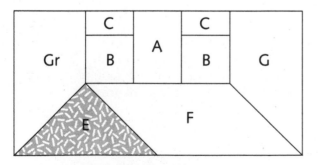

Diagram 11

12. Sew the bottom of the schoolhouse (the unit completed in Step 5) to the lower edge of the unit completed in Step 11. Refer to **Diagram 12.**

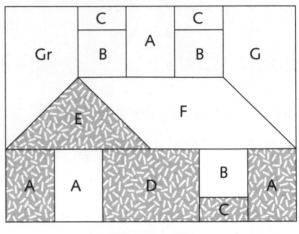

Diagram 12

13. For the grassy strip, sew a green print H rectangle to the house unit, completing the block, as shown in **Diagram 13.**

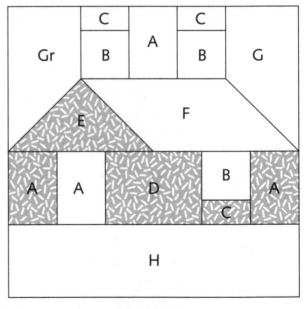

Diagram 13

14. Repeat Steps 1 through 13 to make a total of 15 Schoolhouse blocks.

Assembling the Quilt

1. For all of the steps that follow in this section, refer to the **Quilt Assembly Diagram.** Sew a navy H lattice strip to the lower edges of 12 of the Schoolhouse blocks.

2. Referring to the **Quilt Assembly Diagram,** sew 5 Schoolhouse blocks together to form a vertical row. Be sure each block is separated by a navy H lattice strip. Make 3 of these rows.

3. Sew together the 3 vertical rows of Schoolhouse blocks with the 3½ × 72½-inch navy lattice strips between them.

4. Sew a 9 × 72½-inch navy border to each side of the quilt.

5. Sew 9 × 65½-inch navy borders to the top and bottom of the quilt.

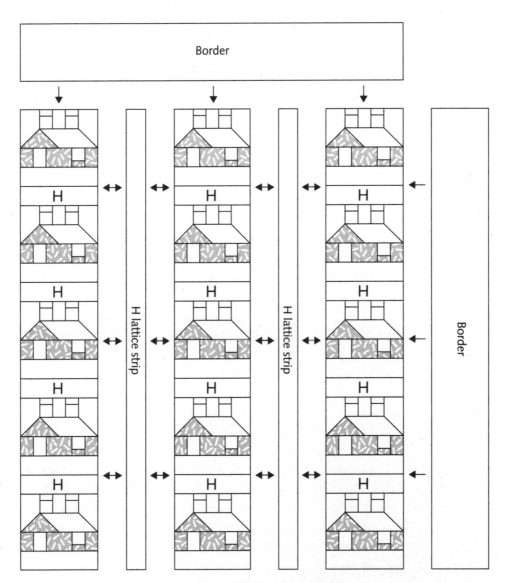

Quilt Assembly Diagram

Quilting

1. Mark the borders with the **Large Cable Quilting Design** on page 111.

2. Mark the lattice strips with the **Small Cable Quilting Design** on page 110.

3. Sew the 2 pieces of backing fabric together with a ¼-inch seam allowance. Press this seam open.

4. Layer the quilt top, batting, and backing and baste together. Refer to page 239 for pointers on how to layer and baste.

5. Quilt ¼ inch from each of the seams in the Schoolhouse blocks. (See page 239 for details on the quilting stitch.)

6. Quilt the marked cable designs in the lattice strips and borders.

Finishing

1. To make the binding, sew the short ends of the 8 binding strips together with diagonal seams. Trim the excess fabric and press these

S N I P P E T S

Children's coloring books can be a wonderful source for creative quilting designs. These simple line drawings are often funny and cute, and the bold dark lines are easy to trace directly onto a quilt. You may find many things in a coloring book that would complement this Schoolhouse theme. If some designs are too large or too small, you can often reduce or enlarge them to exactly the right size on a copy machine.

seams open. (For more details on how to make and attach binding, see page 240.)

2. Fold the binding in half lengthwise, wrong sides together, and press.

3. Sew the binding to the quilt.

4. Sign and date your quilt.

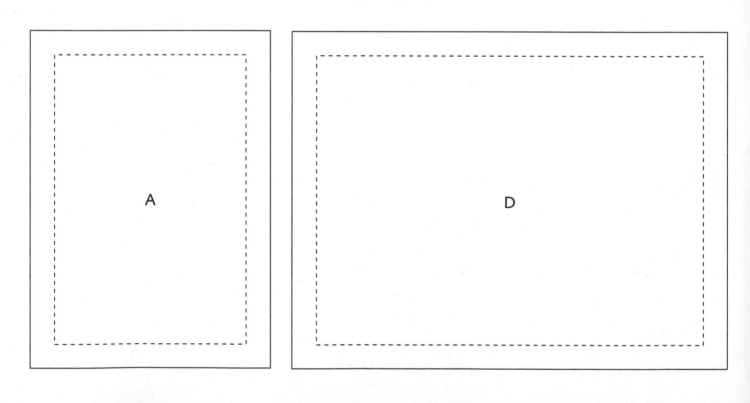

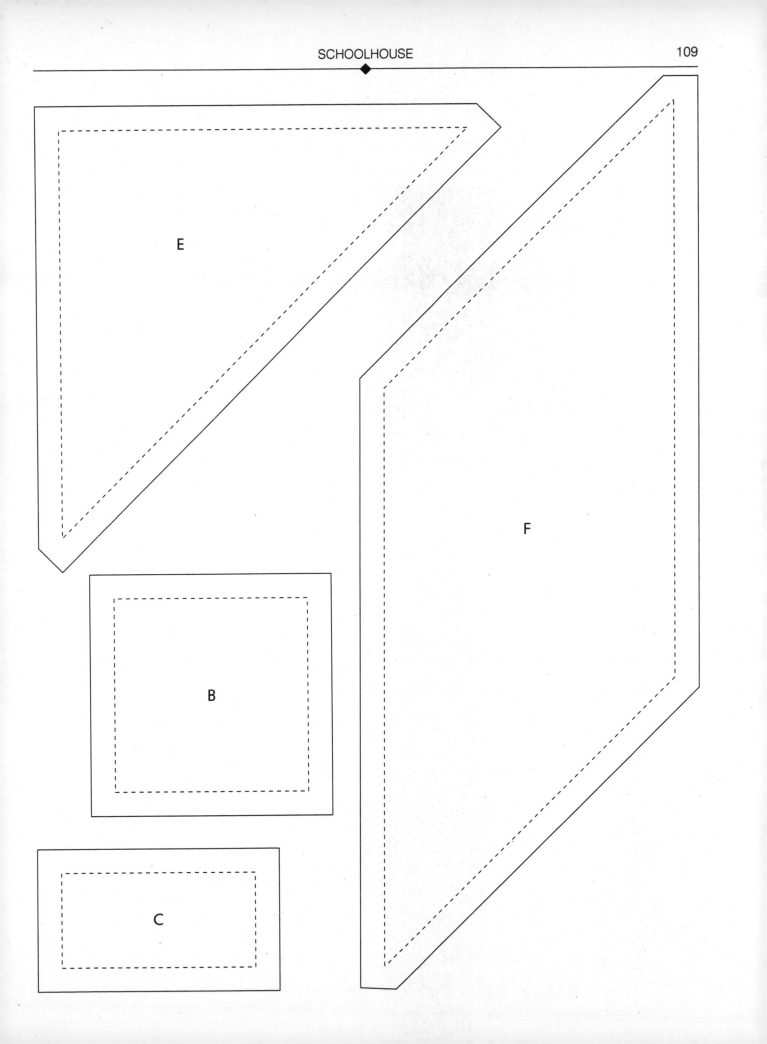

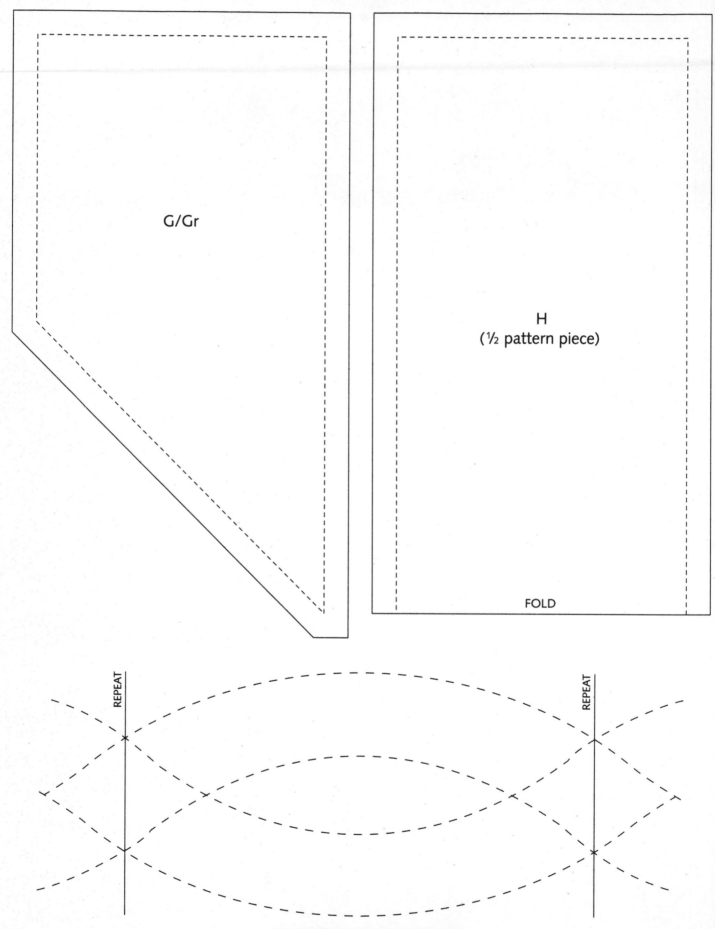

G/Gr

H
(½ pattern piece)

FOLD

REPEAT

REPEAT

Small Cable Quilting Design

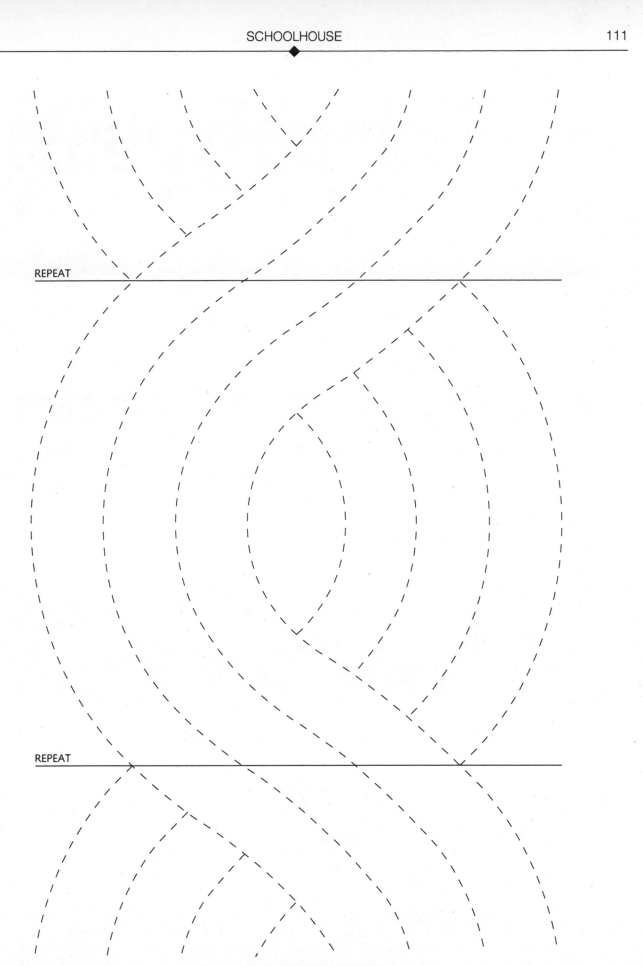

REPEAT

REPEAT

Large Cable Quilting Design

• *SUNSHINE AND SHADOWS* •

*S*ubtle gradations of pink cast a shimmering glow throughout this miniature Sunshine and Shadows quilt. Traditionally thought of as Amish in origin, such a design could just as easily be made in prints. This easy-to-piece quilt doesn't take very long to finish and would make an extra-special gift for a lucky friend or member of your family.

Skill Level: Easy

SIZE

Finished quilt is 27⅛ inches square
Quilt consists of 1 pieced center square,
    4 setting triangles, and inner and outer
    borders

FABRIC REQUIREMENTS AND SUPPLIES

❖ ⅛ yard dark pink (pieced center section)
❖ ⅛ yard medium pink (pieced center section)
❖ ⅛ yard light pink (pieced center section)
❖ ⅛ yard green (pieced center section)
❖ ⅛ yard tan (pieced center section)
❖ ⅜ yard medium-light pink (corner triangles)
❖ ½ yard rust (inner border, binding)
❖ ½ yard brown (pieced center section and outer border)
❖ ⅞ yard backing fabric
❖ ¼ yard for binding (if other than rust)
❖ Crib-size batting (45 × 60 inches)

CUTTING CHART

Pattern pieces on page 117

FABRIC	PATTERN PIECES	
	A	B
Dark pink	28	
Medium pink	28	
Light pink	28	
Green	28	
Tan	28	
Medium-light pink		4
Brown	29	

✄ Cut 2 rust inner border strips,
    each 1⅞ × 18⅞ inches
✄ Cut 2 rust inner border strips,
    each 1⅞ × 21⅝ inches
✄ Cut 2 brown outer border strips,
    each 3½ × 21⅝ inches
✄ Cut 2 brown outer border strips,
    each 3½ × 27⅝ inches
✄ Cut backing to 31 inches square
✄ Cut 3 rust binding strips,
    each 3 × 44 inches
✄ Cut batting to 31 inches square

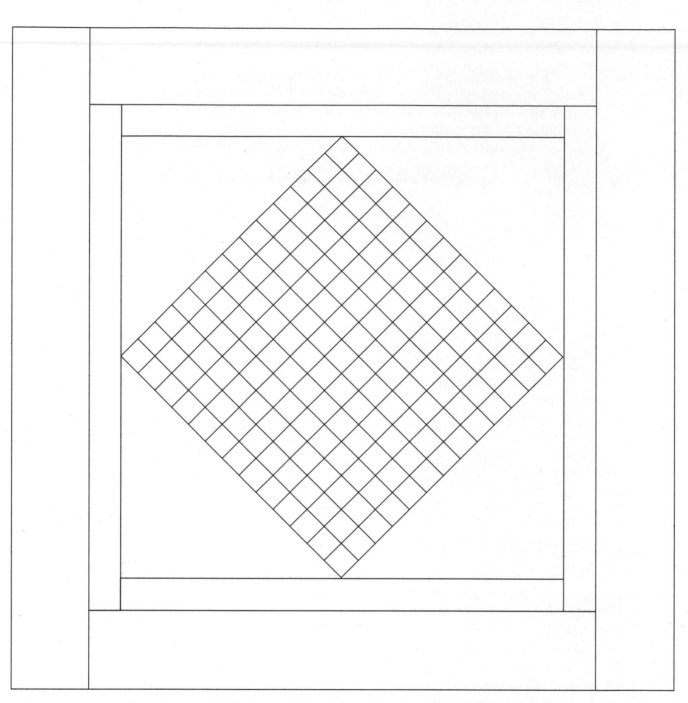

Sunshine and Shadows Color Plan: You may photocopy this page
and use it to experiment with color schemes for your quilt.

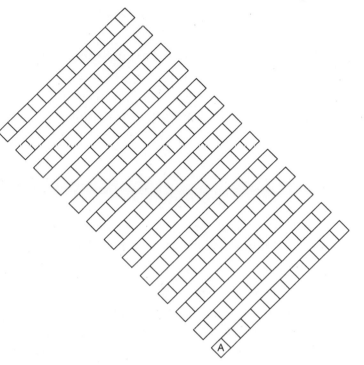

Piecing the Block

1. The center pieced section of the quilt is made of 13 rows, each containing 13 A squares. Referring to the photograph on page 112 for color placement, lay out all the A squares in rows, as shown in **Diagram 1.** Sew the A pieces in each row together, then join the 13 rows to complete the top.

2. For rest of the steps in this section, refer to the **Quilt Assembly Diagram.** Sew a medium-light pink B triangle to each side of the center pieced section.

Diagram 1

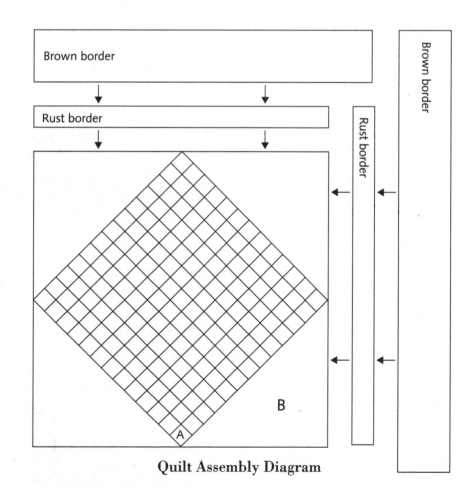

Quilt Assembly Diagram

3. Sew the 1⅞ × 18⅞-inch rust inner borders to the top and bottom of the quilt.

4. Sew the 1⅞ × 21⅝-inch rust inner borders to the sides of the quilt.

5. Sew the 3½ × 21⅝-inch brown outer borders to the top and bottom of the quilt.

6. Sew the 3½ × 27⅝-inch brown outer borders to the sides of the quilt.

Quilting

1. Mark the B corner triangles with the **Floral Vine Quilting Design** on page 118.

2. Mark the rust inner border with the **Tulip Quilting Design** on page 119.

3. Mark diagonal lines in both directions through each of the squares in the center pieced section.

4. Mark a single floral motif from the **Floral Vine Quilting Design** in each corner of the brown outer border.

5. Mark diagonal lines at 1-inch intervals in all the brown outer borders.

6. Layer the quilt top, batting, and backing and baste together. Refer to page 239 for pointers on how to layer and baste.

7. Quilt all the marked lines. (See page 239 for details on the quilting stitch.)

Finishing

1. To make the binding, sew the short ends of the 3 binding strips together with diagonal seams. Trim the excess fabric and press these seams open. (For more details on how to make and attach binding, see page 240.)

2. Fold this long strip in half, wrong sides together, and press, creating a lengthwise fold.

3. Sew the binding to the quilt.

4. Sign and date your quilt.

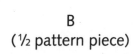

A

B
(½ pattern piece)

FOLD

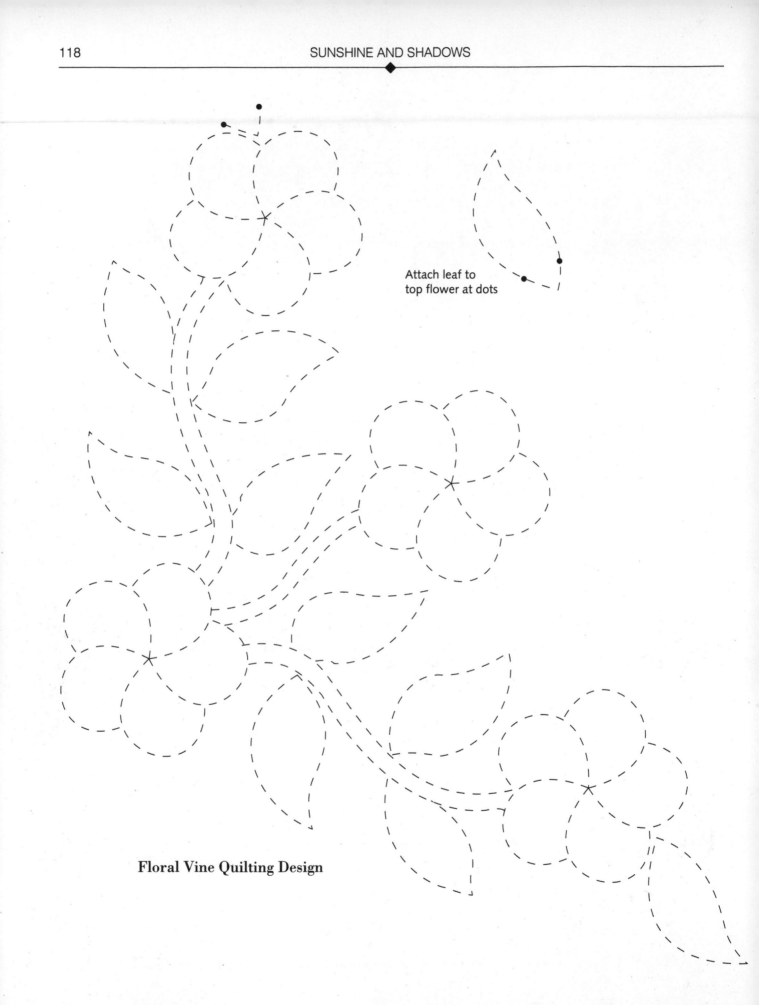

Attach leaf to
top flower at dots

Floral Vine Quilting Design

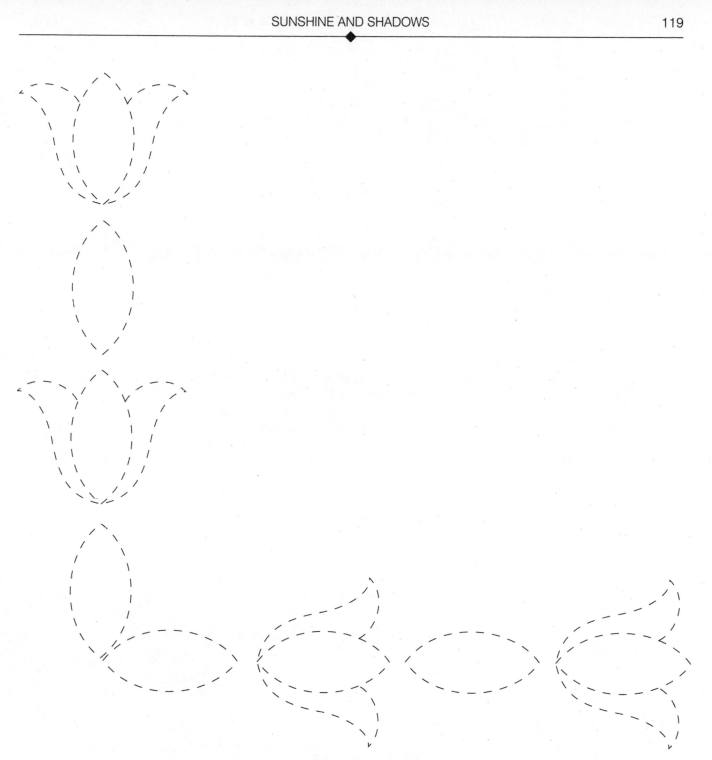

Tulip Quilting Design

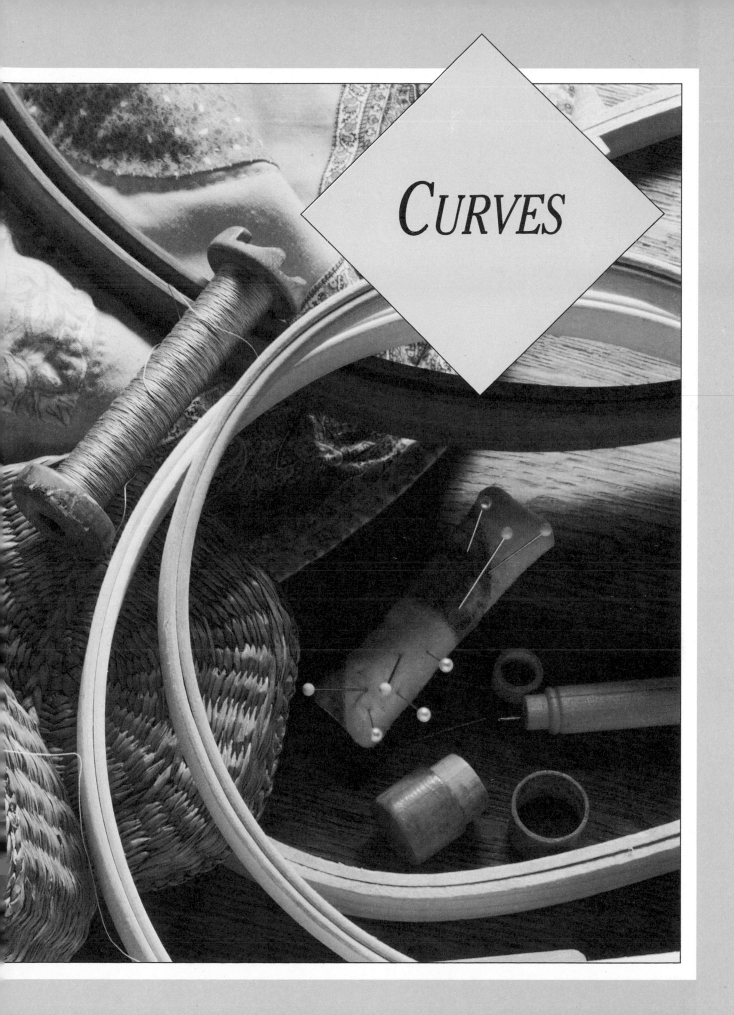

CURVES

• BEAUTY EVERLASTING •

*A*t first glance, this quilt looks very much like the New York Beauty or Rocky Mountain Road pattern, but close inspection reveals that it is unique in the way its triangles are arranged. Some of its elements may remind you of Tree Everlasting and Circular Saw, but Beauty Everlasting seems to be an original design by a creative quiltmaker who may have been inspired by these other quilts. Try making it in some of the wonderful period reproduction prints available now, or create a colorful scrap quilt from your own stash of prints and solids.

Skill Level: Challenging

SIZE

Finished block is 10½ inches square
Finished quilt is 84 × 97½ inches
Quilt consists of 42 pieced blocks, 97 pieced lattice strips, and 56 pieced cornerstones

FABRIC REQUIREMENTS AND SUPPLIES

- ❖ 5 yards muslin (block centers and binding)
- ❖ 5½ yards assorted light prints (pieced blocks, lattice strips)
- ❖ 6¾ yards assorted medium to dark red and blue prints (pieced blocks, lattice strips, cornerstones)
- ❖ 5¾ yards muslin for backing
- ❖ ⅝ yard for binding (if other than muslin)
- ❖ Queen-size batting (90 × 102 inches)

CUTTING CHART

Pattern pieces on pages 128 and 129

FABRIC										PATTERN PIECES
	A	B	C	D	Dr	E	F	G	H
Muslin	42								
Assorted light prints			336	84	84			1358	
Assorted medium to dark red and blue prints		420				84	791	112	28

✂ Cut 2 pieces of fabric for backing, each 44 × 101 inches

✂ Cut 9 muslin binding strips, each 2 × 44 inches

✂ Cut batting to 88 × 101 inches

Beauty Everlasting Color Plan: You may photocopy this page
and use it to experiment with color schemes for your quilt.

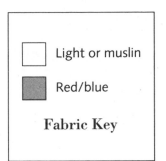

Light or muslin

Red/blue

Fabric Key

Piecing the Block

Note: Be sure to vary the red and blue prints you use in piecing each of the blocks for this quilt. Choose a mixture that pleases you from your collection of red and blue prints.

1. Sew a red/blue print B triangle to a light C triangle, as shown in **Diagram 1.** Make a total of 336 of these BC units for each block.

Diagram 1

2. Referring to **Diagram 2,** sew a curved row of 4 of these BC units and add one more B triangle at the lower edge.

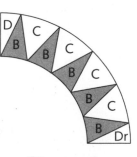

Diagram 2

3. Sew a light D triangle to one end of the curved BC row and a light D reverse (Dr) triangle to the other end, as shown in **Diagram 2.** Make a total of 84 of these curved BCD rows.

4. Sew a red/blue print E piece to the inner curve of *each* BCD row, as shown in **Diagram 3.** Place the BCD unit on top and the E piece on the bottom, right sides together, and place a pin at the midpoint of each. Place another pin at the beginning and a third pin at the end of the seam. As you sew, ease the inner curve of the BCD row to meet the curved edge of the E piece.

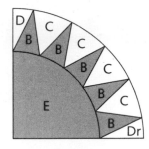

Diagram 3

5. Pin the curved edge of a muslin A piece to a BCDE unit, right sides together, with the A piece on top. Place a pin at the beginning, another pin at the midpoint, and a third pin at the end of the seam. Sew the two pieces together, easing the edge of the A piece to meet the BCDE unit. Sew the other curved edge of this A piece to another BCDE unit. Repeat to make a total of 42 blocks, as shown in **Diagram 4.**

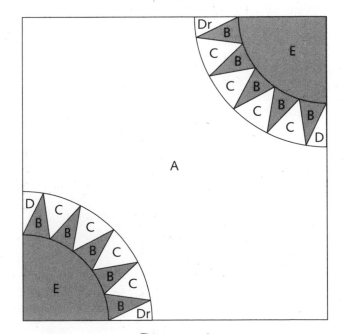

Diagram 4

Piecing the Lattice Strip

1. Sew light G triangles to two sides of a red/blue F triangle, as shown in **Diagram 5.** Make 679 of these GFG units.

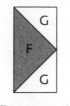

Diagram 5

2. Sew 7 of the GFG units together to create a lattice strip, as shown in **Diagram 6.** Make a total of 97 of these lattice strips.

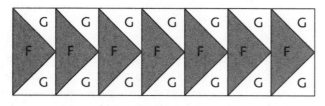

Diagram 6

Piecing the Cornerstones

1. Sew together 4 red/blue print F triangles, as shown in **Diagram 7.** Give some thought to color placement as you sew these pieces together. In the quilt shown in the photo on page 122, you will notice that the red/blue prints match on opposite sides of the cornerstone. (**Diagram 7** also shows this.) Make a total of 28 of these F cornerstones.

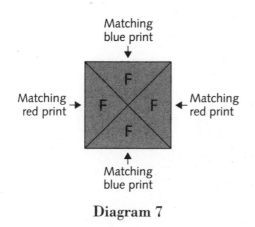

Matching blue print

Matching red print

Matching red print

Matching blue print

Diagram 7

2. Sew 4 red/blue print G triangles to a red/blue print H square, as shown in **Diagram 8.** In the quilt shown in the photo, all of the G triangles within the same cornerstone match. Make a total of 28 of these GH cornerstones.

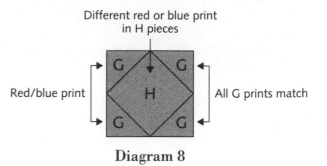

Different red or blue print in H pieces

Red/blue print

All G prints match

Diagram 8

Assembling the Quilt

1. Sew together a row of 6 pieced blocks alternating with 7 pieced lattice strips, as shown in **Diagram 9.** Note that the triangles in the lattice strips face in different directions. Make a total of 7 of these block rows.

2. Sew a horizontal row of 6 lattice strips with 4 F and 3 GH cornerstones placed as shown in **Diagram 10.** Make 4 of these rows.

3. Sew a horizontal row of 6 lattice strips with 3 F and 4 GH cornerstones placed as shown in **Diagram 11.** Make 4 of these rows.

4. Referring to the **Quilt Assembly Diagram,** sew together the block rows and horizontal rows of lattice strips. Be sure to alternate the placement of lattice strip rows, as shown.

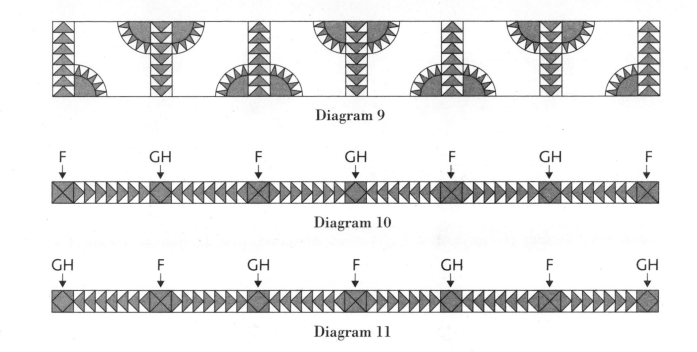

Diagram 9

Diagram 10

Diagram 11

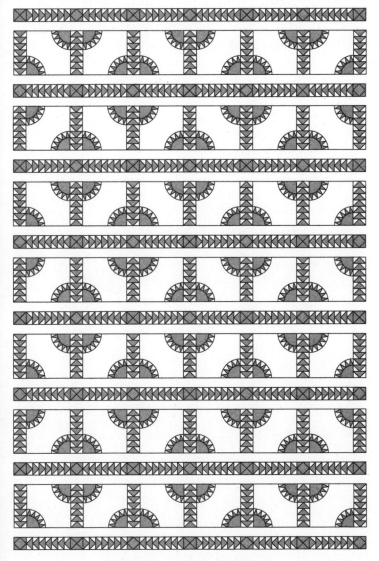

Quilt Assembly Diagram

Quilting

1. Beginning at the outer edges and working inward, mark echo quilting lines at ½-inch intervals in the center (A) portion of each pieced block, as shown in **Diagram 12.**

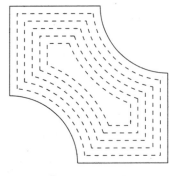

Diagram 12

2. Sew the 2 pieces of backing fabric together with a ¼-inch seam allowance. Press this seam open.

3. Layer the quilt top, batting, and backing and baste together. Refer to page 239 for pointers on how to layer and baste.

4. Quilt in the ditch of each seamline in the pieced areas of the quilt. (See page 239 for details on the quilting stitch.)

S N I P P E T S

When your quilting thread just won't go through the eye of your needle, try clipping it at a sharp angle to make it slip through the needle more easily. Or hold the thread still and "put" the needle onto the thread. Here's a third trick that works with quilting thread only: Pinch a strand of thread hard between your left thumb and forefinger (reverse this, if you're left-handed), with a couple of inches extending out the top. With your other hand, pull the thread gently down between your fingers, so that all you can see from the top is the tiniest little "dot" of thread. Then take your needle and simply "swoop" the eye of it down between your finger and thumb—your needle will be threaded!

Finishing

1. To make the binding, sew the short ends of the 9 binding strips together with diagonal seams. Trim the excess fabric and press these seams open. (For more details on how to make and attach binding, see page 240.)

2. Fold the binding lengthwise, wrong sides together, and press.

3. Sew the binding to the front side of the quilt with a ¼-inch seam allowance, checking to see that the seam lies next to the points of each side F triangle.

4. Bring the binding *and seam allowance* completely around to the back side of the quilt so that the binding will not be visible from the front when sewn. Blindstitch it in place. From the front of the quilt, none of the binding will be visible.

5. Sign and date your quilt.

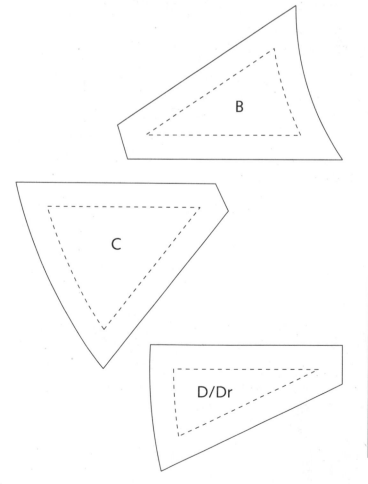

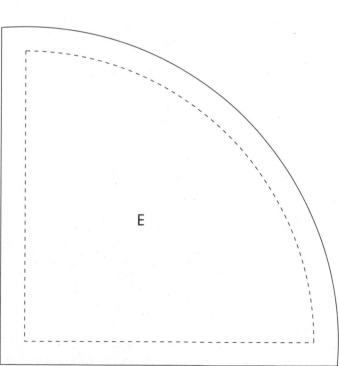

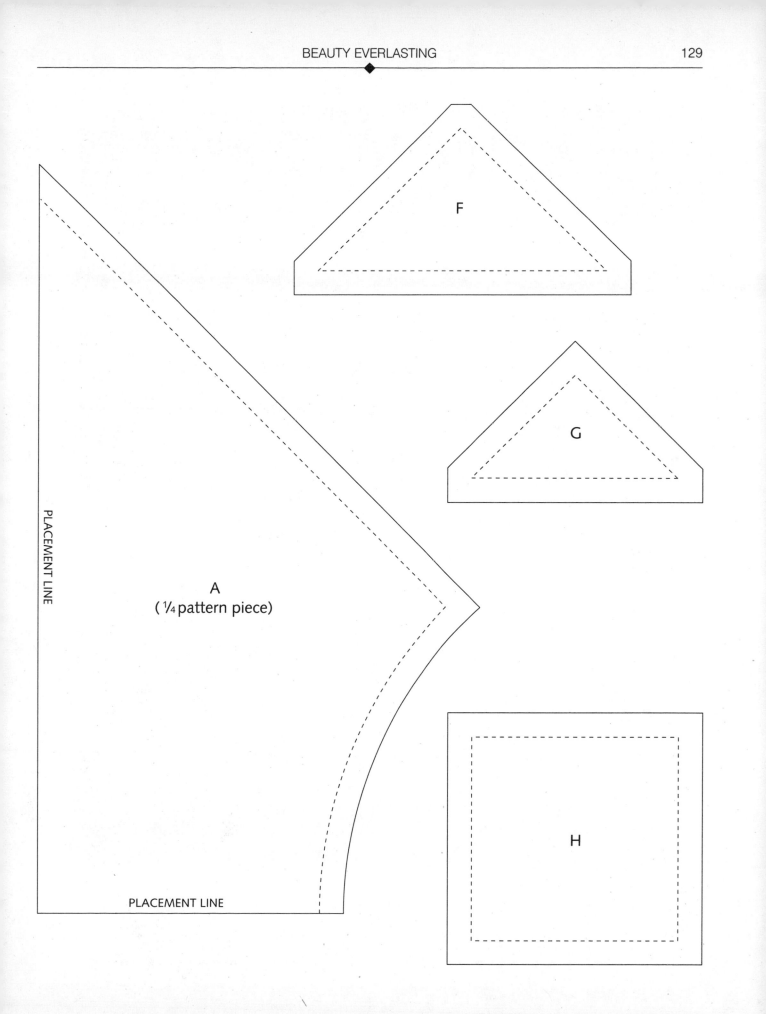

F

G

A
(¼ pattern piece)

PLACEMENT LINE

PLACEMENT LINE

H

◆ *DOUBLE WEDDING RING* ◆

*T*he Double Wedding Ring is an instantly recognizable symbol of American patchwork. It was popular during the lean years of the 1920s and 1930s, probably because it was something most people could afford to make—a scrap quilt. As versatile now as it was in those days, the Double Wedding Ring is still one of the most beloved of all quilt patterns.

Skill Level: Intermediate

SIZE

Finished ring unit is 12 inches in diameter
Finished quilt is 55 × 72 inches
Quilt consists of 48 interlocking blocks

FABRIC REQUIREMENTS AND SUPPLIES

❖ 4¾ yards assorted prints (A and B pieces)
❖ ¾ yard assorted solids (A pieces)
❖ 5 yards off-white solid (C and D pieces, binding)
❖ 4⅜ yards for backing
❖ ⅞ yard for binding (if other than off-white)
❖ Twin-size batting (72 × 90 inches)

CUTTING CHART

Pattern pieces on pages 139 and 140

FABRIC	PATTERN PIECES			
	A	B	C	D
Assorted prints	126	1320		
Assorted solids	126			
Off-white solid			110	48

✂ Cut 2 pieces of fabric for backing, each 30 × 76 inches
✂ Cut binding fabric to 30 inches square
✂ Cut batting to 59 × 76 inches

The pattern pieces for C and D have matching notches indicated on each side. As you cut these pieces, either make a tiny clip into the seam allowance at each of the notches or cut around each notch mark outside the seam allowance.

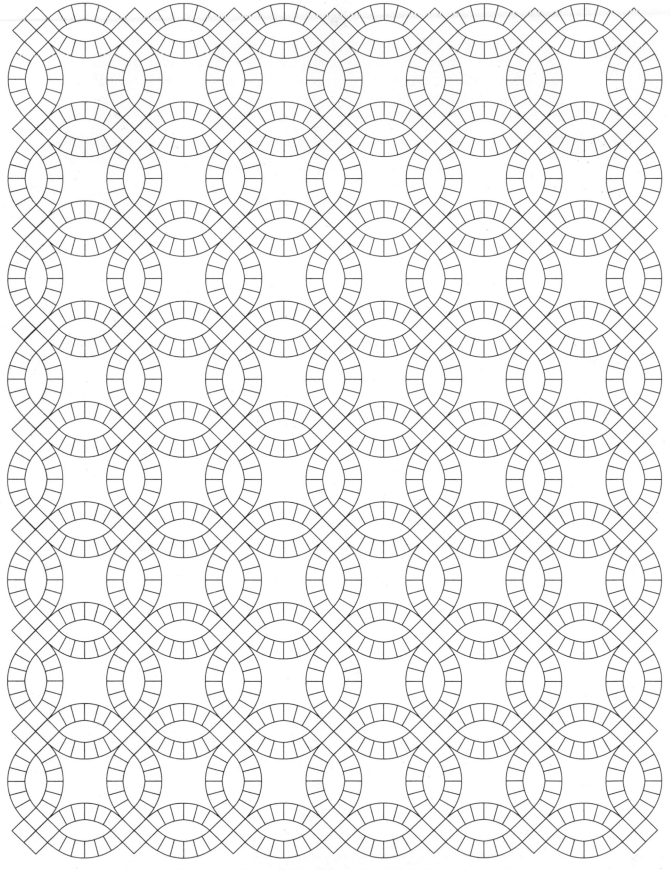

Double Wedding Ring Color Plan: You may photocopy this page
and use it to experiment with color schemes for your quilt.

Print fabric

Solid fabric

Fabric Key

Piecing the Block

1. Sew a row of 6 B pieces, as shown in **Diagram 1,** each of a different print. Make a total of 220 of these B rows, varying the combination of prints in each row.

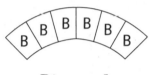

Diagram 1

2. Sew a solid A piece to each end of a B row, creating an ABA row, as shown in **Diagram 2.** (Bright pink solid and purple solid fabrics are used as examples in the text and diagrams.)

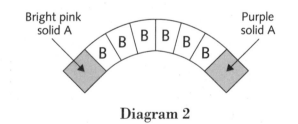

Bright pink solid A

Purple solid A

Diagram 2

3. Make a total of 56 ABA rows, making sure that the first solid A piece in each row is the same color as the last solid you used in the previous ABA row. An example of the color progression in the A pieces is shown in **Diagram 3.** Stack these rows in the order in which you sew them to keep the color progression in order.

4. Place a B row from Step 1 and an off-white C piece right sides together with the B row on top. Pin the middle and the end points of the B row to the C piece, as shown in **Diagram 4** on page 134, and match the notches. Sew the B row to the off-white C piece, easing the edge of the B row to meet the curved edge of the C piece.

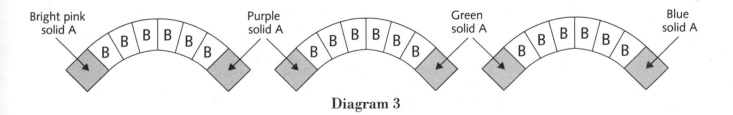

Bright pink solid A

Purple solid A

Green solid A

Blue solid A

Diagram 3

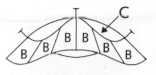

Diagram 4

5. Repeat Step 4 to make a total of 110 of these BC units, shown finished in **Diagram 5.**

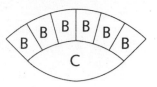

Diagram 5

6. Sew the 56 ABA rows with solid A pieces to 56 of the BC units, as shown in **Diagram 6.** As you sew, keep the ABA row on top and match the midpoint of the inner curve to the notch on the BC unit. These eye-shaped units will be placed *vertically* in the quilt.

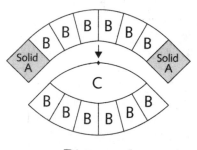

Diagram 6

7. Sew a print A piece to each end of a B row, as shown in **Diagram 7.**

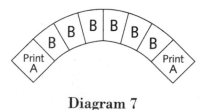

Diagram 7

8. Make a total of 54 ABA rows, making sure that the first print A piece in each row is the same as the last A piece in the previous ABA row. Stack these ABA rows in the order in which you sew them to keep the color progression in order.

9. Sew these 54 ABA rows with print A pieces to 54 of the BC units, as shown in **Diagram 8.** As in Step 6, sew with an ABA row on top and match the midpoint of the inner curve to the notch on the BC unit. These eye-shaped units will be placed *horizontally* in the quilt. Stack the units in the same order in which you sew them.

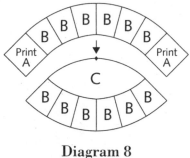

Diagram 8

10. Referring to **Diagram 9** and the photo on page 130, place the eye-shaped units with solid A pieces in 7 *vertical* rows of 8 units each, making sure that the solid A pieces in adjacent vertical units are the same color.

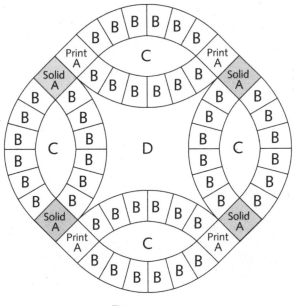

Diagram 9

11. Referring to the photo, place the eye-shaped units with print A pieces in 9 *horizontal* rows of 6 units each. Place these units between the vertical rows of units, making sure that the print A pieces in adjacent horizontal units follow the correct progression of color.

12. Place an off-white D piece between each of the eye-shaped units. This completes the layout of the quilt top. Before assembling the pieces, double-check the color placement to be sure that all the print and solid A pieces are where they should be. It will also help to mark the dots at the ends of each seam allowance on the D pieces.

Assembling the Quilt

1. Beginning at the lower left corner of the quilt, sew 4 eye-shaped units to a D piece, as shown in **Diagram 9,** making sure that the print and solid A pieces are in the proper positions.

2. Moving to the right of the quilt layout, sew the next 3 eye-shaped units to the next D piece, as shown in **Diagram 10.** Check to see that each A piece is in the correct position for the proper color sequence.

3. Sew the free side of this D piece to the first completed "ring," as shown in **Diagram 11,** leaving ¼ inch free at the beginning and end of the seam.

4. Continue sewing 3 eye-shaped units to each succeeding D piece and sewing the free side of the D piece to the previously completed ring. Before sewing each seam, make sure that the solid and print A pieces are placed correctly to maintain the proper color sequence. As you sew, be sure to leave ¼ inch free at the beginning and end of the seam. This completes the bottom row of the quilt top, as shown in the **Quilt Assembly Diagram** on page 136.

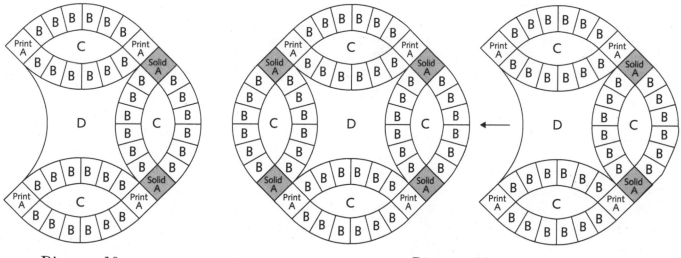

Diagram 10   Diagram 11

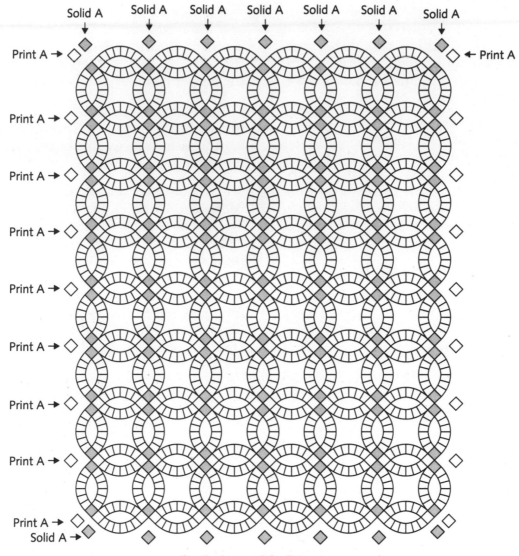

Solid A   Solid A   Solid A   Solid A   Solid A   Solid A   Solid A

Print A →   ← Print A

Print A →

Print A →

Print A →

Print A →

Print A →

Print A →

Print A →

Print A →
Solid A →

Quilt Assembly Diagram

5. Referring to **Diagram 12,** assemble the first ring of the second row by sewing 3 eye-shaped units to a D piece, checking the color placement of each A piece.

6. Referring to **Diagram 13,** sew this ring to the top of the first ring in the bottom row. This seam should begin and end at the point where the 2 lower A pieces come together. This will leave ¼ inch free at the beginning and end of this seam.

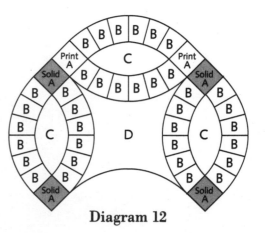

Diagram 12

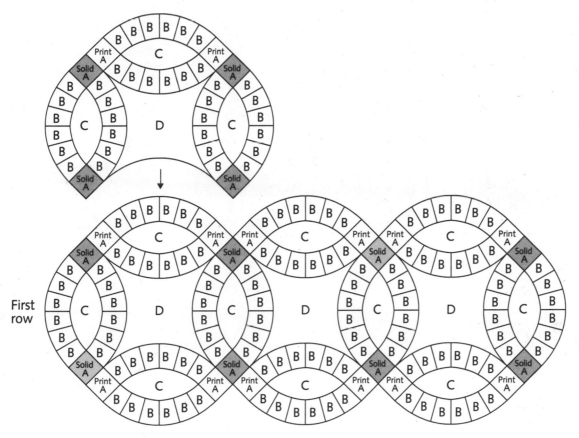

Diagram 13

7. Referring to **Diagram 14,** assemble the second ring of the second row by sewing 2 eye-shaped units to a D piece, checking the color placement of each A piece and leaving ¼ inch free at the beginning and end of the seam.

8. Referring to **Diagram 15** on page 138, sew this ring to the first ring of the second row. Match the dot on the D piece to the juncture of the A pieces in the row below. Then sew the bottom of this ring to the ring below it in the first row.

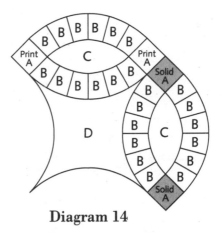

Diagram 14

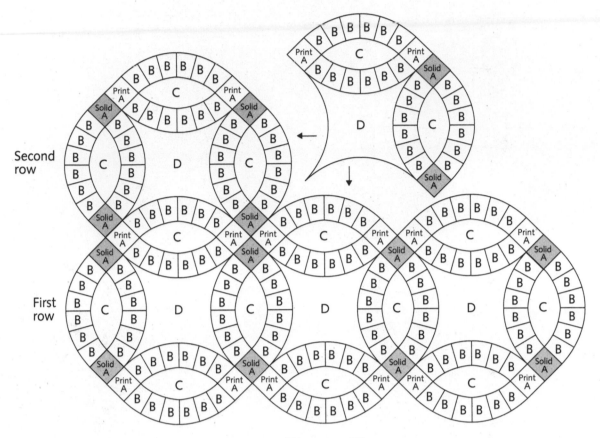

Diagram 15

9. Continue sewing rings and attaching them to the rings in the first row. After this point, each of the remaining 6 rows in the quilt are sewn in the same manner.

10. When all of the rings are sewn together to complete the 8 rows, refer to the **Quilt Assembly Diagram** on page 136 and set in a print A piece at the beginning and end of each horizontal row. Check to see that the print or solid of each of these A pieces matches the opposite A piece.

11. Referring to the **Quilt Assembly Diagram,** set in a solid A piece at the beginning and end of each vertical row, checking to see that the color of each A piece matches the opposite A piece. There will be both a print and a solid A piece at each corner of the quilt.

Quilting

1. Mark each off-white D piece with the **Floral Quilting Design** on page 141.

2. Mark each off-white C piece with the **Leaf Quilting Design** on page 141.

3. Sew the 2 pieces of backing fabric together with a ¼-inch seam allowance. Press this seam open.

4. Layer the quilt top, batting, and backing and baste together. Refer to page 239 for pointers on how to layer and baste.

5. Quilt all marked designs. (See page 239 for details on the quilting stitch.)

6. Quilt ¼ inch from the edge of each A piece and each B piece.

Finishing

1. Cut the 30-inch square of binding fabric into 2-inch bias strips, referring to page 242 for instructions on cutting bias binding.

2. Sew the binding strips together with diagonal seams. Trim these seams to ¼ inch and press them open.

3. Fold the binding in half, wrong sides together, and press.

4. Referring to page 242 for instructions on how to apply bias binding, match the cut edge of the binding to the cut edge of the quilt and sew the binding to the front of the quilt with a ⅜-inch seam. Beginning at an outer curve, ease in the fullness of the binding and sew to the next inside corner point. At the inside corner point, leave the needle in the quilt, pivot, and sew to the next outer point. At the outer point, miter the binding strip and sew to the next inside corner point. Repeat this process around the entire edge of the quilt, finishing this seam by overlapping the ends of the binding.

5. Bring the binding to the back of the quilt and blindstitch it in place, mitering each inner corner and outer corner.

6. Sign and date your quilt.

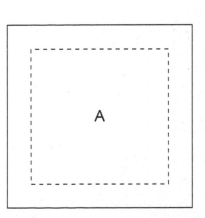

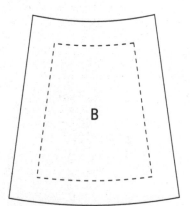

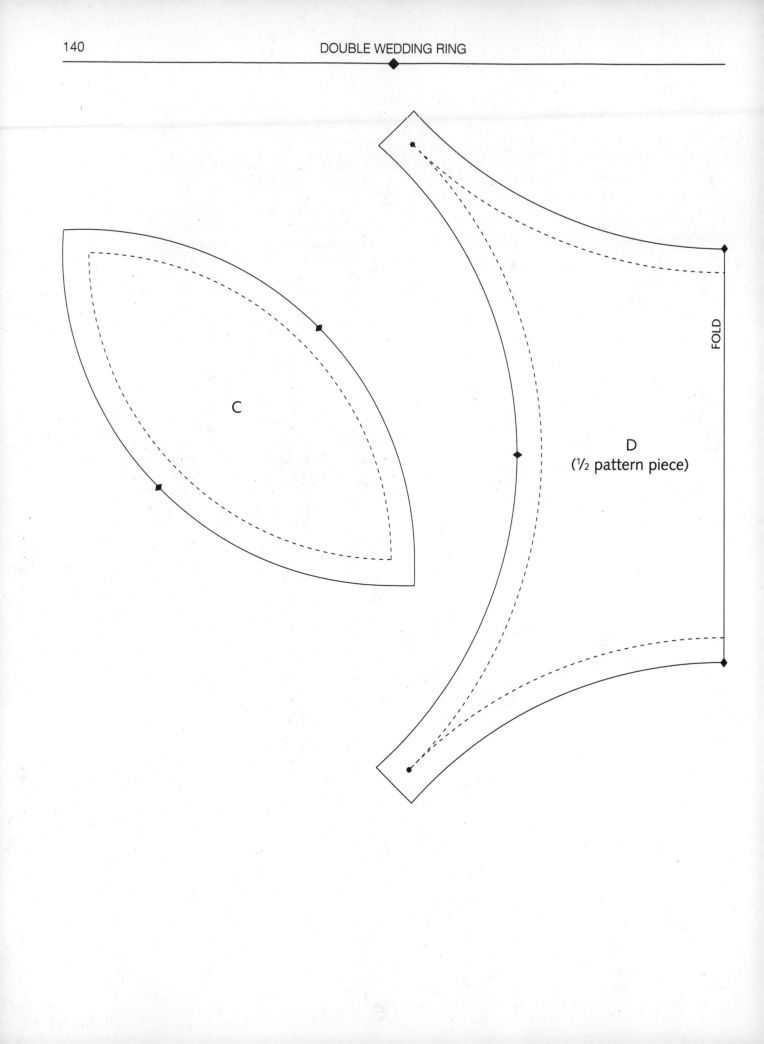

C

D
(½ pattern piece)

FOLD

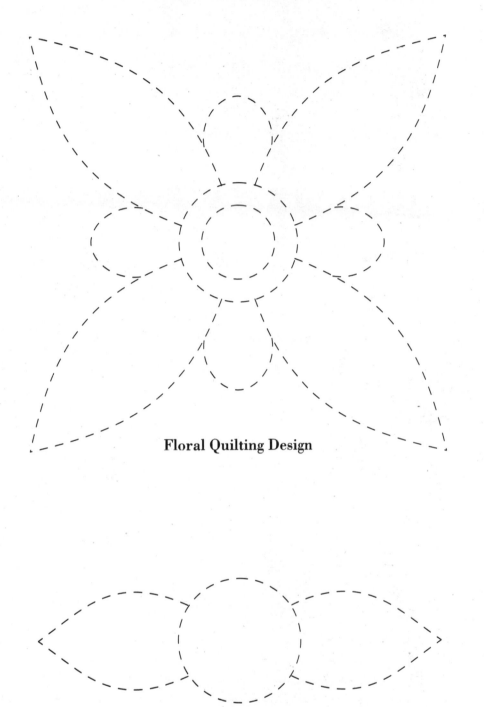

Floral Quilting Design

Leaf Quilting Design

◆ DRESDEN PLATE ◆

*T*his delicate Dresden Plate quilt was the top prizewinner in the antique category at the 1974 Kutztown Folk Festival in Pennsylvania. The soft pastel and delicate green shades are typical of quilts made in the 1920s. You can copy the color scheme of this antique, or you can come up with your own blend of colors to complement the decor in your home. And if your scrap basket is overflowing, this is a great quilt for using up bits of fabric.

Skill Level: Intermediate

SIZE

Finished block is 15 inches square
Finished quilt is 72 × 87 inches
Quilt consists of 20 Dresden Plate blocks,
    quilted border, and dogtooth binding

FABRIC REQUIREMENTS
AND SUPPLIES

- 6⅞ yards white solid (blocks, borders)
- 3¼ yards assorted prints (plate sections)
- ¾ yard green print (center diamonds, binding)
- 5¼ yards for backing
- ⅜ yard for binding (if other than green print)
- Full-size batting (81 × 96 inches)

CUTTING CHART

Pattern pieces on page 148

FABRIC	PATTERN PIECES	
	A	B
Assorted prints	400	
Green print		80

- ✂ Cut 20 white solid background squares, each 15½ inches square
- ✂ Cut 2 white solid border strips, each 6½ × 73 inches
- ✂ Cut 2 white solid border strips, each 6½ × 88 inches
- ✂ Cut 2 backing pieces, each 38½ × 91 inches
- ✂ Cut 8 green print binding strips, each 1½ × 44 inches
- ✂ Cut batting to 76 × 91 inches

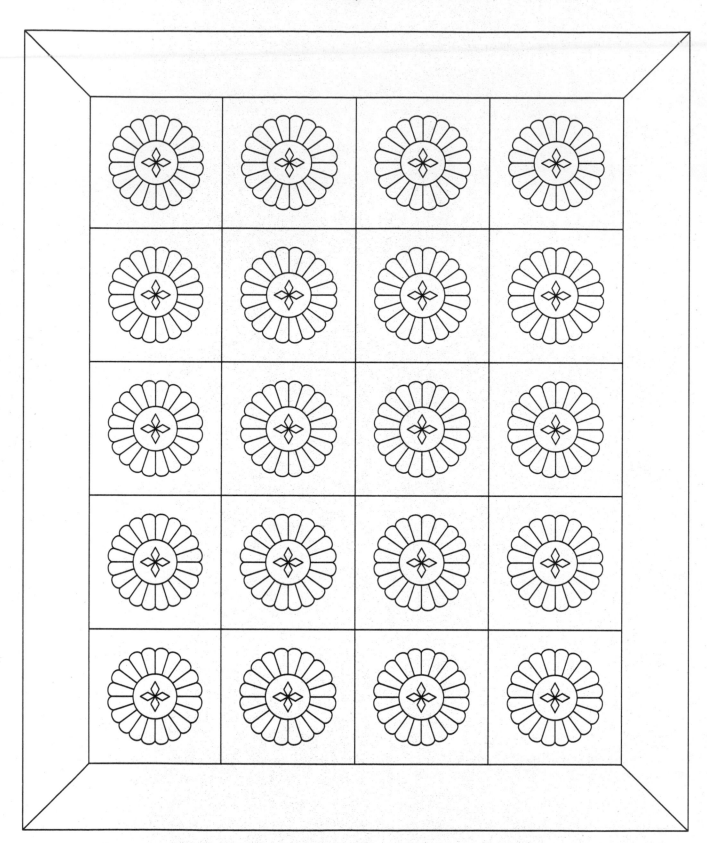

Dresden Plate Color Plan: You may photocopy this page
and use it to experiment with color schemes for your quilt.

Piecing and Appliquéing the Blocks

1. Sew 20 A pieces into a circle, as shown in **Diagram 1.** Begin and end the seams at the dots that are ¼ inch from each edge.

Diagram 1

2. Center the circle on a background block, as shown in **Diagram 2,** and appliqué the inner and outer edges. Refer to page 235 for guidelines on how to appliqué.

Diagram 2

3. With black thread or embroidery floss, appliqué 4 B diamonds in the center of the circle with short, decorative stitches, as shown in **Diagram 3.** Use the decorative stitch featured in "Snippets", or choose your own embroidery stitch.

4. Repeat Steps 1 through 3 to make a total of 20 Dresden Plate blocks.

Diagram 3

S N I P P E T S

Try using this decorative stitch on the center diamonds and the binding. Using black thread or embroidery floss, bring the point of your needle up through an appliqué patch, about ¹⁄₁₆ inch in from the folded edge. Insert the needle into the background fabric directly above this point and you'll create a short, vertical stitch to use as an embellishment on your quilt.

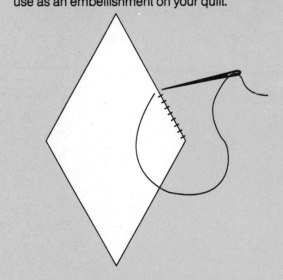

Assembling the Quilt

1. Referring to the **Quilt Assembly Diagram,** sew the blocks together in 5 rows of 4 blocks. Sew together the 5 rows.

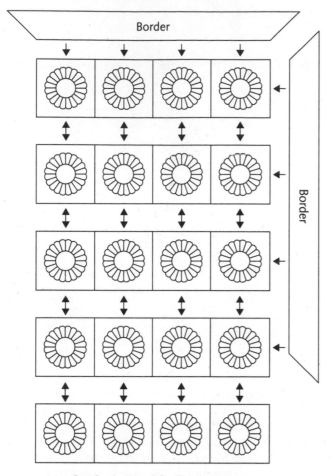

Quilt Assembly Diagram

2. Sew the 6½ × 73-inch white solid top and bottom borders to the quilt, beginning and ending the seams ¼ inch from each edge of the quilt.

3. Sew the 6½ × 88-inch white solid side borders to the quilt, beginning and ending the seams ¼ inch from each edge.

4. Miter the corner seams; trim the excess fabric to ¼ inch and press the seams open. For instructions on how to miter, see page 237.

Quilting

1. Mark the center of each block with the **Circular Quilting Design** on page 148.

2. Mark one oval motif from the **Circular Quilting Design** at the midpoint of each seam between blocks, as shown in **Diagram 4.**

3. Mark the area between adjoining blocks with the **Diamond Quilting Design** on page 149. Use **Diagram 4** as a reference for placement.

4. Referring to **Diagram 4,** mark a scalloped quilting line around each Dresden Plate. Also mark echoing lines that fill the areas between the Dresden Plates and the **Diamond Quilting Designs.** Be sure these echoing lines do not fill in the ovals marked in Step 2.

5. Mark diagonal lines at 1-inch intervals in each border. Use the photograph on page 142 as a guide for placing these lines.

6. Mark another set of diagonal lines in each border, ¼ inch away from the previous lines.

7. Sew the 2 pieces of backing fabric together with a ¼-inch seam allowance. Press this seam open.

8. Layer the quilt top, batting, and backing and baste together. Refer to page 239 for pointers on how to layer and baste.

9. Quilt ¼ inch from each seam in the Dresden Plates, around the B diamonds, and along all marked designs. See page 239 for details on the quilting stitch.

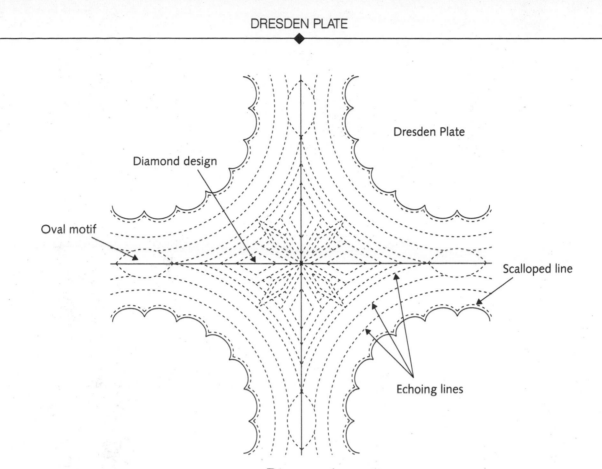

Diagram 4

Finishing

1. To make the binding, sew the short ends of the 8 green print binding strips together with ¼-inch seams and press these seams open.

2. With right sides together, sew a binding strip to the *back* of one edge of the quilt with a ¼-inch seam allowance. Begin and end this seam ¼ inch in from each edge. Trim the fabric even with the edges of the quilt. Repeat this for the other three edges of the quilt.

3. Bring each of the binding strips around to the front of the quilt and pin in place.

4. On each binding strip, mark clipping lines at 2½-inch intervals, as shown in **Diagram 5.** Each clipping line should be ½ inch deep.

5. Clipping only two or three lines at a time, turn under the binding strip ⅛ inch at the highest point on the binding and appliqué, as shown in **Diagram 6.** This forms the "dogtooth" shape in the binding. Adjust each corner as needed so that the binding strips meet symmetrically and form miters on the front and back sides of the quilt.

6. Sign and date your quilt.

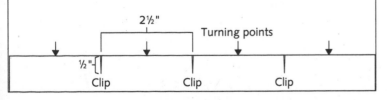

Diagram 5

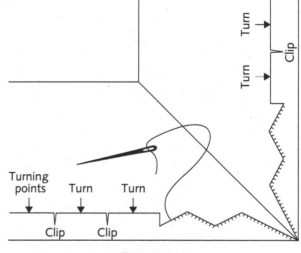

Diagram 6

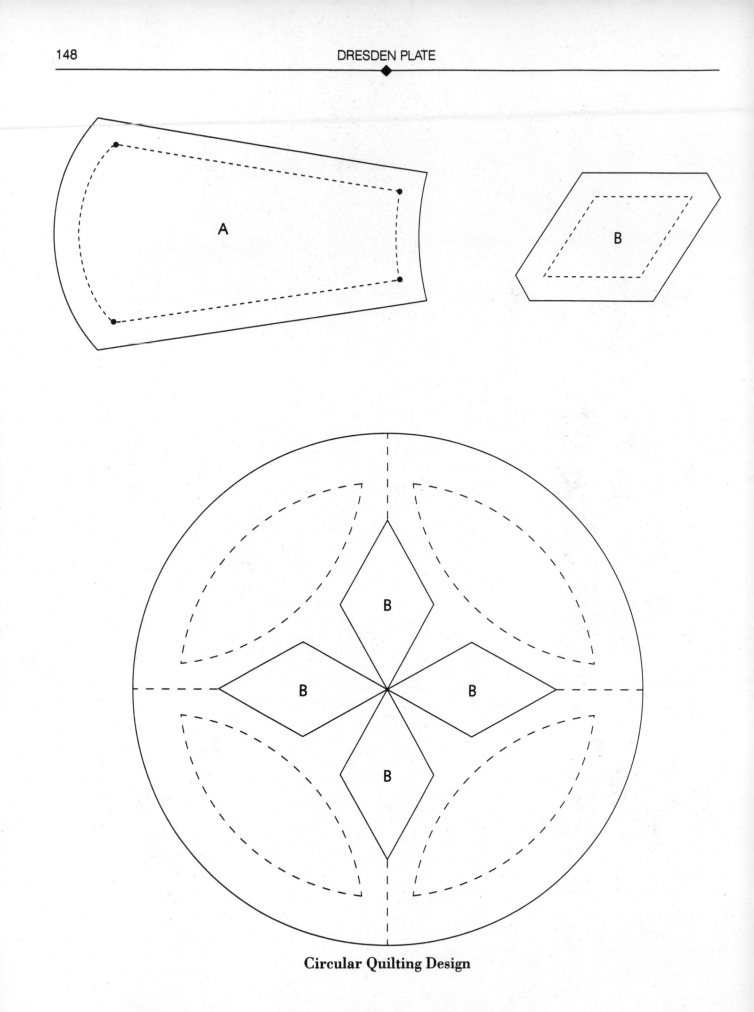

Circular Quilting Design

Diamond Quilting Design

· DRUNKARD'S PATH ·

*T*his two-patch block offers many creative design possibilities and is often known by other names, such as Pebble in a Pond, Around the World, Snake Trail, Snowy Windows, and Country Husband. One particularly popular version, often called Robbing Peter to Pay Paul, has been widely used since the late 1800s. The gentle blue meandering curves of the quilt shown in the photograph are arranged in a commonly used configuration of the classic Drunkard's Path pattern.

Skill Level: Intermediate

SIZE

Finished Drunkard's Path unit is 4 inches
    square
Finished quilt is 72 × 80 inches
Quilt consists of 288 Drunkard's Path units
    and border

FABRIC REQUIREMENTS AND SUPPLIES

❖ 4 yards medium blue solid (pieced blocks,
    binding)
❖ 4⅜ yards white solid (pieced blocks, border)
❖ 4¾ yards for backing
❖ ¾ yard binding (if other than medium blue)
❖ Full-size batting (81 × 96 inches)

CUTTING CHART

Pattern pieces on page 157

FABRIC	PATTERN PIECES	
	A	B
Medium blue solid*	144	144
White solid*	144	144

*Mark the notch on *each* pattern piece as you cut it out of the blue and white fabrics.

✂ Cut 8 white border strips,
        each 4½ × 44 inches
✂ Cut 2 pieces of fabric for backing,
        each 39 × 84 inches
✂ Cut 8 medium blue binding strips,
        each 3 × 44 inches
✂ Cut batting to 76 × 84 inches

Drunkard's Path Color Plan: You may photocopy this page
and use it to experiment with color schemes for your quilt.

White

Medium blue

Fabric Key

Piecing the Drunkard's Path Units

1. With the white B piece on top and right sides facing, pin a medium blue A to a white B at the notch, as shown in **Diagram 1.**

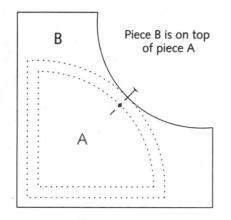

B

Piece B is on top of piece A

A

Diagram 1

2. With the B piece still on top, pin the left edge of B to the left edge of A. Place another pin midway between the first pin and the pin at the notch, as shown in **Diagram 2.** Sew from the edge of the seam to the notch, gradually adjusting the fabric of the B piece as you sew to meet the edge of the A piece, referring to **Diagram 2.** Stop the seam at this point.

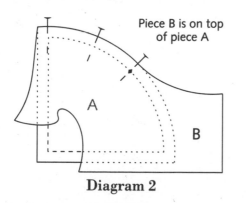

Piece B is on top of piece A

A

B

Diagram 2

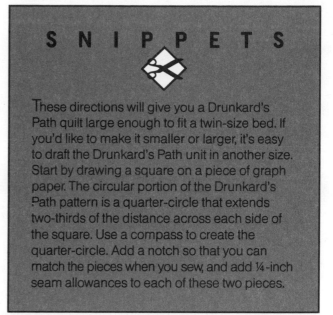

S N I P P E T S

These directions will give you a Drunkard's Path quilt large enough to fit a twin-size bed. If you'd like to make it smaller or larger, it's easy to draft the Drunkard's Path unit in another size. Start by drawing a square on a piece of graph paper. The circular portion of the Drunkard's Path pattern is a quarter-circle that extends two-thirds of the distance across each side of the square. Use a compass to create the quarter-circle. Add a notch so that you can match the pieces when you sew, and add ¼-inch seam allowances to each of these two pieces.

3. Lift the presser foot and match and pin the other edges of the A and B pieces. Complete the seam, easing the edge of the B piece to meet the edge of the A piece.

4. Repeat Steps 1 through 3 to make a total of 144 of these Drunkard's Path units, shown completed in **Diagram 3.** You will use 112 of these units to construct Block I, 30 to make Half-Block A, and 2 will serve as Corner Block I in the quilt.

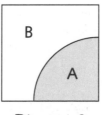

B

A

Diagram 3

5. In the same manner, repeat Steps 1 through 3 to sew a white A piece to a medium blue B piece, reversing the color scheme of the 144 units you just completed in Step 4. Make a total of 144 of these Drunkard's Path units, shown completed in **Diagram 4.** You will use 112 of these units to construct Block II, 30 to make Half-Block B, and 2 will serve as Corner Block II in the quilt.

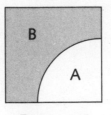

Diagram 4

Assembling the Blocks

1. Sew together 4 Drunkard's Path units (medium blue A and white B), referring to **Diagram 5** for color placement. Make a total of 28 of these blocks, which will be called Block I.

Block I

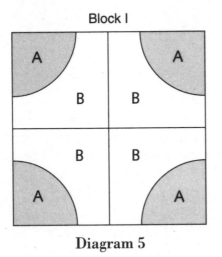

Diagram 5

2. Sew together 4 Drunkard's Path units (white A and medium blue B), referring to **Diagram 6** for color placement. Make a total of 28 of these blocks, which will be called Block II.

Block II

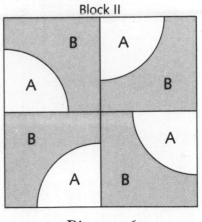

Diagram 6

3. Sew together 2 Drunkard's Path units (medium blue A and white B), placing the colors as shown in **Diagram 7.** Make a total of 15 of these half-blocks, which will be called Half-Block A.

Half-Block A

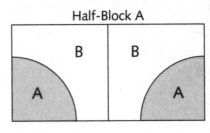

Diagram 7

4. Sew together 2 Drunkard's Path units (white A and medium blue B), placing the colors as shown in **Diagram 8.** Make a total of 15 of these half-blocks, which will be called Half-Block B.

Half-Block B

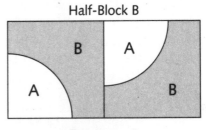

Diagram 8

Assembling the Quilt

1. Arrange and sew the blocks, half-blocks, and corner blocks in rows, referring to the **Quilt Assembly Diagram** for block placement and the photograph on page 150 for color placement. Sew the rows together.

2. Sew together 2 white $4\frac{1}{2} \times 44$-inch border strips to make a border. Repeat this step to make 4 pieced borders.

3. Sew a pieced border to the top of the quilt, matching the border seam to the middle of that edge of the quilt. Trim the excess border fabric. Repeat for the bottom edge of the quilt.

4. Sew a border to each side of the quilt, matching the border seam to the middle of the edge of the quilt. Trim the excess border fabric.

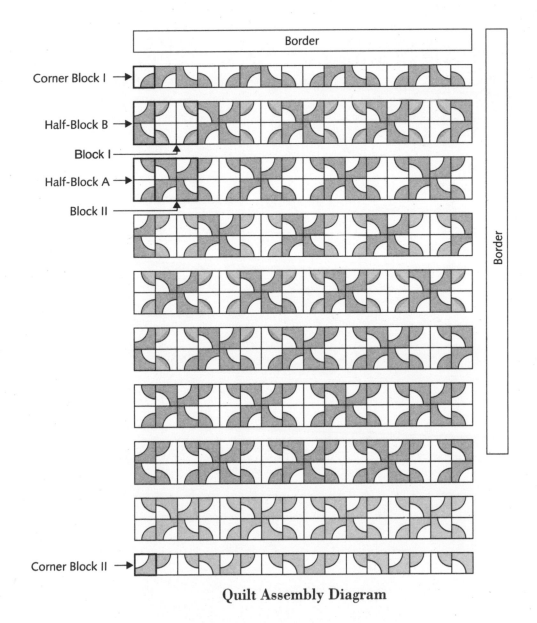

Quilt Assembly Diagram

Quilting

1. Mark diagonal lines in both directions at 1-inch intervals through each block and half-block in the quilt top.

2. Mark diagonal lines at 1-inch intervals in each border.

3. Mark a second set of diagonal lines in each border that are ¼ inch from each of the previous lines.

4. Sew the 2 pieces of backing fabric together with a ¼-inch seam allowance. Press this seam open.

5. Layer the quilt top, batting, and backing and baste together. Refer to page 239 for pointers on how to layer and baste.

6. Quilt all marked lines. (See page 239 for details on the quilting stitch.)

Finishing

1. To make the binding, sew together the short ends of the 8 binding strips with diagonal seams. Trim the excess fabric and press these seams open. (For more details on how to make and attach binding, see page 240.)

2. Fold the binding in half lengthwise, wrong sides together, and press.

3. Sew the binding to the quilt.

4. Sign and date your quilt.

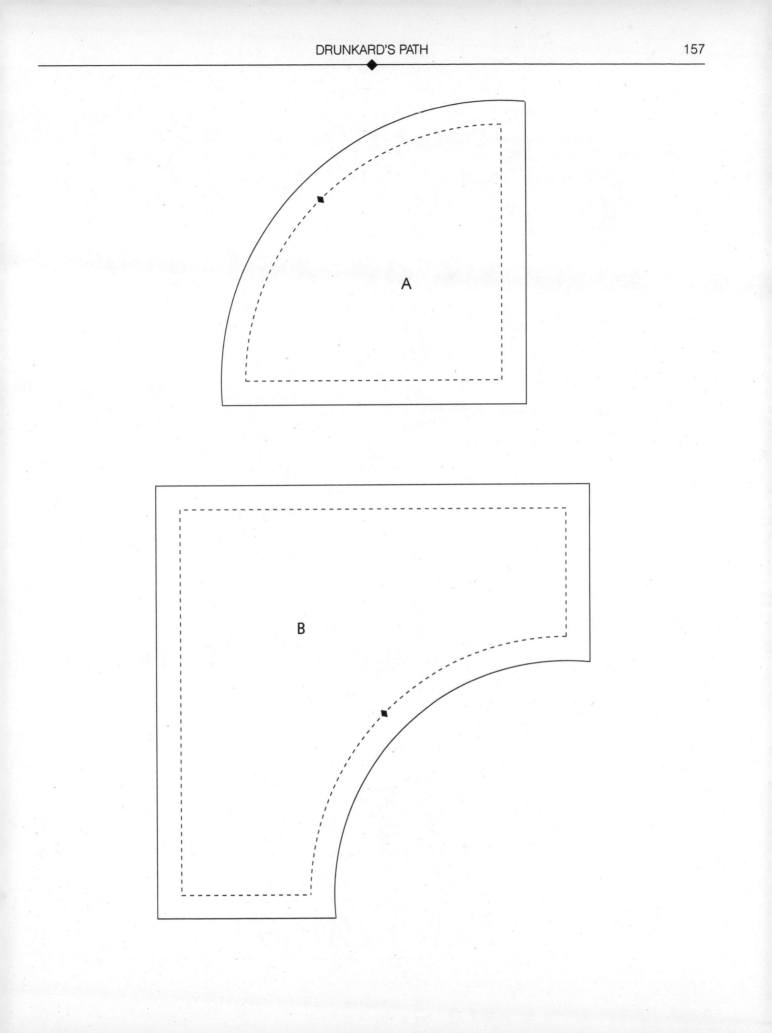

• FANCY PATCH •

A *contemporary, well-balanced color scheme gives a very struc-tured look to this charming fan quilt, but the pattern would also lend itself to a more traditional scrap look. Surprisingly, the nine-patches in each border are appliquéd over the curves of the corner fans rather than pieced, as they are in the lattice strips. If you relish the idea of expressing yourself through designing, use this block to develop other creative fan quilts.*

Skill Level: Challenging

SIZE

Finished block is 16 inches square
Finished quilt is 87½ inches square
Quilt consists of 13 fan blocks, 8 side blocks, 4 corner blocks, 32 lattice strips, 12 nine-patch blocks, and a border

FABRIC REQUIREMENTS AND SUPPLIES

❖ 6¾ yards light-blue-and-cream print (fan blocks, nine-patch blocks, lattice strips, and borders)

❖ ⅝ yard pink solid (small curved corner pieces)
❖ ⅞ yard light blue print (fan pieces)
❖ 1⅝ yards multicolored print (fan pieces, binding)
❖ ⅞ yard dark blue print (fan pieces)
❖ ⅞ yard pink print (fan pieces)
❖ ⅞ yard paisley print (fan pieces)
❖ 1 yard medium blue print (fan pieces, nine-patch blocks)
❖ 7¾ yards for backing
❖ ⅞ yard for binding (if other than multicolored print)
❖ Queen-size batting (90 × 102 inches)

CUTTING CHART

Pattern pieces on pages 166 and 167   Instructions for cutting pattern pieces A, B, and C on page 161

FABRIC	PATTERN PIECES										
	A	B	C	D	E	F	G	H	I	J	K
Light-blue-and-cream print	13	8	4	28	80						4
Pink solid						60		8			
Light blue print							64		8		
Multicolored print							64		8		
Dark blue print							64		8		
Pink print							64		8		
Paisley print							64			4	
Medium blue print				100			64				

(continued)

Fancy Patch Color Plan: You may photocopy this page
and use it to experiment with color schemes for your quilt.

CUTTING CHART—
Continued

✂ For pattern piece A, cut 13 light-blue-and-cream print 16½-inch squares

✂ For pattern piece B, cut 4 light-blue-and-cream print 16⅞-inch squares. Cut each square in half diagonally to make 2 B triangles, for a total of 8 B triangles

✂ For pattern piece C, cut 2 light-blue-and-cream print 16⅜-inch squares. Cut each square in half diagonally to make 2 C triangles, for a total of 4 C triangles

✂ Cut 8 light-blue-and-cream print border strips, each 3½ × 44 inches

✂ Cut 3 pieces of fabric for backing, each 31 × 92 inches

✂ Cut 9 multicolored print binding strips, each 3 × 44 inches

✂ Cut batting to 92 inches square

Piecing the Fan Blocks

1. Sew together 6 different print G pieces, as shown in **Diagram 1**. Be sure to press all seams of these fan pieces in the same direction.

Diagram 1

2. Place the G fan unit and a pink solid F piece right sides together, pinning the beginning, middle, and end points. Sew the pieces together with the G fan unit on top, easing the curved edge to meet the edge of the F piece. This creates a GF unit, as shown in **Diagram 2**. Make a total of 60 of these GF units.

Diagram 2

3. Appliqué the outer curved edge of a GF unit onto each corner of a light-blue-and-cream print A background square, as shown in **Diagram 3**.

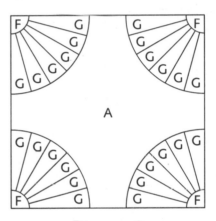

Diagram 3

4. Trim the background fabric to a ¼-inch seam allowance beneath the curved appliquéd seam of each of the GF units.

5. Repeat Steps 1 through 4 to make a total of 13 fan blocks.

Piecing Side Block I

1. In the same manner, appliqué a GF unit onto one corner of a light-blue-and-cream print B triangle, as shown in **Diagram 4** on page 162, and trim out the background fabric to ¼ inch, as before.

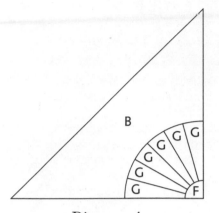

Diagram 4

2. Sew 3 different print G pieces together and sew a pink solid H at the inner curve, as shown in **Diagram 5.** Make 8 of these GH units.

Diagram 5

3. Appliqué one of these GH units at the lower *left* corner of the same B triangle, as shown in **Diagram 6,** trimming out the background fabric below to ¼ inch, as before.

Side Block I

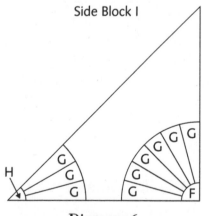

Diagram 6

4. Repeat Steps 1 through 3 to make a total of 4 Side Block I units.

Piecing Side Block II

Following the directions above for Side Block I, make a total of 4 Side Block II units, each with a GH unit at the lower *right* corner, as shown in **Diagram 7.**

Side Block II

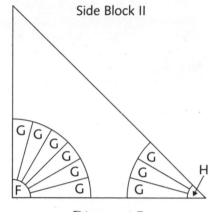

Diagram 7

Piecing the Corner Block

1. Sew together 4 different print I pieces, as shown in **Diagram 8.** Make 2 of these I units.

Diagram 8

2. Finger-press the center fold of a light-blue-and-cream print C triangle and place an I unit on each side, aligning the lower edges with the C triangle and making sure that the curved outer edges will lie 5½ inches from the fold after they are appliquéd, as shown in **Diagram 9.**

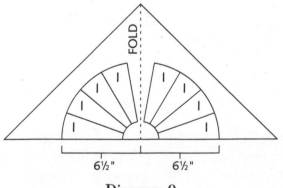

Diagram 9

3. Appliqué the outer curves of these two I units.

4. Place a J piece over the two I units, matching the notches on the J piece to the finished edges of the adjacent I pieces, as shown in **Diagram 10.** Appliqué the two long sides and outer curved edge of the J piece. Baste the outer straight edges of the I pieces to the background triangle, and baste the inner curves of the I and J pieces to the background triangle. The cut edges of the inner curves of the I and J pieces will be covered later by pieced nine-patch blocks.

Corner Block

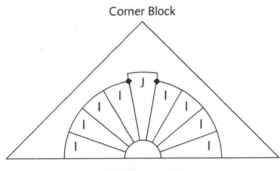

Diagram 10

5. Repeat Steps 1 through 4 to make a total of 4 corner blocks.

Piecing the Nine-Patch Block

Sew together 4 light-blue-and-cream print E squares and 5 medium blue print E squares, alternating colors, as shown in **Diagram 11.** Make a total of 20 nine-patch blocks.

E	E	E
E	E	E
E	E	E

Diagram 11

Assembling the Quilt

Note: This quilt consists of 5 diagonal rows of fan blocks that are surrounded by D and K lattice strips, nine-patch blocks, Side Blocks I and II, and corner blocks. As you sew the quilt together, refer closely to the **Quilt Assembly Diagram** on page 164 for each of the 5 rows.

1. For Row 1: Sew a light-blue-and-cream D lattice strip to the top and bottom of a fan block. Sew a Side Block I to the top D lattice strip and a Side Block II to the bottom D lattice strip. Then sew a corner block at the lower left side of the fan block. This completes Row 1.

2. For Row 2: Sew a row of 3 fan blocks with D lattice strips between them. Then sew a vertical row of 3 D lattice strips with nine-patch blocks between them. Sew this vertical row of D lattice strips and nine-patches to the left side of the row of fan blocks. Now sew a light-blue-and-cream K lattice strip to the top and bottom of this row of blocks, D lattice strips, and nine-patches. Now sew a Side Block II to the top and a Side Block I to the bottom of this unit. This completes Row 2.

3. For Row 3: Sew a row of 5 fan blocks with D lattice strips between them. Then sew a vertical row of 5 D lattice strips with nine-patch blocks between them. Repeat this to make another row of D lattice strips and nine-patches. Sew one of these rows on either side of the row of fan blocks. Finally, sew a corner block at the top and bottom of this row. This completes Row 3.

4. For Row 4: Sew a row of 3 fan blocks with D lattice strips between them. Then sew a vertical row of 3 D lattice strips with nine-patch blocks between them. Sew this vertical row of D lattice strips and nine-patch blocks to the right side of the row of fan blocks. Sew K lattice strips to the top and bottom of this row. Sew a Side Block I to the top and a Side Block II to the bottom, completing Row 4.

5. For Row 5: Sew 2 D lattice strips to the top and bottom of a fan block. Sew a Side Block II to the top D lattice strip and a Side Block I to the bottom D lattice strip. Sew a corner block to the top right side of this unit, completing Row 5.

6. Sew the 5 diagonal rows of the quilt together and trim the edges of the K lattice strips even with the edges of the quilt.

7. Place a nine-patch block over the center area of one corner block so that the inner edges of the I and J pieces are covered, as shown in **Diagram 12** on page 164. Appliqué, using a ¼-inch seam allowance. Repeat for each of the three remaining corners.

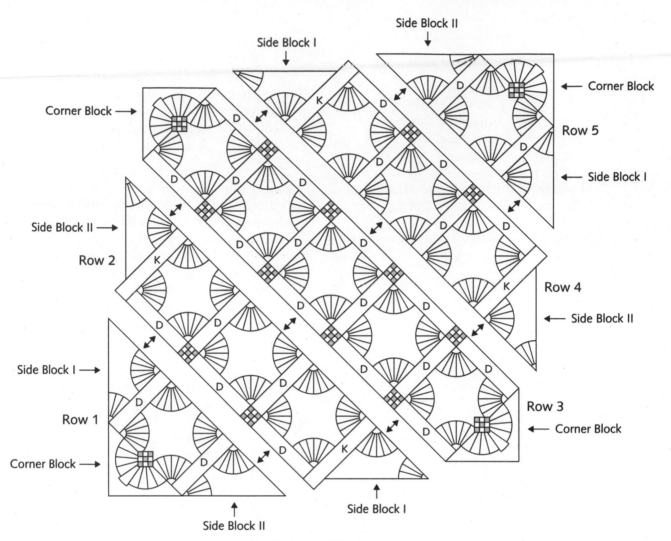

Side Block II

Side Block I

Corner Block

Corner Block

Row 5

Side Block I

Side Block II

Row 2

Row 4

K

Row 1

Side Block II

Side Block I

Side Block I

Corner Block

K

Row 3

Corner Block

Side Block II

Side Block I

Quilt Assembly Diagram

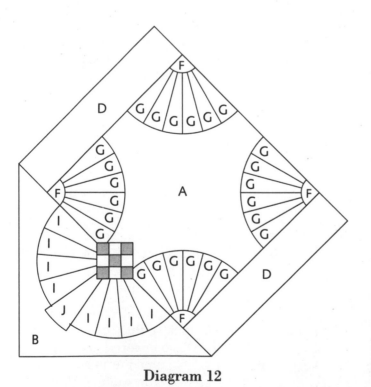

Diagram 12

Adding the Borders

1. Sew together the short ends of 2 light-blue-and-cream 3½ × 44-inch border strips. Press this seam open. Make 4 of these border strip units.

2. Placing the border seam at the center of each side of the quilt, sew the border strips to the quilt. Begin and end each seam ¼ inch from the edge of the quilt.

3. Miter the corner seams, trim the excess fabric to ¼ inch, and press the seams open. For instructions on how to miter, see page 237.

4. Center a nine-patch block on each side of the quilt, over the midpoint of each border, as shown in **Diagram 13**. The nine-patch block should lie across the border seam and a corner of it should meet the pink solid F piece of the fan block next to it.

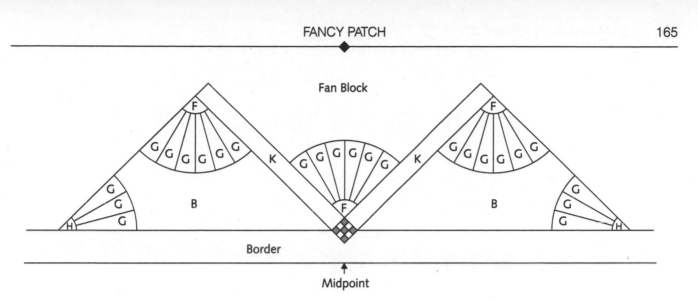

Diagram 13

Quilting

1. Mark diagonal lines at 1-inch intervals in each direction through the center of each square, lattice strip, and border.

2. Sew the 3 pieces of backing fabric together with ¼-inch seam allowances. Press these seams open.

3. Layer the quilt top, batting, and backing and baste together. Refer to page 239 for pointers on how to layer and baste.

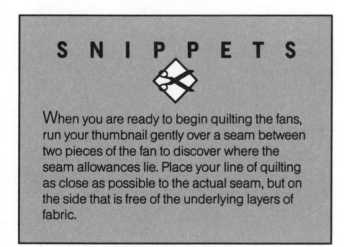

When you are ready to begin quilting the fans, run your thumbnail gently over a seam between two pieces of the fan to discover where the seam allowances lie. Place your line of quilting as close as possible to the actual seam, but on the side that is free of the underlying layers of fabric.

4. Quilt the diagonal lines in the lattice strips and in the middle of each fan block. In the corners of the fan blocks, quilt lines that radiate from the corner and continue through the ditch of the seams between pieces of the fans. Also quilt in the ditch of each of the nine-patch blocks. (See page 239 for details on the quilting stitch.)

Finishing

1. To make the binding, sew the short ends of the 9 binding strips together with diagonal seams. Trim the excess fabric and press these seams open. (For more details on how to make and attach binding, see page 240.)

2. Fold the binding in half lengthwise, wrong sides together, and press.

3. Sew the binding to the quilt.

4. Sign and date your quilt.

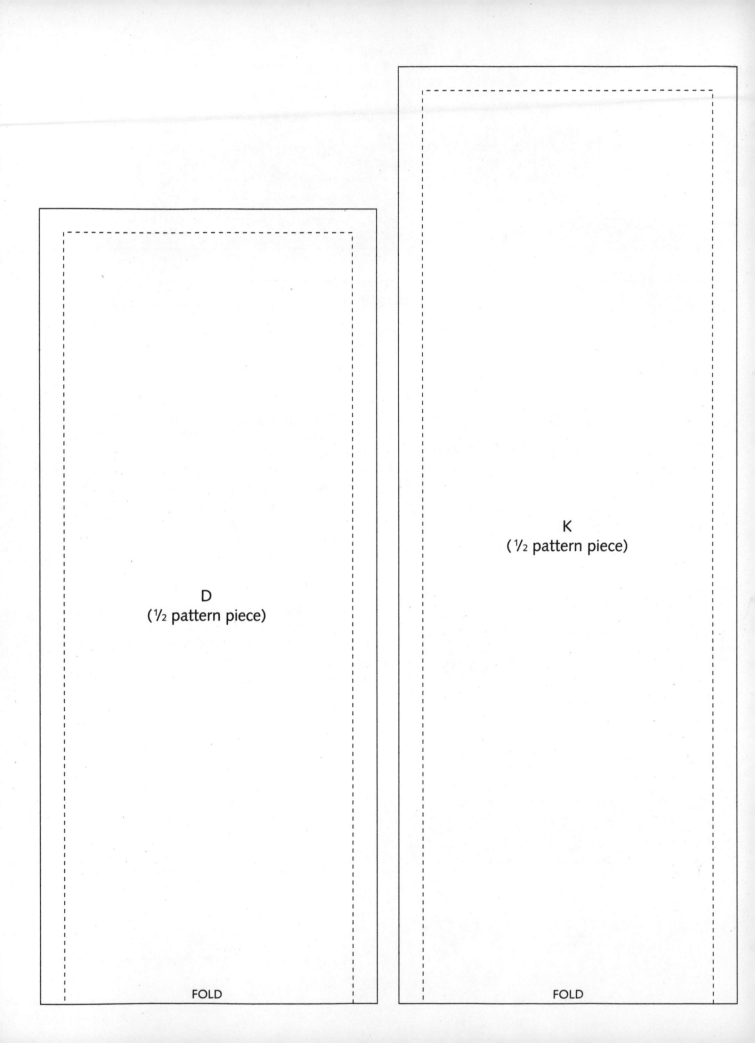

D
(½ pattern piece)

K
(½ pattern piece)

FOLD

FOLD

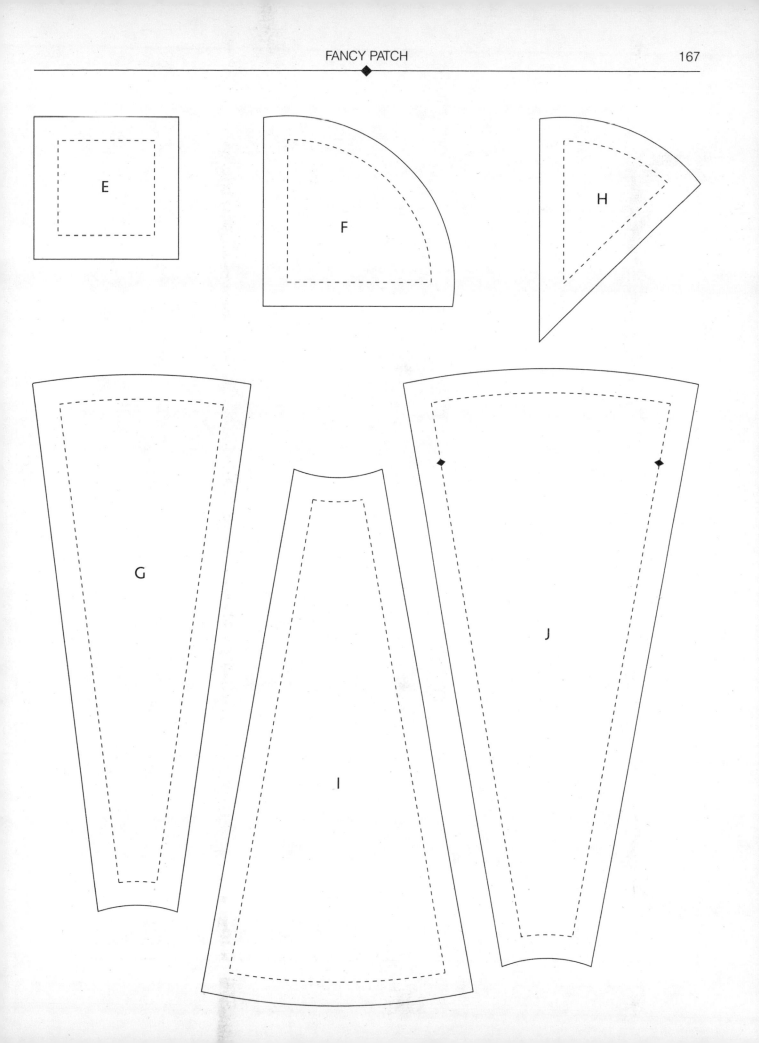

• *GRANDMOTHER'S FLOWER GARDEN* •

*G*randmother's Flower Garden, often associated with the quilt revival of the 1930s, is a perennial favorite that offers plentiful variations, along with the comfort and security of using only one pattern piece. The 1930s pastels, peaches, pinks, greens, and yellows make this quilt a true classic of that time period. Why not explore your scrap bag and plant an array of today's colorful prints and solids in a country garden quilt of your own?

Skill Level: Intermediate

SIZE

Finished quilt is 78½ × 104½ inches
Quilt consists of 95 hexagonal flowers and 8 half-flowers made of concentric rounds of hexagons

FABRIC REQUIREMENTS AND SUPPLIES

❖ ½ yard yellow solid (centers)
❖ 2⅜ yards assorted medium solids (first circle of hexagons)
❖ 4⅜ yards assorted light prints (second circle of hexagons)
❖ 6¾ yards white solid (third circle of hexagons)
❖ 5¼ yards green solid (outer circle of hexagons, binding)
❖ 6¼ yards for backing
❖ 1 yard for binding (if other than green solid)
❖ King-size batting (120 inches square)

CUTTING CHART

Pattern pieces on page 175

FABRIC	HEXAGONS
Yellow	103
Assorted medium solids	602 (cut in groups of 6)
Assorted light prints	1196 (cut in groups of 12)
White solid	1790
Green solid	1202

✂ Cut 2 pieces of fabric for backing, each 42 × 109 inches
✂ Cut binding fabric to 36 inches square
✂ Cut batting to 83 × 109 inches

Grandmother's Flower Garden Color Plan: You may photocopy this page
and use it to experiment with color schemes for your quilt.

Fabric Key

Solid

Print

Green

Piecing the Block

Note: Paper piecing is the traditional method for constructing a Grandmother's Flower Garden quilt. To do paper piecing, you will need 1 paper hexagon for each fabric hexagon in the quilt. From good quality paper, such as postcards or index cards, cut each paper hexagon using pattern piece B on page 175, which is the size of the finished piece. Cut each fabric hexagon using pattern piece A on page 175, which has seam allowances added.

1. Baste the ¼-inch seam allowance of a yellow solid A hexagon around a paper B hexagon, as shown in **Diagram 1,** tucking in the corners as you work around the sides of the hexagon. Press lightly. From this point on, each hexagon in the quilt must be prepared in this way before sewing it to the others. (You can remove a paper hexagon from inside its fabric hexagon after it is completely surrounded by other hexagons, or you may remove all of the paper hexagons at one time when the quilt is completed. To remove a paper hexagon, pull out the basting stitches and gently lift out the piece of paper.)

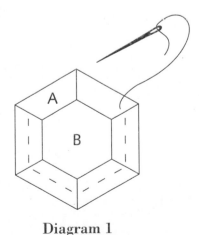

Diagram 1

2. Place a medium solid A hexagon next to the yellow A hexagon so that two sides are aligned, as shown in **Diagram 2.**

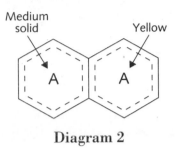

Diagram 2

3. Beginning and ending with a backstitch, sew the 2 hexagons together with a whipstitch, as shown in **Diagram 3,** taking care not to catch the edge of the paper in the seam.

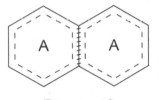

Diagram 3

4. Using the same stitching method for each seam, join 5 more medium solid A hexagons (all the same color) to the center yellow A hexagon, as shown in **Diagram 4.** If desired, remove the paper from the center yellow A hexagon after all 5 hexagons are stitched in position.

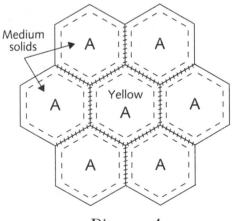

Diagram 4

5. Add a round of 12 light print A hexagons (all the same print), as shown in **Diagram 5,** stitching each seam in the same manner. If desired, remove the paper from the previous round of medium solid A hexagons.

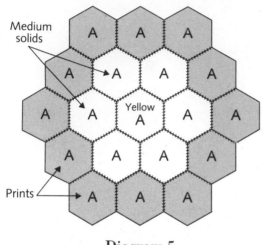

Diagram 5

6. Add a round of 18 white A hexagons, as shown in **Diagram 6,** stitching each seam in the same manner. If desired, remove the paper from the previous round of print hexagons. This round of white A hexagons completes the basic flower unit of the quilt. Make 95 of these flower units.

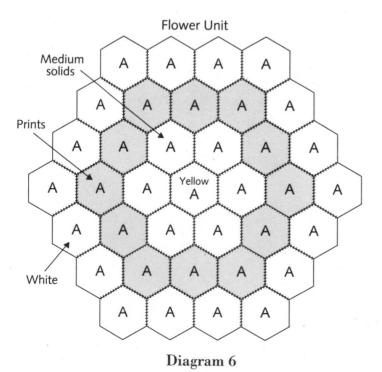

Diagram 6

7. Make 8 half-flower units, as shown in **Diagram 7.**

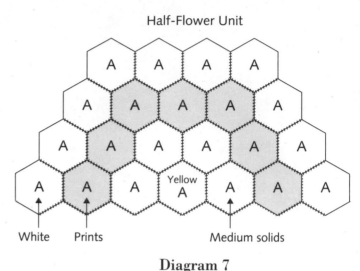

Diagram 7

Assembling the Quilt

1. Sew a row of 3 green A hexagons together, as shown in **Diagram 8.** Make a total of 104 of these rows.

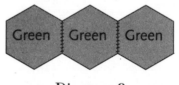

Diagram 8

2. Sew a vertical row of 11 flower units with a row of 3 green A hexagons between each and one at each end, as shown in **Diagram 9.** Make a total of 5 of these rows.

3. Sew a round of green A hexagons around each of the remaining white A hexagons in the 5 vertical rows, as shown in **Diagram 10.**

4. Sew a vertical row of 10 flower units with 3 green hexagons between them and a half-flower unit at each end, as shown in **Diagram 11.** Make a total of 4 of these rows.

5. For the steps that follow in this section, refer to the **Quilt Assembly Diagram** on page 174. Sew the vertical rows together, alternating rows of 11 flower units with rows of 10 flower units and 2 half-flower units.

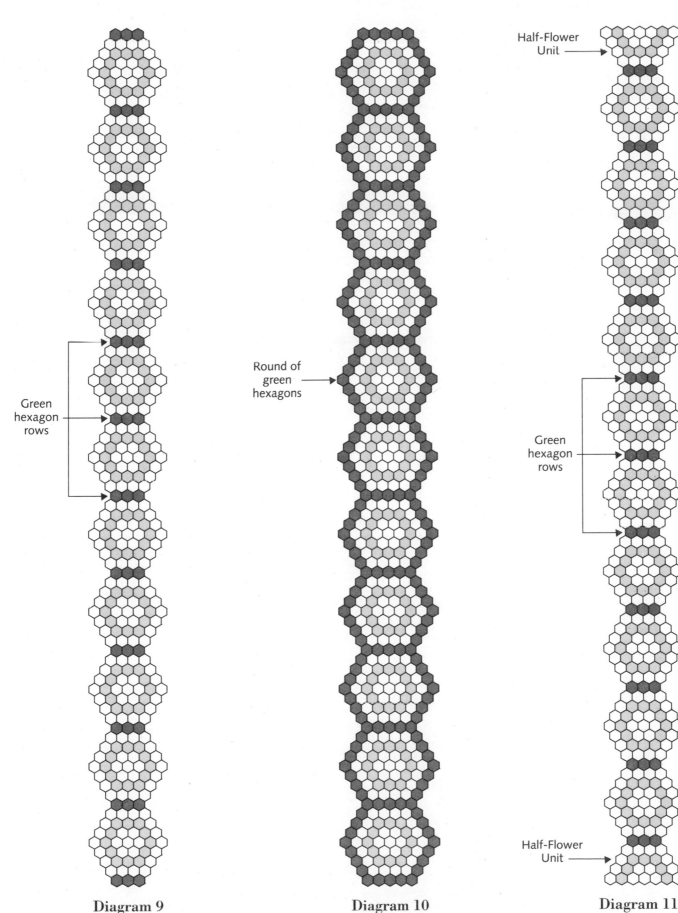

Half-Flower Unit

Green hexagon rows

Round of green hexagons

Green hexagon rows

Half-Flower Unit

Diagram 9

Diagram 10

Diagram 11

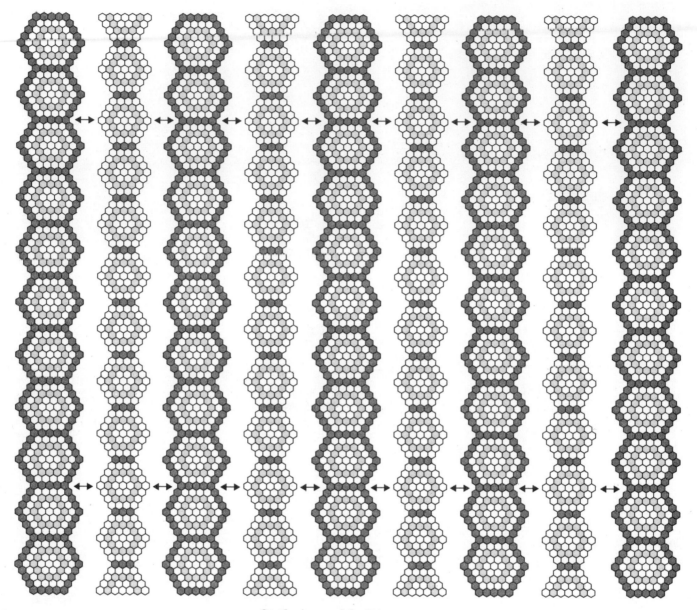

Quilt Assembly Diagram

6. Trim the points from the hexagons at the top and bottom of the quilt, creating straight edges.

7. Trim the hexagons at the sides of the quilt, creating straight edges along the sides of each flower unit.

Quilting

1. Sew the 2 pieces of backing fabric together with a ¼-inch seam allowance and press the seam open.

2. Layer the quilt top, batting, and backing and baste together. Refer to page 239 for pointers on how to layer and baste.

3. Quilt ¼ inch from each seam in each hexagon. (See page 239 for details on the quilting stitch.)

Finishing

1. From the 36-inch square of green solid, cut 2-inch bias strips, referring to page 242 for instructions on cutting bias binding.

2. Sew the bias strips together with ¼-inch seams and press these diagonal seams open.

3. Fold the binding in half lengthwise, wrong sides together, and press.

4. Sew the binding to the quilt, as discussed on page 242, mitering the inner and outer corners on the sides of the quilt.

5. Sign and date your quilt.

S N I P P E T S

The hexagon shape of the classic Grandmother's Flower Garden quilt can also make a beautiful embellishment for garments. Try it out on a small scale and create some "flowers" to appliqué on a child's collar. Use a red or yellow center hexagon for each blossom and surround it with an array of hexagons in colorful prints. Appliqué one or more of these on a purchased white collar and add some embroidered stems and leaves to create a bright spring or summer accessory.

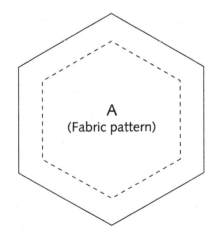

A
(Fabric pattern)

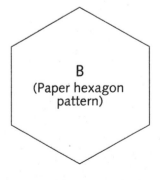

B
(Paper hexagon pattern)

◆ *HEARTS GALORE* ◆

*W*hat could be prettier than a profusion of hearts floating on a delicate pink background? If you've never done appliqué before, this is a wonderful quilt on which to begin. The classic heart shape has three features that can help perfect your appliqué skills: outer curves, an outer point, and an inner point. Practice your favorite stitching techniques in this quilt and you'll be ready for more advanced appliqué in your next project!

Skill Level: Easy

SIZE

Finished block is 6 inches square
Finished quilt is 42 × 48 inches
Quilt consists of 42 appliquéd blocks and a
  border

FABRIC REQUIREMENTS AND SUPPLIES

- ❖ 1⅜ yards pink solid (background blocks)
- ❖ ¼ yard *each* of 7 different pink prints (hearts)
- ❖ 1⅜ yards pink stripe (border)
- ❖ 1⅜ yards for backing
- ❖ ½ yard pink print for binding
- ❖ Crib-size batting (45 × 60 inches)

CUTTING CHART

Pattern pieces on page 181

FABRIC	PATTERN PIECES	
	A	B
Pink solid	42	
7 assorted pink prints* (cut in groups of 6)		42

*Read "Appliquéing the Blocks" on page 179 before cutting out these pieces.

- ✂ Cut 2 pink stripe border strips, each 3 × 43 inches
- ✂ Cut 2 pink stripe border strips, each 3 × 49 inches
- ✂ Cut backing fabric, 44 × 50 inches
- ✂ Cut 5 strips of fabric for binding, each 3 × 44 inches
- ✂ Cut batting to 44 × 50 inches

Note: To speed up the process of cutting background squares, use your rotary cutter! Instead of tracing and cutting around pattern piece A, cut squares from strips of fabric. From 1⅜ yards pink solid, cut 7 strips, each 6½ × 44 inches. Cut each of these strips into six 6½-inch background squares, to give you the total of 42 that you will need.

Hearts Color Plan: You may photocopy this page
and use it to experiment with color schemes for your quilt.

Appliquéing the Blocks

1. To prepare each heart for appliqué, trace **Pattern Piece B** on page 181 onto the right side of the assorted pink fabrics. In the quilt shown, 6 hearts were cut from each of the 7 fabrics.

2. Cut out each heart with a 3⁄16-inch seam allowance.

3. Referring to the **Block Placement Diagram,** position each heart in the center of a block. Make a fold through the center of the background block. Align the inner and outer points of the heart with this guide. The inner point of the finished heart should be 1½ inches from the top edge of the background block. The outer point of the finished heart should be 1 inch from the bottom edge of the background block. When the heart is pinned in position, blindstitch it onto the block.

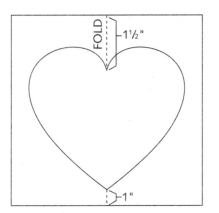

Block Placement Diagram

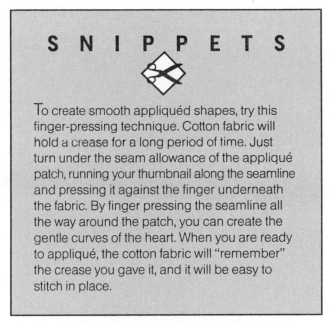

To create smooth appliquéd shapes, try this finger-pressing technique. Cotton fabric will hold a crease for a long period of time. Just turn under the seam allowance of the appliqué patch, running your thumbnail along the seamline and pressing it against the finger underneath the fabric. By finger pressing the seamline all the way around the patch, you can create the gentle curves of the heart. When you are ready to appliqué, the cotton fabric will "remember" the crease you gave it, and it will be easy to stitch in place.

Assembling the Quilt

1. Sew together a row of 6 heart blocks, as shown in **Diagram 1.** Make 7 of these rows.

Diagram 1

2. Referring to the **Quilt Assembly Diagram** on page 180, sew together the 7 rows of the quilt.

3. Sew the 3 × 43-inch pink stripe borders to the top and bottom of the quilt, beginning and ending each seam ¼ inch from the cut edges.

4. Sew the 3 × 49-inch pink stripe borders to the sides of the quilt, beginning and ending each seam ¼ inch from the cut edges.

5. Miter the corner seams, trim the excess fabric to ¼ inch, and press the seams open. For instructions on how to miter, see page 237.

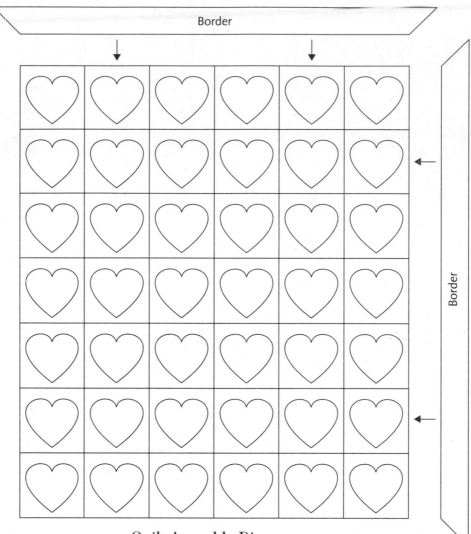

Quilt Assembly Diagram

Quilting

1. Mark the border with the **Cable Quilting Design.**

2. Layer the quilt top, batting, and backing and baste together. Refer to page 239 for pointers on how to layer and baste.

3. Quilt ¼ inch inside and outside each of the hearts and quilt the marked design in the borders. (See page 239 for details on the quilting stitch.)

Finishing

1. To make the binding, sew together the short ends of the 5 binding strips with diagonal seams. Trim the excess fabric and press these seams open. (For more details on how to make and attach binding, see page 240.)

2. Fold the binding in half lengthwise, wrong sides together, and press.

3. Sew the binding to the quilt.

4. Sign and date your quilt.

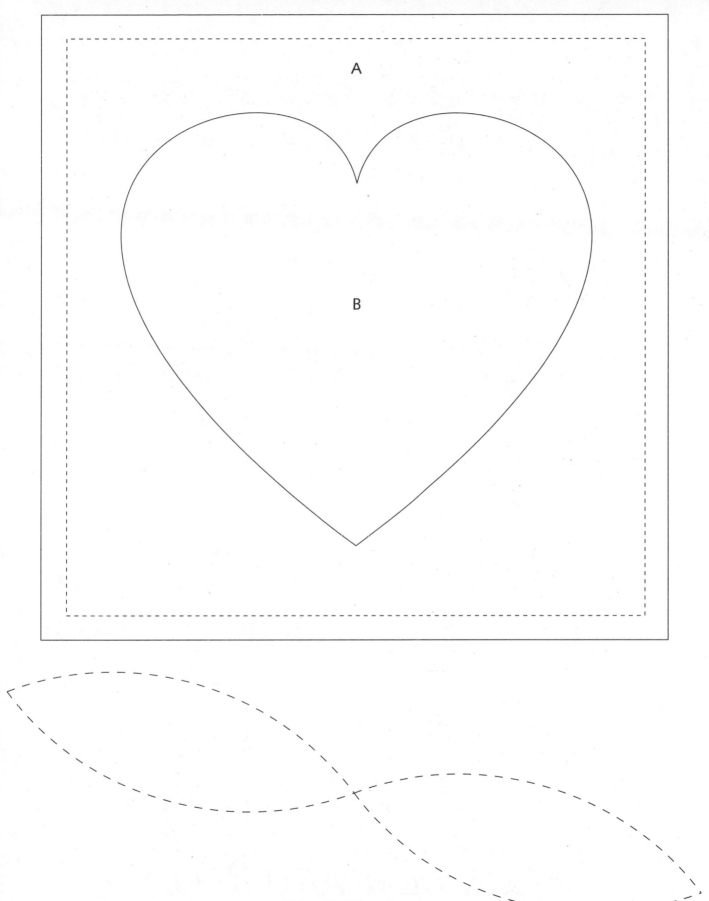

A

B

Cable Quilting Design

• OAK LEAF AND REEL •

*T*his exquisite appliqué Quaker friendship quilt has no batting between the top and bottom layers. Only the cornerstones are quilted, which probably means that this was made as a summer quilt, or possibly as a bedcover intended for display only at special occasions. There is ample space in the background blocks and lattice strips, however, for creative quilting, and you'll find instructions here for duplicating the edge finish of the original as well as a traditional double-fold French binding.

Skill Level: Intermediate

SIZE

Finished block is 11 inches square
Finished quilt is 95 inches square
Quilt consists of 48 Oak Leaf and Reel blocks, 1 Center Leaf Wreath block, 112 lattice strips, and 64 cornerstones

FABRIC REQUIREMENTS AND SUPPLIES

- ❖ 6¼ yards muslin (background blocks, cornerstones)
- ❖ 4½ yards red print (lattice strips, small leaves, center motifs)
- ❖ 2 yards green print (large and small leaves, corner leaves)
- ❖ 8½ yards for backing
- ❖ ⅞ yards for binding (red or green print)
- ❖ King-size batting (120 inches square)

CUTTING CHART

Pattern pieces on page 190

FABRIC	PATTERN PIECES						
	A	B	C	D	E	F	G
Red print*		48	192	1		4	
Green print*	192		384		44		4

*Read "Appliquéing the Oak Leaf and Reel Block" on page 185 before cutting out these pieces.

- ✂ Cut 49 muslin background squares, each 11½ inches square
- ✂ Cut 112 red print lattice strips, each 2¾ × 11½ inches
- ✂ Cut 64 muslin cornerstones, each 2¾ inches square
- ✂ Cut 3 pieces of fabric for backing, each 33½ × 99 inches
- ✂ Cut 10 binding strips, each 3 × 44 inches
- ✂ Cut batting to 99 inches square

Oak Leaf and Reel Color Plan: You may photocopy this page
and use it to experiment with color schemes for your quilt.

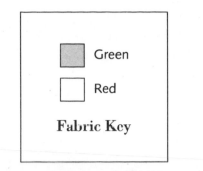

Fabric Key

Green

Red

Appliquéing
the Oak Leaf and Reel Block

1. Referring to page 235 for basic appliqué instructions, prepare templates for appliqué pieces A, B, and C. For each block, you will need 4 green A corner leaves, 1 red B center motif, 8 green C leaves, and 4 red C leaves.

2. Press horizontal, vertical, and diagonal folds in an 11½-inch muslin background square, as shown in **Diagram 1.**

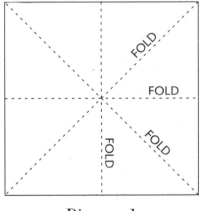

Diagram 1

3. Place 4 green A leaves on the diagonal folds and place a red B center motif in the middle of the block so that it will overlap the A leaves when stitched, as shown in **Diagram 2.**

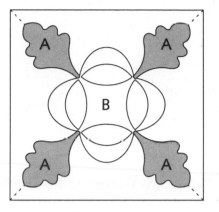

Diagram 2

4. Remove the red B center motif and appliqué the 4 green A leaves.

5. Referring to **Diagram 2,** appliqué the red B center motif, checking to see that it overlaps the lower edge of each green A leaf.

6. Appliqué 1 red and 2 green C leaves at each scalloped edge of the red B center motif (on the horizontal and vertical folds), as shown in **Diagram 3.**

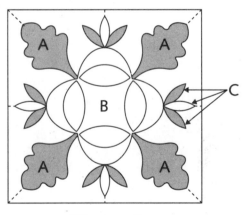

Diagram 3

7. Repeat Steps 1 through 6 to make a total of 48 Oak Leaf and Reel blocks. After you have completed the appliqué, place the finished block face down on a terry towel and spritz with water. Press with a dry iron on the cotton setting.

Appliquéing the Leaf Wreath Block

1. For this block you will need 1 red D patch, 44 green E leaves, 4 red F leaves, and 4 green G leaves.

2. Referring to **Diagram 1,** press horizontal, vertical, and diagonal folds in an 11½-inch muslin background square.

3. Place a red D motif at the center of the block, as shown in **Diagram 4,** and appliqué it in place.

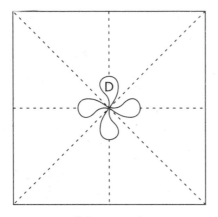

Diagram 4

4. Using the **Leaf Placement Guide** on page 191, mark the circle guideline *lightly* on the background square (or use a removable marker). Match the center of the placement guide with the center of the block. Place 17 green E leaves inside the circle, as shown in **Diagram 5,** so that they slant diagonally and are evenly spaced. Appliqué each E leaf.

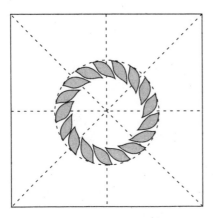

Diagram 5

5. Place 27 green E leaves outside the circle so that they are evenly spaced and slant diagonally, as shown in **Diagram 6.** Appliqué each E leaf.

Diagram 6

6. Place a red F leaf on each diagonal fold so that the inner tip of the leaf is 3¼ inches from the corner, as shown in **Diagram 7.** Appliqué each F leaf.

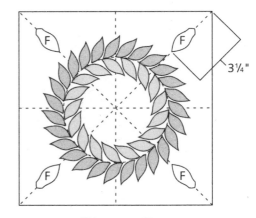

Diagram 7

7. Place a green G leaf over each of the red F corner leaves, as shown in **Diagram 8,** and appliqué.

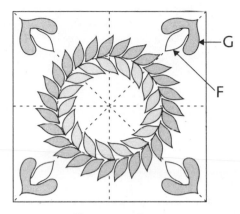

Diagram 8

8. After you have completed the appliqué, press this block in the same manner as you did for the Oak Leaf and Reel blocks.

Assembling the Quilt

1. Sew a horizontal row of 7 Oak Leaf and Reel blocks and 8 red 2¾ × 11½-inch lattice strips, as shown in **Diagram 9.** Make a total of 6 of these block rows.

2. Sew 1 block row with the Leaf Wreath block in the center, as shown in **Diagram 10.**

3. Sew a row of 7 red horizontal lattice strips and 8 muslin cornerstones, as shown in **Diagram 11.** Make a total of 8 of these lattice rows.

4. Sew together the 7 block rows and 8 lattice rows, referring to the **Quilt Assembly Diagram** on page 188.

Diagram 9

Leaf Wreath Block

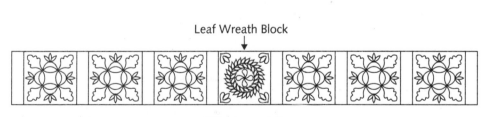

Diagram 10

Cornerstones

Lattice strip

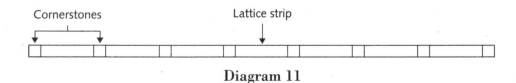

Diagram 11

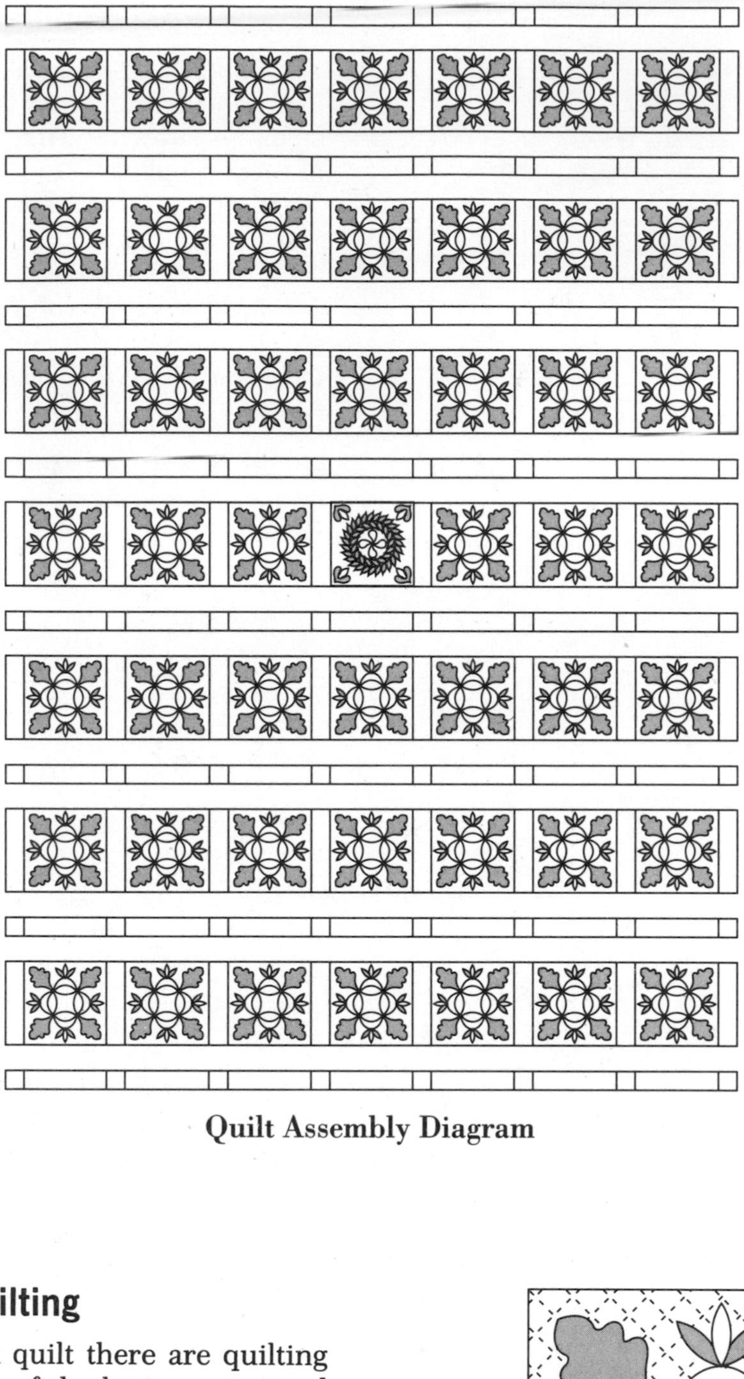

Quilt Assembly Diagram

Quilting

1. In the original quilt there are quilting lines only in the ditch of the lattice strips and cornerstones to hold the layers of this "batting-less" quilt together. If you like, however, you can mark and quilt diagonal lines in each direction at ¾-inch intervals around the appliquéd shapes in each block, as shown in **Diagram 12.**

Diagram 12

2. If desired, mark and quilt the **Leaf Quilting Design** on page 191 in each of the red lattice strips.

3. Sew the 3 pieces of backing fabric together with ¼-inch seam allowances. Press these seams open.

4. Layer the quilt top, batting, and backing and baste together. Refer to page 239 for pointers on how to layer and baste.

5. Quilt all marked designs. (See page 239 for details on the quilting stitch.)

Finishing

1. To make the binding, sew the short ends of the 10 binding strips together with diagonal seams. Trim the excess fabric and press these seams open. (For more details on how to make and attach binding, see page 240.)

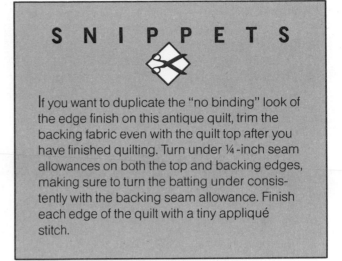

S N I P P E T S

If you want to duplicate the "no binding" look of the edge finish on this antique quilt, trim the backing fabric even with the quilt top after you have finished quilting. Turn under ¼-inch seam allowances on both the top and backing edges, making sure to turn the batting under consistently with the backing seam allowance. Finish each edge of the quilt with a tiny appliqué stitch.

2. Fold the binding lengthwise, wrong sides together, and press.

3. Sew the binding to the quilt.

4. Sign and date your quilt.

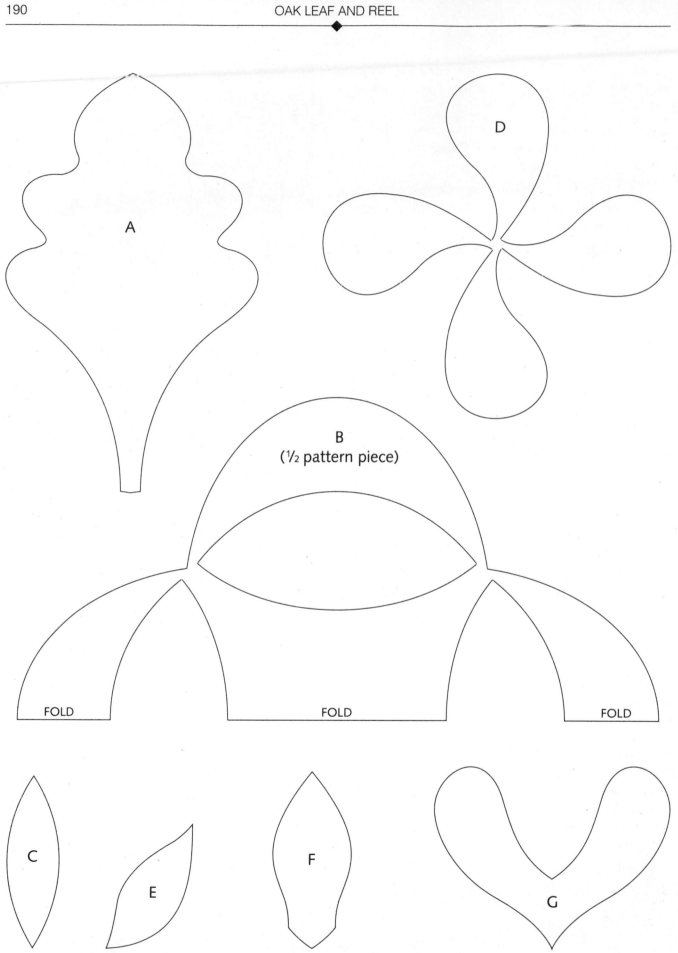

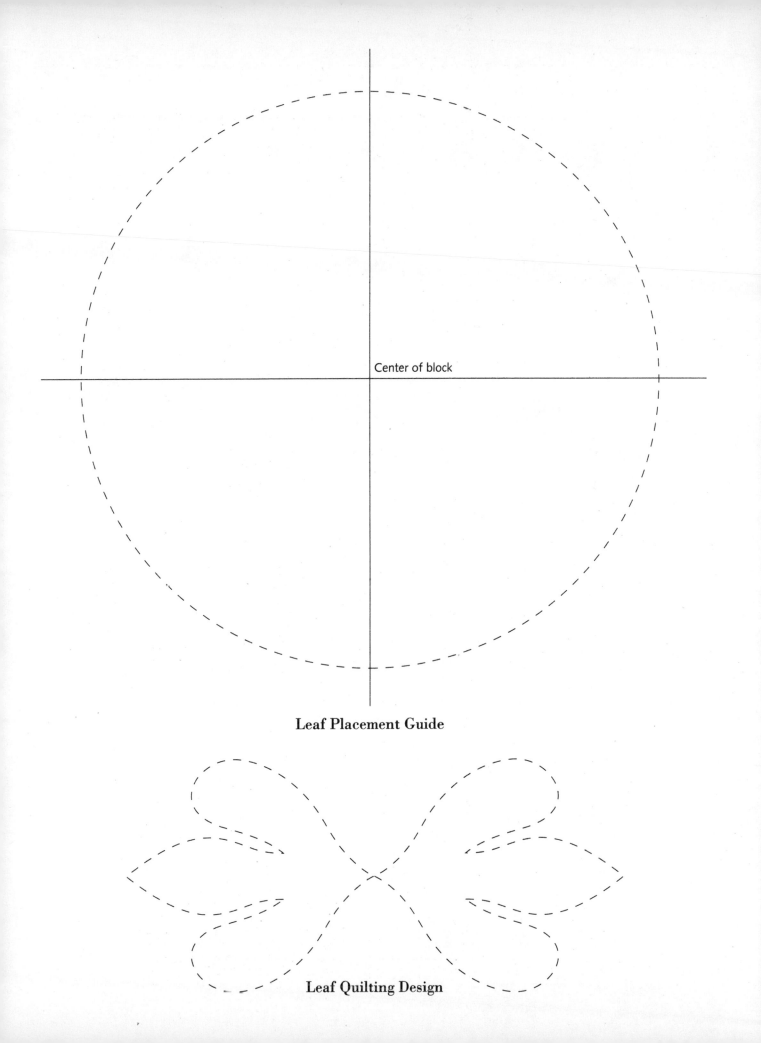

Center of block

Leaf Placement Guide

Leaf Quilting Design

♦ ROSE OF SHARON ♦

R ose of Sharon is one of the oldest and most favored of all appliqué designs. Perhaps that is why so many variations of this pattern have been developed by creative quiltmakers throughout the years. This pastel version is particularly appealing, with its gently curved scallops and delicate buds surrounding the large central blossoms.

Skill Level: Challenging

SIZE

Finished block is 12 inches square
Finished quilt is 83 inches square
Quilt consists of 13 appliquéd blocks, 12
   quilted blocks, and appliquéd border

FABRIC REQUIREMENTS AND SUPPLIES

❖ 7⅜ yards white solid (background blocks and border)

❖ 2¼ yards dark pink print (appliqué and binding)
❖ 1½ yards light pink solid (appliqué)
❖ ⅛ yard yellow solid (appliqué)
❖ 1 yard green solid (appliqué)
❖ 5 yards white solid for backing
❖ ¾ yard for binding (if other than dark pink print)
❖ Queen-size batting (90 × 102 inches)

CUTTING CHART

Pattern pieces on pages 199 and 200

FABRIC	PATTERN PIECES											
	A	B	C	D	E	F	G	H	I	J	K	L
Dark pink print*		13					102	20		4		
Light pink solid*	13					102			20		4	
Yellow solid*			13									
Green solid*				13	102							126

*Read "Appliquéing the Blocks" on page 195 before cutting out these pieces.

✂ Cut 3 yards total of green solid bias
   strips, each 1½ inches wide
✂ Cut 25 white solid background blocks,
   each 12½ inches square
✂ Cut 4 white solid border strips,
   each 11¾ × 84 inches

✂ Cut 2 pieces of fabric for backing,
   each 44 × 87 inches
✂ Cut 8 dark pink binding strips,
   each 3 × 44 inches
✂ Cut batting to 87 inches square

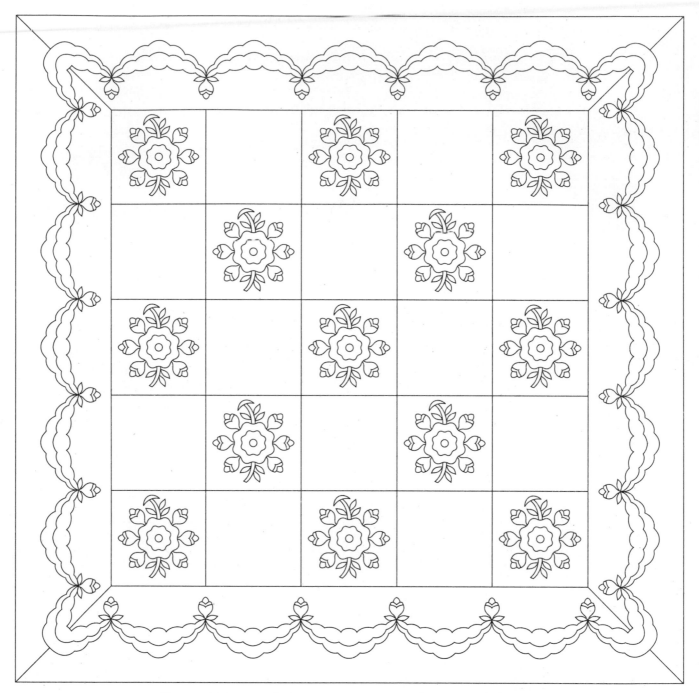

Rose of Sharon Color Plan: You may photocopy this page
and use it to experiment with color schemes for future quilts.

Appliquéing the Blocks

1. Make templates for pattern pieces A through L. (See page 235 for guidelines on making appliqué templates.)

2. To prepare a background block for placement of the pattern pieces, fold and finger press it horizontally, vertically, and diagonally, as shown in **Diagram 1**.

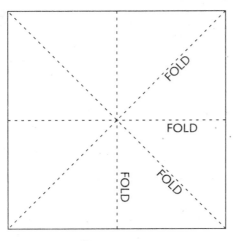

Diagram 1

3. Referring to the **Block Placement Diagram,** position pattern piece A in the center of the block. Trace lightly around pattern piece A with a quilter's silver pencil or removable marker. This line will be a guide for positioning the bias stems and pattern pieces E, F, and G on the background block.

Block Placement Diagram

4. To make the stems, fold each strip of green bias in half lengthwise, wrong sides together. Stitch a ¼-inch seam, creating a bias tube. Press this tube with the seam allowances on the bottom, as shown in **Diagram 2**.

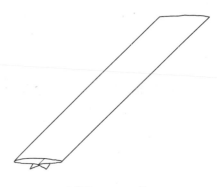

Diagram 2

5. Cut two 4-inch bias strips for the stems. Position the base of one stem at a vertical fold so that it will lie underneath pattern piece A. Then curve it 1 inch toward the left side of the block, as shown in **Diagram 3**. Position the second stem so that it curves in the same direction as the first. Appliqué the stems in place. (Also refer to the **Block Placement Diagram** for help in placing these curved stems.)

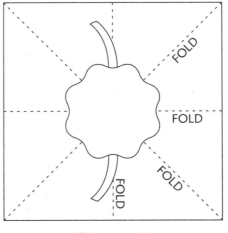

Diagram 3

6. Position 2 leaves next to the outer curve and 1 leaf next to the inner curve of each stem, as shown in the **Block Placement Diagram**, and appliqué.

7. Appliqué a D piece over the tip of the bias stem at the top of each block.

8. Position the E, F, and G pieces of each flower bud on the horizontal and diagonal folds around piece A, as shown in the **Block Placement Diagram.** Appliqué each flower bud in this order: G first, F second, and E last.

9. For the center of the rose, appliqué piece C to the center of piece B. Then appliqué this unit to the center of piece A.

10. Appliqué the rose center to the center of the block, making sure that it overlaps the lower ends of each flower bud and stem. After you have completed the appliqué, place the finished block face down on a terry towel and spritz it with water. Press with a dry iron on the cotton setting.

11. Repeat Steps 1 through 10 to make a total of 13 appliquéd blocks.

Appliquéing the Borders

1. Divide a white 11¾ × 84-inch border strip into 12-inch sections, as shown in **Diagram 4.** Mark each division with basting thread or pins.

2. Position a G piece at each division, placing the point of the G piece 1⅜ inches away from the cut edge of the border, referring to **Diagram 4.**

3. Appliqué a flower bud at each of these divisions, placing the pieces on in the same order as on the quilt blocks: G first, F second, and E last. Refer to the **Swag Border Placement Diagram** for reference.

4. Appliqué an L piece (leaf) on either side of each flower bud.

5. Position light pink I pieces in each border section. Appliqué the outer curves of the swags, making sure that the points of each swag lie at the bottom of each flower bud.

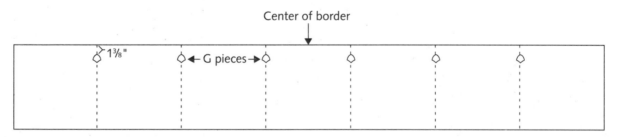

Diagram 4

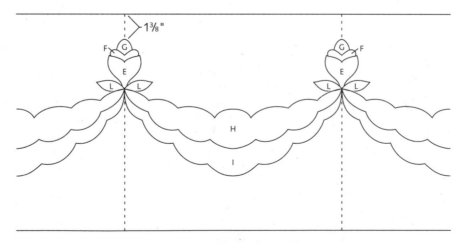

Swag Border Placement Diagram

6. Position H pieces in each border section, making sure that the outer curve of each swag overlaps the inner curve of the I swag. Appliqué both the inner and outer curves of the H pieces, checking that the points meet those of the I pieces directly at the bottom of the flower buds.

7. Appliqué each of the 3 remaining borders in this manner.

Assembling the Quilt

1. Stitch the 25 quilt blocks together, alternating appliqué blocks with solid blocks, as shown in the **Quilt Assembly Diagram.** Press the seams to one side.

2. Referring to the **Quilt Assembly Diagram,** stitch a border section to each side of the quilt top, starting and stopping each line of stitching ¼ inch from the corner. Make sure that the edge of the border with the flower buds is the edge you attach to the quilt.

3. Miter the corner seams, trim the excess fabric to ¼ inch, and press the seams open. For instructions on how to miter, see page 237. After the borders are mitered, press the borders and corners from the wrong side, making sure that the seams lie flat.

4. Refer to the **Corner Swag Placement Diagram** on page 198 to position the four K swag pieces in each corner of the quilt. Make

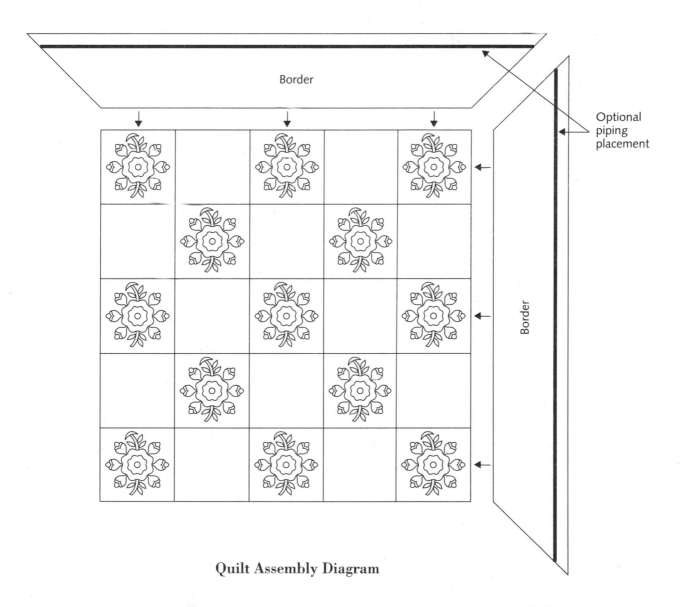

Quilt Assembly Diagram

sure that the points of each swag meet the adjacent swag directly below the flower bud. Appliqué the outer curves only, leaving the inner curves unstitched.

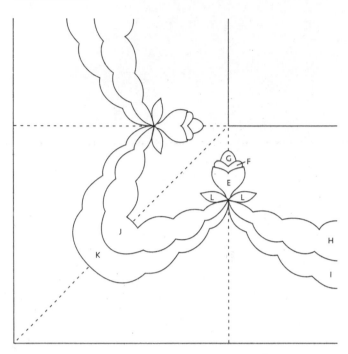

Corner Swag Placement Diagram

5. Position the four J swag pieces in each corner of the quilt. Overlap the inner curves of the K swags and make sure that the points meet the adjacent swag directly below the flower bud. Appliqué both the inner and outer curves of these J pieces. When all four corner swags are complete, press the corners from the wrong side.

Quilting

1. Mark each solid block with the **Scroll Quilting Design** on page 201, or select any quilting motif suitable for a 12-inch block.

2. If desired, mark straight lines at 2-inch intervals above and below the swags in each of the borders.

3. Sew the 2 pieces of backing fabric together with a ¼-inch seam allowance. Press this seam open.

4. Layer the quilt top, batting, and backing and baste together. (Refer to page 239 for pointers on how to layer and baste.)

5. Quilt along all marked lines and around each of the appliqué shapes in the quilt. (See page 239 for details on the quilting stitch.)

Finishing

1. To make the binding, stitch the short ends of the 8 binding strips together with diagonal seams. Trim the excess fabric and press these seams open. (For more details on how to make and attach binding, see page 240.)

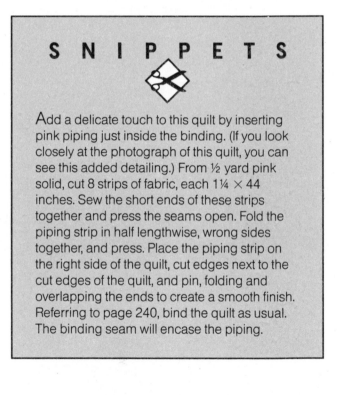

Add a delicate touch to this quilt by inserting pink piping just inside the binding. (If you look closely at the photograph of this quilt, you can see this added detailing.) From ½ yard pink solid, cut 8 strips of fabric, each 1¼ × 44 inches. Sew the short ends of these strips together and press the seams open. Fold the piping strip in half lengthwise, wrong sides together, and press. Place the piping strip on the right side of the quilt, cut edges next to the cut edges of the quilt, and pin, folding and overlapping the ends to create a smooth finish. Referring to page 240, bind the quilt as usual. The binding seam will encase the piping.

2. Fold this strip in half, wrong sides together, and press to create a lengthwise fold.

3. Stitch the binding to the quilt.

4. Sign and date your quilt.

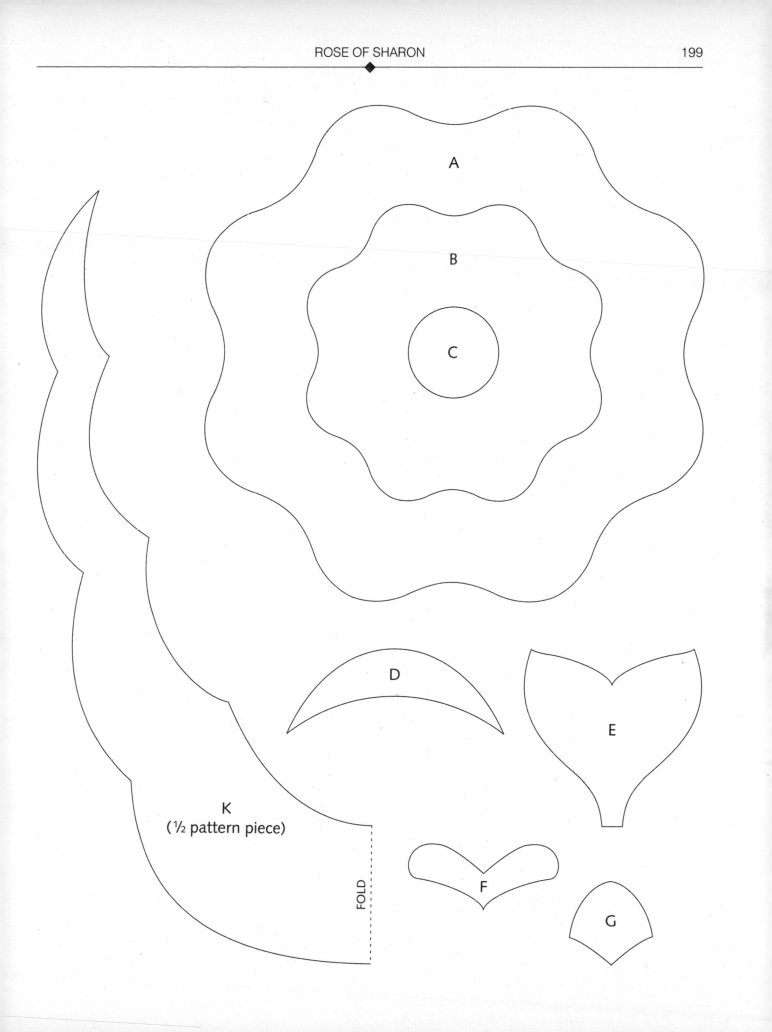

A

B

C

D

E

K
(½ pattern piece)

FOLD

F

G

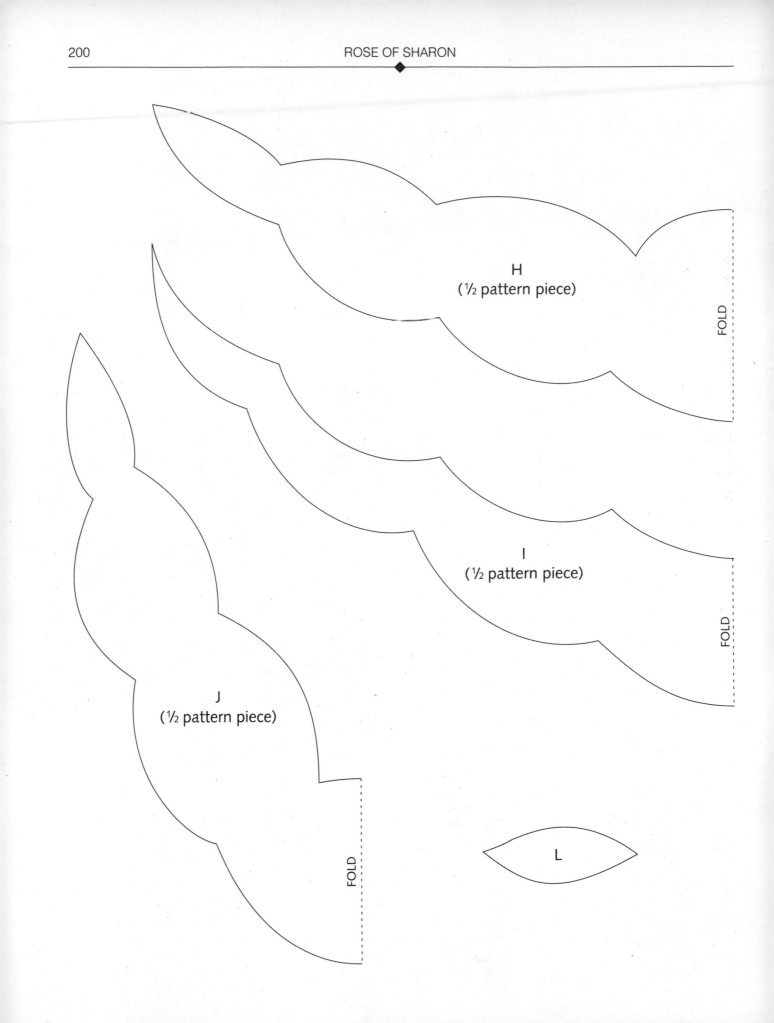

H
(½ pattern piece)

FOLD

I
(½ pattern piece)

FOLD

J
(½ pattern piece)

FOLD

L

FOLD

FOLD

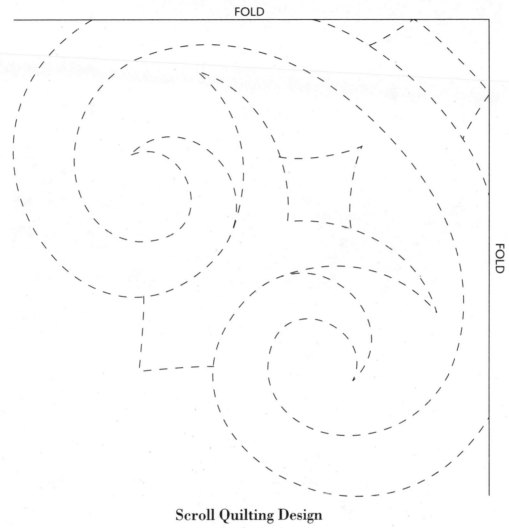

Scroll Quilting Design
(¹/₄ design)

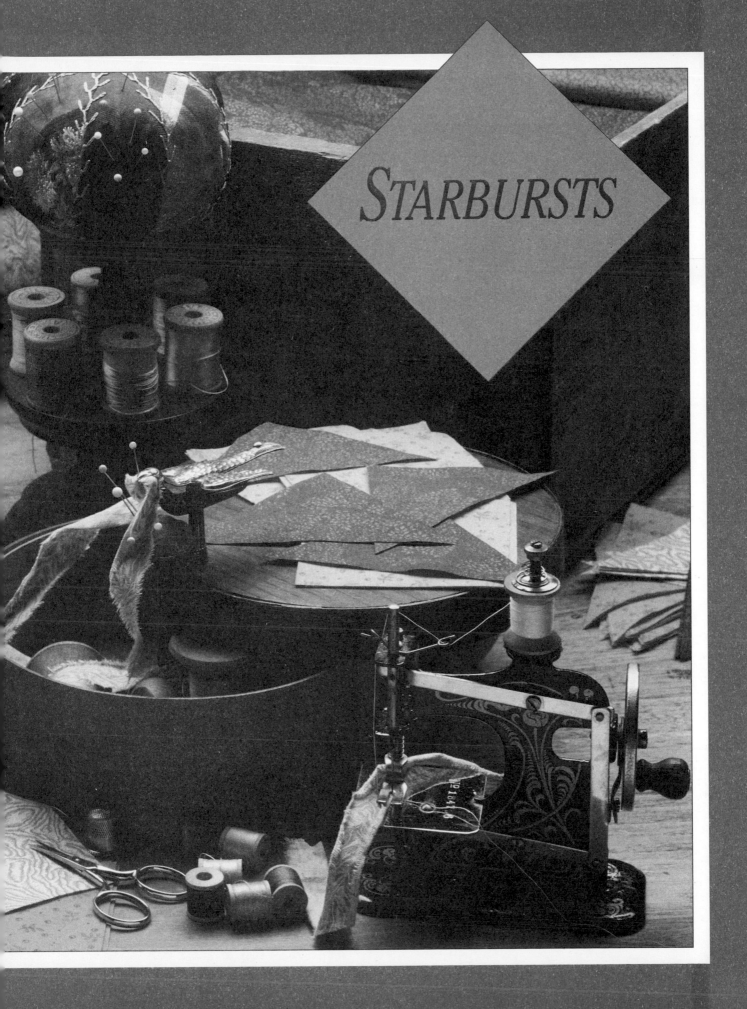

STARBURSTS

· AROUND THE STARS ·

*T*he stars in this scrap quilt are the traditional Doris's Delight pattern. The cream-colored squares in the pieced lattice strips connect the triangles in the blocks, creating the optical illusion of a circular design, even though only straight lines are used.

Skill Level: Easy

SIZE

Finished block is 12 inches square
Finished quilt is 64 × 80 inches
Quilt consists of 12 pieced blocks, 4 long pieced lattice strips, 15 short pieced lattice strips, and inner and outer borders

FABRIC REQUIREMENTS AND SUPPLIES

- ❖ 1⅝ yards cream print (pieced blocks, pieced lattice strips)
- ❖ ⅝ yard assorted beige scraps (pieced blocks)
- ❖ 1 yard medium rust print (pieced lattice strips)
- ❖ ⅜ yard assorted bright scraps (pieced blocks)
- ❖ ⅝ yard assorted medium scraps (pieced blocks)
- ❖ 1⅛ yards assorted dark scraps (pieced blocks)
- ❖ ½ yard dark brown dot (pieced lattice strips)
- ❖ 2¾ yards tan dot (inner border)*
- ❖ 2⅜ yards dark brown print (outer border)*
- ❖ 4¾ yards for backing
- ❖ ¾ yard dark brown solid for binding
- ❖ Twin-size batting (72 × 90 inches)

Refer to "Snippets" on page 210 for yardages for optional pieced border.

CUTTING CHART

Pattern pieces on page 211

FABRIC	PATTERN PIECES						
	A	B	C	Cr	D	E	F
Cream print					48		31
Assorted beige scraps						48	
Medium rust print							62
Assorted bright scraps		48					
Assorted medium scraps						48	
Assorted dark scraps	12		48	48			
Dark brown dot							20

(continued)

205

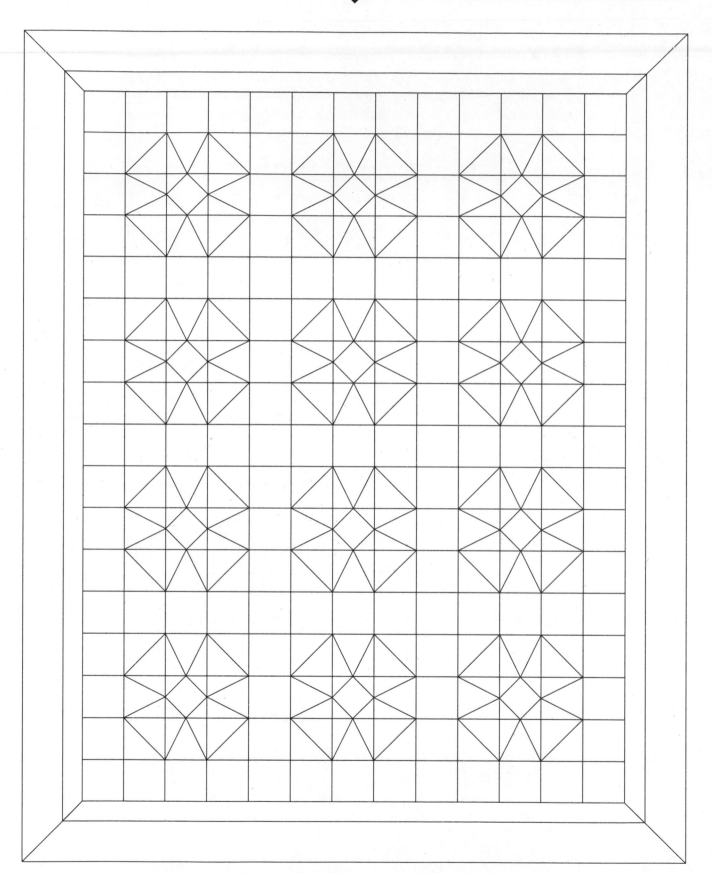

Around the Stars Color Plan: You may photocopy this page
and use it to experiment with color schemes for your quilt.

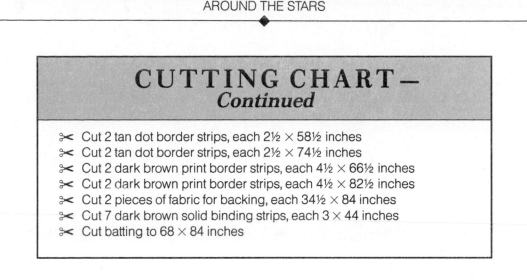

CUTTING CHART—
Continued

- ✂ Cut 2 tan dot border strips, each 2½ × 58½ inches
- ✂ Cut 2 tan dot border strips, each 2½ × 74½ inches
- ✂ Cut 2 dark brown print border strips, each 4½ × 66½ inches
- ✂ Cut 2 dark brown print border strips, each 4½ × 82½ inches
- ✂ Cut 2 pieces of fabric for backing, each 34½ × 84 inches
- ✂ Cut 7 dark brown solid binding strips, each 3 × 44 inches
- ✂ Cut batting to 68 × 84 inches

Bright/beige/cream

Medium/rust

Dark/brown

Fabric Key

Piecing the Block

Note: Contrast is an important element in the look of this block. You'll create a balanced effect in your quilt if you keep the following in mind: The center A square is dark; the surrounding B triangles are bright shades; the C and C reverse (Cr) triangles are dark; the D triangles are light; the corner E triangles are a medium and a light.

1. Sew 4 bright B triangles to the sides of a dark A square, as shown in **Diagram 1.**

Diagram 1

2. Sew a dark C triangle and a dark Cr triangle to a cream D triangle, as shown in **Diagram 2.** Make 4 of these CD units.

Diagram 2

3. Sew a medium E triangle to a beige E triangle, as shown in **Diagram 3.** Make 4 of these EE units.

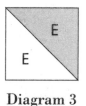

Diagram 3

4. Referring to the **Block Assembly Diagram** on page 208, sew the units together to create horizontal rows. Sew 2 EE units onto opposite sides of each of 2 CD units, making sure to position the medium E blocks as shown in the diagram. Sew a CD unit onto each side of the AB square from Step 1.

5. Join the 3 rows together, as shown in the **Block Assembly Diagram,** positioning the tips of the D triangles so they face toward the center of the block.

6. Repeat Steps 1 through 5 to make a total of 12 blocks.

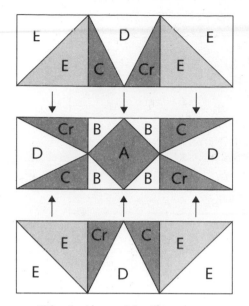

Block Assembly Diagram

Piecing the Lattice Strips

1. Sew together 1 cream F square and 2 medium rust F squares, as shown in **Diagram 4.** Make a total of 31 of these pieced F units. Sixteen F units will be used for the vertical lattice strips; the remaining 15 will be used during quilt assembly.

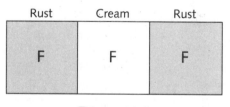

Diagram 4

2. Using the pieced F units from Step 1 and dark brown F squares, sew a vertical lattice strip row, as shown in **Diagram 5.** Make a total of 4 of these rows. For each row you will need 4 F units and 5 brown F squares.

Assembling the Quilt

1. Sew a vertical row of 4 blocks alternating with pieced F units, as shown in **Diagram 6.** Make a total of 3 of these rows.

2. Referring to the **Quilt Assembly Diagram,** sew together the 3 vertical rows of blocks, alternating them with the 4 rows of lattice strips.

3. Referring to **Diagram 7,** prepare the short borders. Fold each border in half and press to mark the center point. Matching these center points, sew a 2½ × 58½-inch tan border strip to a 4½ × 66½-inch dark brown border strip. Repeat this step to make the second short border.

4. In the same manner, fold, press the center points, and sew a 2½ × 74½-inch tan border strip to a 4½ × 82½-inch dark brown border strip and repeat this step to make the second long border.

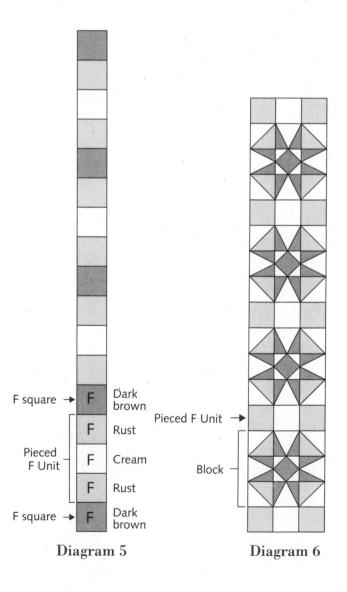

Diagram 5   Diagram 6

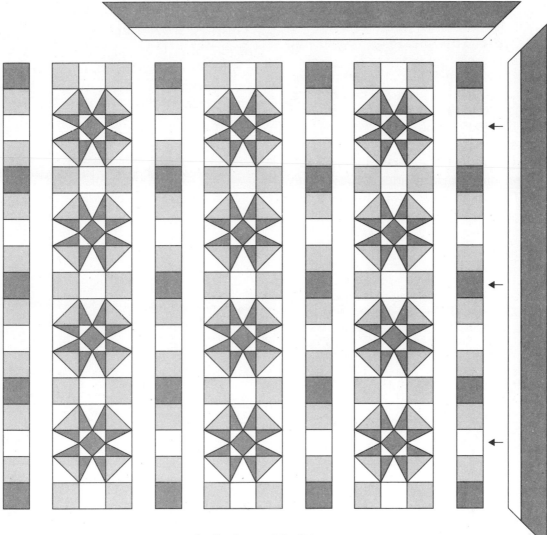

Quilt Assembly Diagram

5. Referring to the **Quilt Assembly Diagram,** sew each of the borders to the quilt, beginning and ending each seam ¼ inch in from the edge of the quilt top.

6. Miter the corner seams, trim the excess fabric to ¼ inch, and press the seams open. For instructions on how to miter, see page 237.

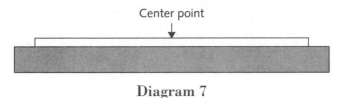

Center point

Diagram 7

Quilting

1. Referring to **Diagram 8** on page 210, mark quilting lines in the cream-colored D triangles ¼ inch in from the two long seamlines. Then measure over ½ inch from these lines and mark another set of quilting lines. There should be 2 inches between the last marked lines, as shown in the diagram.

2. In the borders, mark quilting lines in the light F squares at the same intervals as the lines marked in the D triangles. First extend the lines from the D triangles into the light F squares. Then extend these lines out into the borders.

Because you are marking a line ¼ inch from either side of the seamlines in the D triangles, the intervals between the lines in the border will turn out to be ¾ inch. Referring to **Diagram 8,** mark quilting lines ¼ inch in from each seam of the medium and dark F squares. Then mark a second set of quilting lines ½ inch from each of these lines. Note that all four of these lines run parallel to the borders and that they cross each other in the corner dark F squares. Referring to **Diagram 8,** continue marking lines at these same intervals. At the corner seams, the lines should meet.

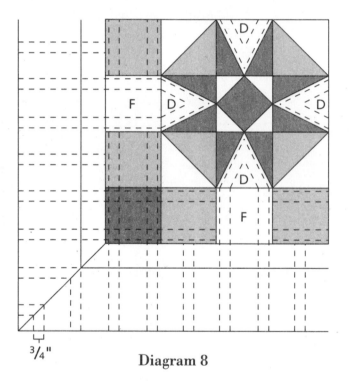

3/4"

Diagram 8

3. Sew the 2 pieces of backing fabric together with a ¼-inch seam allowance. Press this seam open.

4. Layer the quilt top, batting, and backing and baste together. Refer to page 239 for pointers on how to layer and baste.

5. Quilt all marked lines and ¼ inch away from each seam in the blocks. (See page 239 for details on the quilting stitch.)

Finishing

1. To make the binding, sew the short ends of the 7 binding strips together with diagonal seams. Trim the excess fabric and press these seams open. (For more details on how to make and attach binding, see page 240.)

2. Fold the binding lengthwise, wrong sides together, and press.

3. Sew the binding to the quilt.

4. Sign and date your quilt.

S N I P P E T S

You can save fabric if you piece the borders for this quilt. The yardages given under "Fabric Requirements and Supplies" are for solid, nonpieced border strips. However, when borders are pieced from dark fabrics, especially dark prints, very often the seams will not be very noticeable. If you decide pieced borders will work for your quilt, here are some guidelines. From ⅝ yard tan dot fabric, cut 8 border strips, each 2½ inches × 44 inches. Sew 2 of these strips together with ¼-inch seam allowances. Repeat this process to make the other 3 tan dot border strips. From 1⅛ yard dark brown fabric, cut 8 border strips, each 4½ × 44 inches, and sew together as for the tan dot borders. The border strips are now ready to be attached to the quilt, as described starting in Step 3 under "Assembling the Quilt." Just remember to center the seams of the tan/brown border strips on the sides of the quilt top.

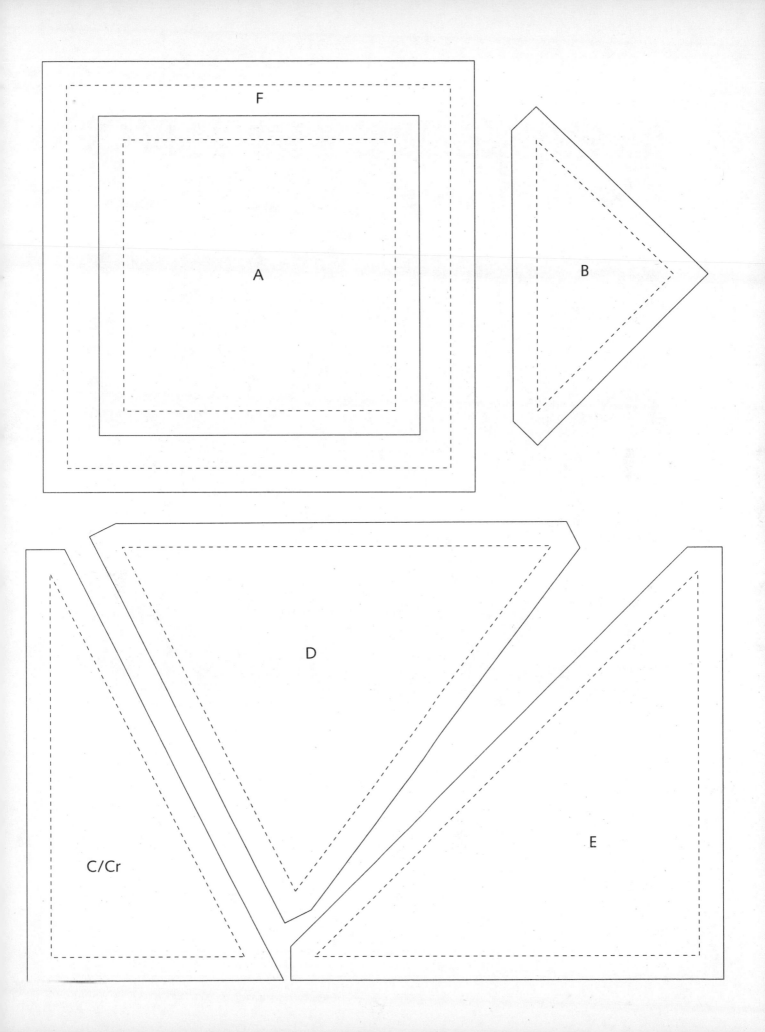

• *GALLOPING STAR* •

*S*tars brighten the night sky, and they'll brighten your quilts, too! In Galloping Star, five Variable Star blocks are surrounded by alternating blocks that create the illusion of an inner frame. This quilt is a perfect size for a lap, baby, or wall quilt.

Skill Level: Easy

SIZE

Finished block is 14 inches square
Finished quilt is 48½ inches square
Quilt consists of 5 star blocks, 4 alternating
　　blocks, and pieced border

FABRIC REQUIREMENTS AND SUPPLIES

❖ 1 yard medium pink print (star blocks, alternating blocks, and border)
❖ ⅞ yard white-and-rust print (star blocks)
❖ ½ yard dark rust print (star blocks and border)
❖ ⅝ yard rust floral print (alternating blocks and border)
❖ ⅞ yard small white print (alternating blocks and binding)
❖ 3 yards for backing
❖ ½ yard for binding (if other than small white print)
❖ Twin-size batting (72 × 90 inches)

CUTTING CHART

Pattern pieces on pages 218 and 219

FABRIC	PATTERN PIECES					
	A	B	C	D	E	Er
Medium pink print	20		12		4	4
White-and-rust print	20	20	20			
Dark rust print	44					
Rust floral print	4		4	16		
Small white print			20			

✂ Cut 2 pieces of fabric for backing, each 27 × 54 inches
✂ Cut 3 binding strips, each 3 × 44 inches
✂ Cut batting to 54 inches square

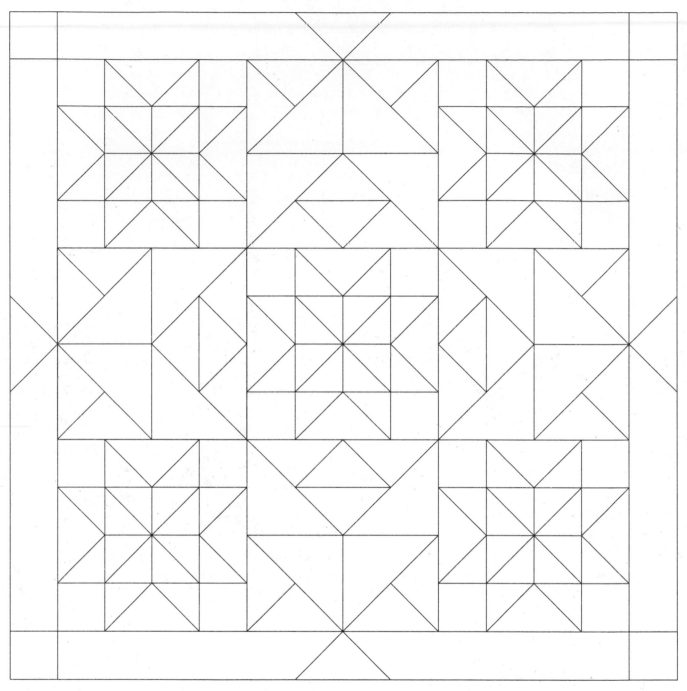

Galloping Star Color Plan: You may photocopy this page
and use it to experiment with color schemes for your quilt.

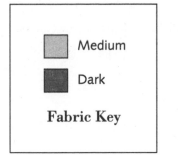

Fabric Key

Medium

Dark

Piecing the Star Block

1. Sew a medium pink A triangle to a white-and-rust A triangle, as shown in **Diagram 1.** Make 4 of these AA units.

Diagram 1

2. Sew the 4 AA triangle units together, as shown in **Diagram 2.**

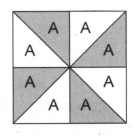

Diagram 2

3. Sew a dark rust A triangle to each side of a white-and-rust C triangle, as shown in **Diagram 3.** Make 4 of these ACA units.

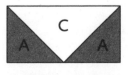

Diagram 3

4. Sew a white-and-rust B square to each side of one of the ACA units, as shown in **Diagram 4.** Repeat, making a total of 2 of these units.

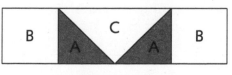

Diagram 4

5. Sew the star block together, as shown in the **Star Block Piecing Diagram.**

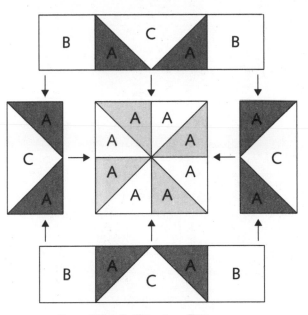

Star Block Piecing Diagram

6. Repeat Steps 1 through 5 to make a total of 5 star blocks.

Piecing the Alternating Block

1. Sew a white print C triangle to a medium pink C triangle, as shown in **Diagram 5.**

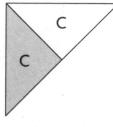

Diagram 5

2. Sew a rust floral D triangle to the CC triangle unit, as shown in **Diagram 6.**

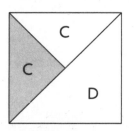

Diagram 6

3. Reversing the position of the C triangles, make another of these CCD units, as shown in **Diagram 7.**

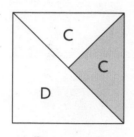

Diagram 7

4. Sew a white print C triangle to a medium pink C triangle, as shown in **Diagram 8.**

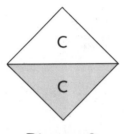

Diagram 8

5. Sew a white print C triangle to each of the remaining sides of the medium pink C triangle, as shown in **Diagram 9.**

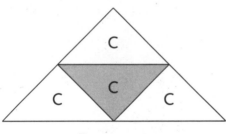

Diagram 9

6. Sew a rust floral D triangle to each side of the unit from Step 5, as shown in **Diagram 10.**

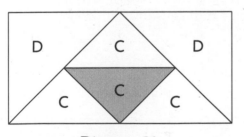

Diagram 10

7. Sew the units of the block together, as shown in the **Alternating Block Piecing Diagram.**

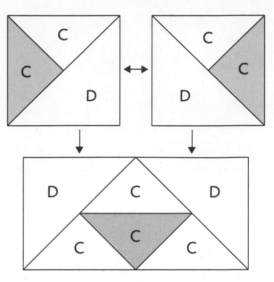

Alternating Block Piecing Diagram

8. Repeat Steps 1 through 7 to make a total of 4 alternating blocks.

Piecing the Border

1. Sew a rust floral A triangle to a dark rust A triangle, as shown in **Diagram 11.** Make 4 of these AA corner units. (These corners will not be added to the border until later, when the quilt is assembled.)

Diagram 11

2. Sew a medium pink E piece to one side of a rust floral C triangle and a medium pink E reverse (Er) piece to the other side of the triangle, as shown in **Diagram 12.** Make a total of 4 of these border units.

Assembling the Quilt

1. For all the steps in this section, refer to the **Quilt Assembly Diagram.** Sew 3 horizontal rows of 3 blocks each. Be sure the star and alternating blocks are positioned correctly.

2. Sew the 3 rows together to complete the center of the quilt top.

3. Sew border units to two opposite sides of the quilt. To check for proper positioning, make sure the point of the C triangle in the border meets the point of the D triangle in the alternating block.

4. Sew an AA corner unit to each of the two remaining border units and sew these borders to the top and bottom of the quilt.

Quilting

1. Beginning at the center of the border and working toward the corners, mark diagonal lines at 1¾-inch intervals. (Use the photograph on page 212 for reference.)

2. Sew the 2 pieces of backing fabric together with a ¼-inch seam allowance. Press this seam open.

3. Layer the quilt top, batting, and backing and baste together. (Refer to page 239 for pointers on how to layer and baste.)

4. Quilt all marked lines and ¼ inch on both sides of each seamline in the quilt. (See page 239 for details on the quilting stitch.)

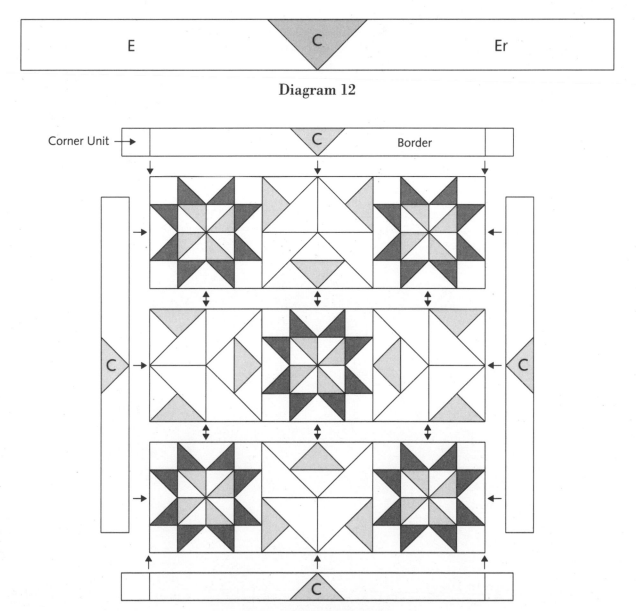

Diagram 12

Quilt Assembly Diagram

Finishing

1. To make the binding, sew the short ends of the three 3-inch binding strips together with diagonal seams. Trim the excess fabric and press these seams open. (For more details on how to make and attach binding, see page 240.)

2. Fold this strip in half, wrong sides together, and press.

3. Sew the binding to the quilt.

4. Sign and date your quilt.

SNIPPETS

Once you've finished your quilt, try viewing the design through a reducing glass (a tool now widely available in quilt shops). It produces the same result as standing back a great distance from a quilt and can tell you much about the visual effects of certain color combinations, print scales, and color values in your quilt.

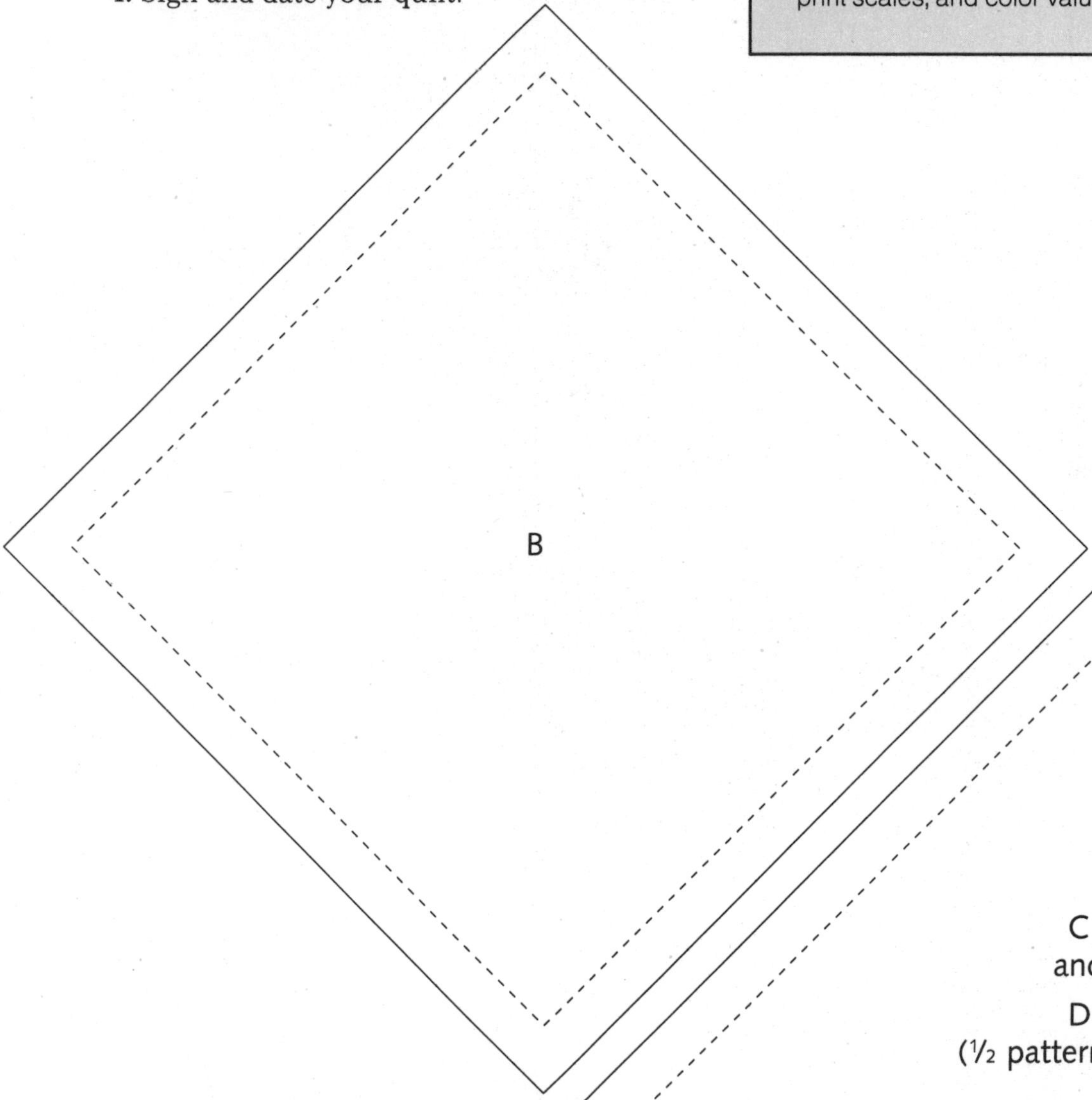
B

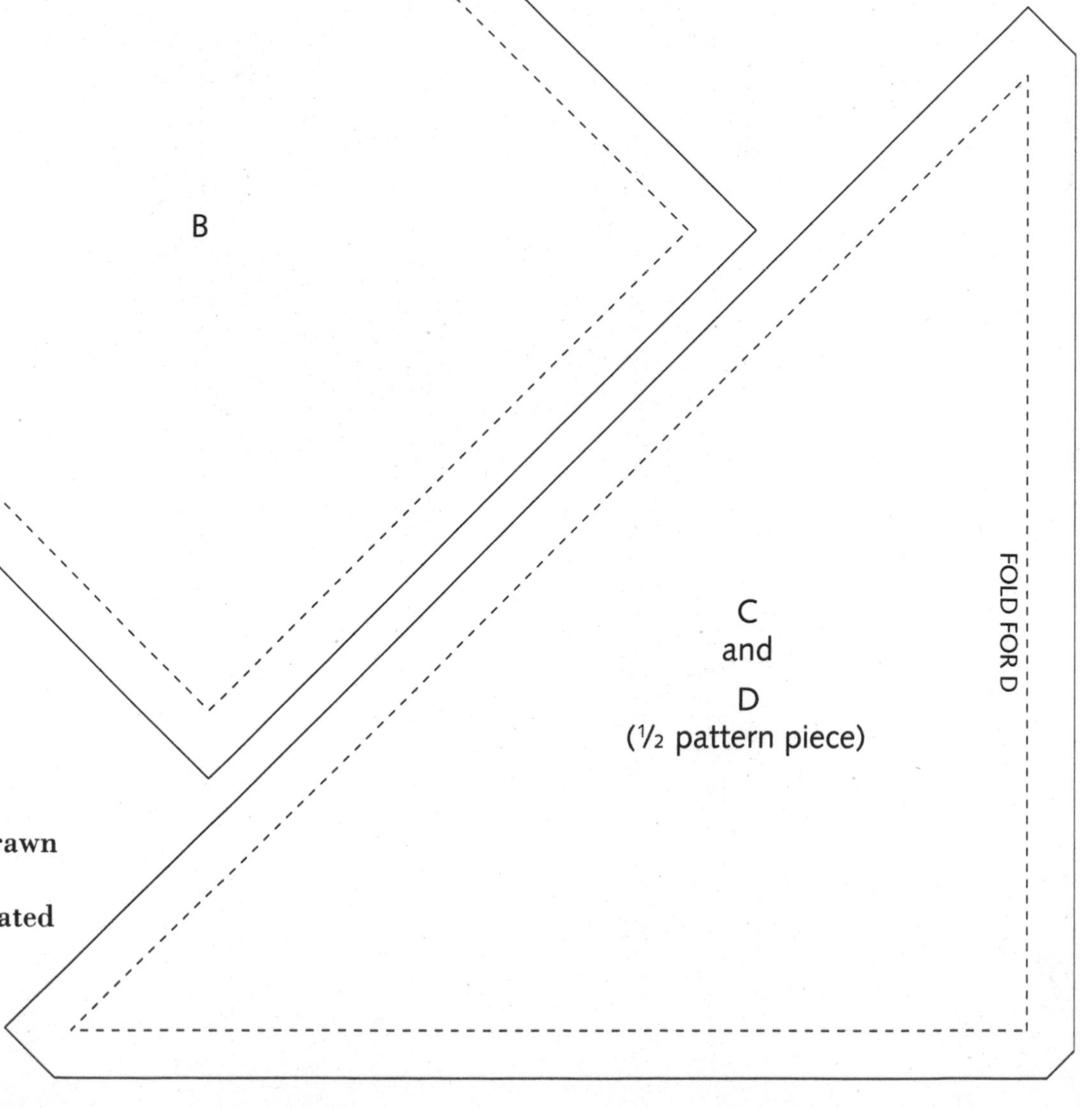
C
and
D
(½ pattern piece)
FOLD FOR D

Use this pattern as drawn for the C triangle; place on fold as indicated for the D triangle.

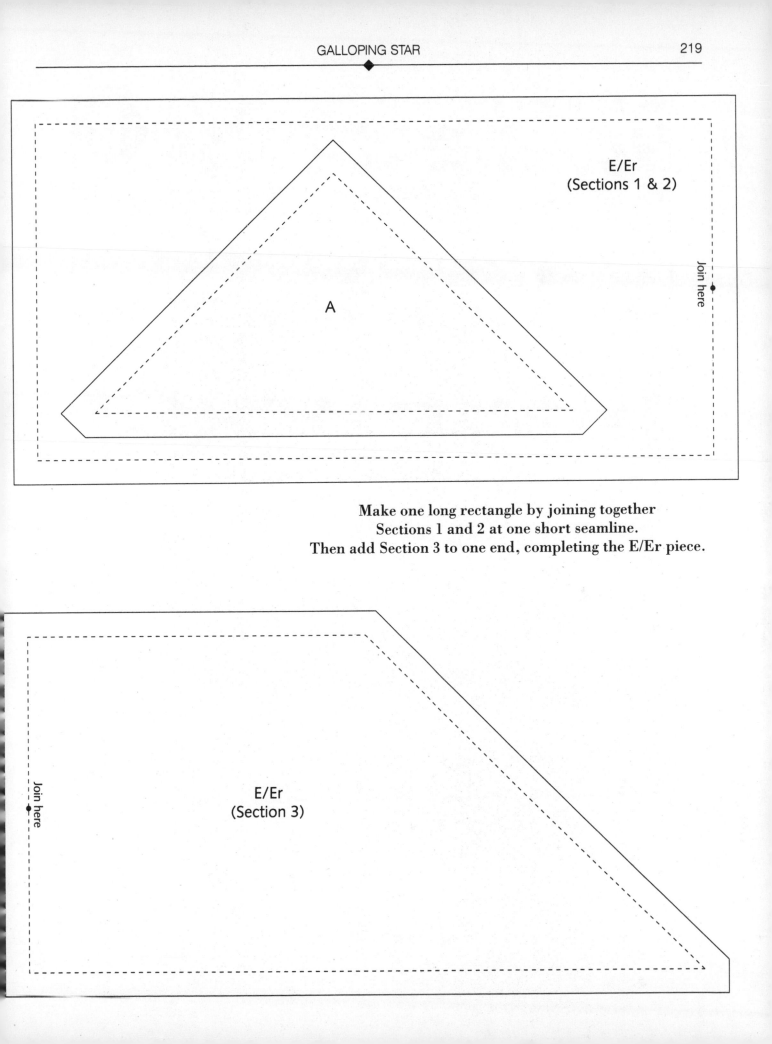

E/Er
(Sections 1 & 2)

Join here

A

Make one long rectangle by joining together
Sections 1 and 2 at one short seamline.
Then add Section 3 to one end, completing the E/Er piece.

E/Er
(Section 3)

Join here

• TEABOX •

*R*ummage through your scrap bag, gather your favorite fabrics, and make a star-studded Teabox quilt. This traditional pattern creates the effect of six-pointed stars and usually features half of a hexagon shape at the ends of alternate rows. Here, however, there are units of 4 diamonds that complete the sides of the design and create almost an argyle-like effect. Whatever color combination you choose to use, your Teabox quilt will be a sparkling beauty!

Skill Level: Challenging

SIZE

Finished quilt is 80 × 96¼ inches
Quilt consists of 12 Unit 1s, 71 Unit 2s, and
   10 Unit 3s

FABRIC REQUIREMENTS AND SUPPLIES

- ❖ 2⅝ yards beige print (triangles)
- ❖ 2½ yards assorted light prints (diamonds)
- ❖ 2½ yards assorted medium prints (diamonds)
- ❖ 5 yards assorted dark prints (diamonds)
- ❖ 5¾ yards for backing
- ❖ ¾ yard brown solid for binding
- ❖ Queen-size batting (90 × 102 inches)

CUTTING CHART

Pattern pieces on page 227

FABRIC	PATTERN PIECES			
	A	B	C	Cr
Beige print	164		22	22
Assorted light prints		269 (cut in groups of 3)		
Assorted medium prints		269 (cut in groups of 3)		
Assorted dark prints		498 (cut in groups of 6)		

✂ Cut 2 pieces of fabric for backing, each 42 × 100 inches
✂ Cut 9 binding strips, each 3 × 44 inches
✂ Cut batting to 84 × 100 inches

Teabox Color Plan: You may photocopy this page
and use it to experiment with color schemes for your quilt.

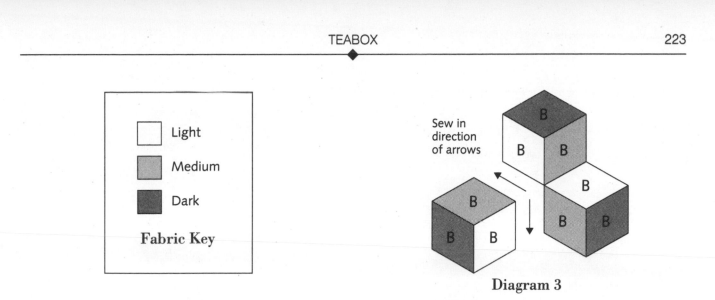

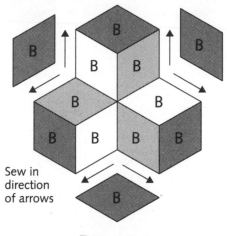

Diagram 3

Piecing Unit 1

Note: Use the same prints within each unit.

1. Sew a light B diamond to a medium B diamond, as shown in **Diagram 1.** Begin and end the seam ¼ inch from each edge.

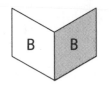

Diagram 1

2. Sew a dark B diamond to the BB unit from Step 1, as shown in **Diagram 2,** beginning each seam at the point where the previous seam ended and sewing outward, ending these seams ¼ inch from the outer edges. (Directions for setting-in are on page 234.) Make 3 of these units.

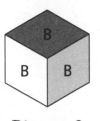

Diagram 2

3. Sew together 2 of these BBB units, as shown in **Diagram 3,** beginning and ending the seam ¼ inch from each edge. Sew a third BBB unit to these 2 units, referring to the diagram for placement of light, medium, and dark fabrics. Begin each of these seams at the point where the first seam ended and sew outward, in the direction of the arrows, to ¼ inch from the outer edge.

4. Sew 3 dark B diamonds to this unit, beginning each seam at the inner point between diamonds and sewing outward to ¼ inch from the outer edge, as shown in **Diagram 4.** This completes the center of Unit 1.

Diagram 4

5. Sew a beige C triangle to the top left side of Unit 1, as shown in **Diagram 5.** Sew this seam from cut edge to cut edge of the B diamonds.

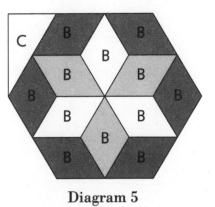

Diagram 5

Unit 1 (complete)

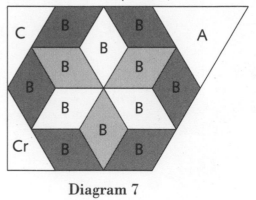

Diagram 7

Piecing Unit 2

1. Following Steps 1 through 4 under "Piecing Unit 1," sew light, medium, and dark B diamonds together to form the center portion of Unit 2.

2. Complete Unit 2 by sewing beige A triangles to opposite sides of the center unit, as shown in **Diagram 8.** Sew these seams from cut edge to cut edge of the B diamonds. Repeat Steps 1 and 2 to make a total of 71 Unit 2s.

6. Sew a C reverse (Cr) triangle to the lower left side of Unit 1, as shown in **Diagram 6.** Sew this seam from cut edge to cut edge of the B diamonds.

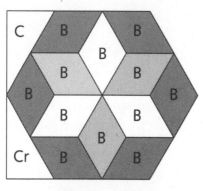

Diagram 6

7. Sew a beige A triangle to the top right side, completing Unit 1, as shown in **Diagram 7.** Sew this seam from cut edge to cut edge of the B diamonds.

8. Repeat Steps 1 through 7 to make a total of 12 Unit 1s.

Unit 2 (complete)

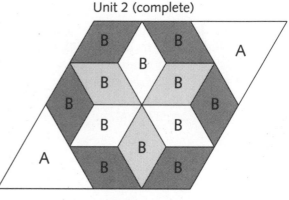

Diagram 8

Piecing Unit 3

1. Sew a medium B diamond to a light B diamond, as shown in **Diagram 9.** Sew this seam from cut edge to cut edge of the B diamond. Make 2 of these BB units.

2. Sew the 2 BB units together, as shown in **Diagram 10.** Sew this seam from cut edge to cut edge of the B diamonds. This completes the center for Unit 3.

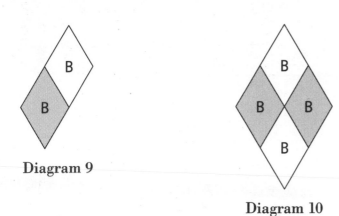

Diagram 9

Diagram 10

5. Complete Unit 3 by sewing a beige A triangle to the top right side, as shown in **Diagram 13.** Sew this seam from cut edge to cut edge of the B diamonds. Repeat Steps 1 through 5 to make a total of 10 Unit 3s.

Unit 3 (complete)

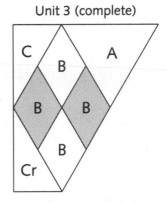

Diagram 13

3. Sew a beige C triangle to the top left side of the center unit, as shown in **Diagram 11.** Sew this seam from cut edge to cut edge of the B diamonds.

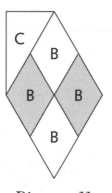

Diagram 11

Assembling the Quilt

1. The quilt consists of alternating A and B rows made of Units 1, 2, and 3 attached in a specific order. For Row A, sew together a row of 6 Unit 2s, with a Unit 1 at each end, as shown in **Diagram 14.** Make a total of 6 A rows.

2. For Row B, sew together a row of 7 Unit 2s, with a Unit 3 at each end, as shown in **Diagram 15.** Make a total of 5 B rows.

3. Sew alternating A and B rows together, as shown in the **Quilt Assembly Diagram** on page 226.

4. Sew a beige Cr triangle to the lower left side of the center unit, as shown in **Diagram 12.** Sew this seam from cut edge to cut edge of the B diamonds.

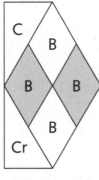

Diagram 12

Row A

| Unit 1 | Unit 2 | Unit 2 | Unit 2 | Unit 2 | Unit 2 | Unit 2 | Unit 1 |

Diagram 14

Row B

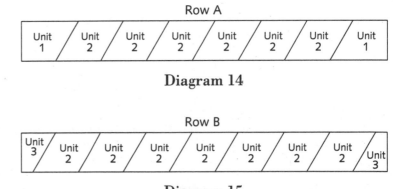

| Unit 3 | Unit 2 | Unit 2 | Unit 2 | Unit 2 | Unit 2 | Unit 2 | Unit 2 | Unit 3 |

Diagram 15

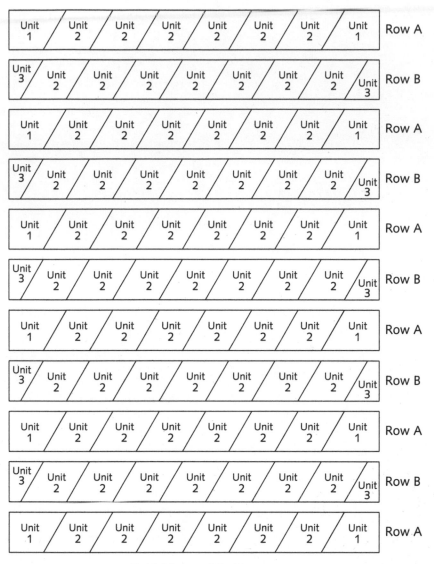

Quilt Assembly Diagram

Quilting

1. Mark each of the beige A triangles with the **Leaf Quilting Design.**

2. Sew the 2 pieces of backing fabric together with a ¼-inch seam allowance. Press this seam open.

3. Layer the quilt top, batting, and backing and baste together. Refer to page 239 for pointers on how to layer and baste.

4. Quilt the marked leaf designs in each of the A triangles and quilt ¼ inch away from each seam in the pieced diamonds. (See page 239 for details on the quilting stitch.)

Finishing

1. To make the binding, sew the short ends of the nine 3-inch binding strips together with diagonal seams. Trim the excess fabric and press these seams open. (For more details on how to make and attach binding, see page 240.)

2. Fold the binding strip in half lengthwise, wrong sides together, and press.

3. Sew the binding to the quilt.

4. Sign and date your quilt.

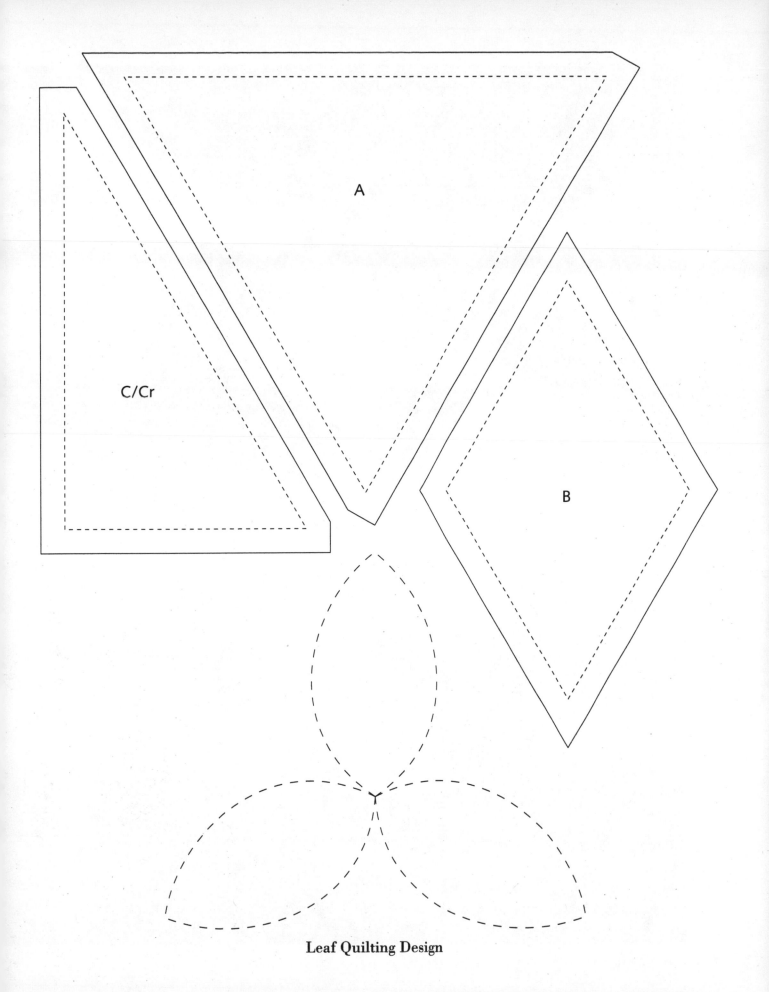

A

C/Cr

B

Leaf Quilting Design

BACK
TO BASICS

• QUILTMAKING ABCs •

These "Quiltmaking ABCs" will give you detailed instructions and information about the general techniques used in making each of the quilts in this book. You'll find it useful for brushing up on the basics you'll need to make wonderful quilts, and a good, quick refresher course for use in your future projects.

Selecting Fabric

Color is one of the most meaningful ways to express yourself in your quilts. You may decide you want to re-create a quilt as it is pictured in this book or combine different hues to produce unique effects. For each of the quilts in the book, you will find a **Fabric Key** with colors listed as lights, mediums, darks, or brights. These terms refer to the level of color contrast. Light refers to the lightest of colors for a quilt. Dark refers to the darkest of the shades used, with medium falling between the two. Where the word bright is used, it refers to a particularly brilliant shade of the color named.

For each quilt in the book there is a page called the **Color Plan,** which is a detailed line drawing of the entire quilt with no color indications. You may make photocopies of these **Color Plans** and use them to experiment with colorations for making the quilts. By creating more than one color scheme, you'll discover how different a design can look by varying its color scheme. Shade in the pieced or appliquéd shapes of a quilt block with children's crayons or Berol Prismacolor pencils, which are available in a veritable rainbow of hues and have thick, soft leads that are great for covering large areas.

Whatever your taste, the **Color Plans** can help you achieve successful results in selecting colors for many quilts to come.

Cotton, the Quilter's Choice

The quilts in this book are made of 100 percent cotton fabrics. Cotton is a good choice for several reasons. It can be manipulated to match tricky points, and it is flexible enough to ease around curves. It is easy to press cotton because its "memory" allows it to retain a crease for some time. Cotton is also soft and lightweight, which makes it easier to quilt through three layers of a quilt sandwich. There are varying amounts of residual shrinkage from fabric to fabric, however, which should be considered before using any given piece of cotton fabric in your quilt. One of the first things to decide after selecting your fabrics is whether to prewash them.

To Pretreat or Not to Pretreat?

There are several benefits to prewashing 100 percent cotton fabrics, but there are also some valid reasons for not doing so. If there is a good chance that the quilts you make will need to be laundered in the future, you might want to pre-wash all of the fabrics you use, especially for bed-size quilts. For smaller projects, such as wall quilts, miniature quilts, or doll quilts, you may decide not to prewash the fabrics, as there is less chance that these kinds of quilts will need cleaning on a regular basis. If you like the crisp finish and new look of just-purchased fabric, you might prefer not to prewash your fabric, especially for small projects.

If you decide to prewash your fabric, plan to treat it now as it will be treated in the future. If there is a chance that the fabric will ever shrink or "bleed," you should know it now and deal with it before using that fabric in a quilt. If you know that you will only launder your quilts in a solution of water and a particular quilt cleanser, such as Orvus Paste, prewash your fabric in that way. In any case, it is probably good to avoid using detergents with fabric softeners in them, which can sometimes produce blotchiness or unevenness in color. Dry the fabrics, removing them while slightly damp, if you wish, and press them with a dry iron on the cotton setting.

Checking for Colorfastness

If you are working with dark fabrics, especially solid greens, blues, and reds, it's a good idea to check for colorfastness before using them in your quilt. Place the fabric in hot water for an hour to see if color seeps into the water. If this happens, you can try to "set" the color by immersing the fabric in undiluted white vinegar for several hours. There is really no correct amount of vinegar to use for this setting process, but it is a good idea to cover the fabric completely so that the vinegar penetrates all of the fibers. A large bowl or tray works well for soaking small amounts of fabric, and a sink or laundry basin is best if you are working with more than a yard or two of fabric.

Salt can also set color in fabric, so if vinegar does not work well by itself, try adding a generous amount of salt. Again, there is not a specific amount to add; be generous and try using up to a cup of salt for a gallon or more of vinegar.

If color bleeds into the vinegar, you can make a second attempt to set it, but if you continue to see the dye, it may be better in the long run to select another fabric for your quilt.

Quiltmaking Supplies

Quilting supplies vary from project to project, but there are some things that you'll want to use in making any quilt. In addition to such basics,

you'll undoubtedly discover that you like other things, as well. Explore the many different types of quilting tools available today and add your own personal list of "must-haves" to these basics.

Pressing Needs: In general, you'll want to use a dry iron on a hot or cotton setting for pressing cotton fabrics. Also, keep a spray bottle of water handy for spritzing seams, blocks, borders, corners, and other key areas.

Marking Time: For marking on fabric, try the Quilter's Choice silver pencil, the Berol silver pencil, a soft graphite pencil such as the Ebony pencil (available in art stores), a removable marker, or a wax-base marking tool. For black or dark fabrics, try the Berol Prismacolor white pencil. For marking on template plastic or drafting patterns on graph paper, you may like the Sharpie ultrafine-point permanent marker, which makes a finer line than many others. For marking quilting designs on fabric, try using a hard lead .5 mm mechanical pencil, a powdered chalk marker, or a silver or white pencil. To sign and date a quilt, permanent Pigma pens are available in six colors.

Template Plastic: Template plastic is a staple in quilting. It's available in large sheets at quilt shops, and each sheet usually has one smooth side and one side that is a bit rougher. When you trace any of the pattern pieces from this book, mark on the smooth side of the template plastic so that when you place the template on the fabric, the rougher side lies next to the fabric. This helps keep the template from slipping.

Quilter's Rules: A plastic quilter's ruler is a must for both traditional cutting and strip-cutting methods. If you have one with markings in ⅛-inch increments as well as lines to indicate 30, 45, and 60 degree angles, you'll find it becomes a much-used piece of your quilting equipment.

The Cutting Edge: Along with a good ruler, you'll need to have a rotary cutter for quick-cutting methods, preferably with a large blade for cutting straight edges. A rotary cutter with a small blade can be effective for cutting curved shapes. Keep extra blades on hand in case a blade becomes dull.

Rotary cutting needs to be done on a special surface. Several brands of rotary cutting mats are now widely available in quilt and fabric shops. Some mats have grid lines marked at 1-inch intervals and lines to indicate various angles, and some mats are unlined. You can find opaque mats or those that are green, burgundy, or gray on one side and white on the other, making it easy to see any color fabric against the cutting surface. Any of these mats will protect your tables or countertops, and they will "self-heal" after each cut you make, which helps keep blades sharp for a longer period of time.

It can be a joy to cut fabric with a pair of scissors that are sharp to the very tip of the blades. If you like having a variety of sizes on hand, keep one pair of 8-inch dressmaker's shears for making large cuts, a 4- or 6-inch pair of embroidery scissors for trimming, and a tiny pair of 2½-inch scissors for clipping threads and making tiny cuts in appliqué seam allowances.

In Stitches: Thread that has the same fiber content as your fabric is the best choice, if it is available. If your fabric is a natural fiber such as 100 percent cotton, use 100 percent cotton thread. Polyester threads or cotton-covered polyester threads may cut the fabric because they're stronger than the cotton fibers of your fabric. And while the colors in your quilt may fade throughout the years, polyester threads may retain enough color so that they no longer match the quilt. Silk thread is a wonderful fiber to use for hand appliqué because it glides through fabric like butter. It is costly, but the ease of stitching with this thread can be worth the higher price. For general hand quilting, the best all-around choice for strength and durability is still 100 percent cotton thread. If you like to do machine quilting, you might enjoy using a clear or smoke-colored nylon thread as the top thread in your machine with cotton thread in the bobbin.

Nimble Thimbles: A thimble that fits well can save your fingers from a lot of pain and allow you to stitch in comfort for longer periods of time. Look for a thimble that fits whichever finger you will use to push the needle. To be a good fit, a thimble should be snug enough that you can shake your hand and it will stay on your finger. There should also be a bit of space between the end of your finger and the inside of the thimble. This space helps to avoid soreness from pushing repeatedly against the top of the thimble. The thimble should lie just above the first knuckle of your finger to be comfortable.

If you find that you tend to resist the very thought of using a thimble but you would like to learn to wear one, this experiment might help. Try wearing a thimble at times when you are not sewing and when you can become engrossed in something, such as watching your favorite television program or reading a good book. These activities will take your mind off the thimble on your finger and allow you to become accustomed very gradually to its presence. Soon you'll find that you don't mind wearing it and you can begin using it to protect your fingers as you stitch.

On Pins and Needles: Good, sharp needles will make your quilting much easier and more fun. Use an 80/12 universal needle in your sewing machine for working with cotton fabrics. For hand appliqué, try Hapco #12 or John James #11 sharps. For hand piecing or hand quilting, Hapco or Hemmings #10 or #12 betweens can all produce beautiful results.

Pins can be valuable in each step of the quilting process. Try straight pins, such as quilter's pins with colored plastic heads, or the finest of all, silk pins, for piecing needs. For hand appliqué, there are short sequin pins that can help avoid tangled thread. When you baste the layers of a quilt together, use a rust-proof nickel-plated brass safety pin, preferably in size 0. This size pin has a very narrow shank, which helps avoid leaving sizable holes in your fabric. And it is a very short pin, which means that the quilt layers will be anchored firmly at each place you pin.

Hoop-la: Whether you stitch with your quilt in a hoop or in a floor frame, put tension on the quilt in some way whenever you work on it. Your stitches and the spaces between them will be more even if there is tension on the quilt as you stitch. Lap quilting can be effective for small projects, but there are so many wonderful hoops and frames on the market today that you can easily find many sizes that meet your own quilting needs.

A standard 14-inch round wooden hoop is useful for most medium and large projects, and there are hoops as tiny as 8 inches for small quilts. Try plastic Q-Snap frames for portability and ease of assembly. For quilting borders, try a D-shaped hoop with a fabric sleeve along the straight side.

Floor frames are possibly the ultimate in quilting accessories. If you are in the market to buy one, make a point to investigate the many features available in floor frames and decide which ones appeal to you and will make your quilting easier. Ask yourself questions like these: How do you insert a quilt into the frame? How much actual quilting space is there between the poles? Are the height and tilt of the quilting surface adjustable? Is it possible to create side tension on your quilt? Can you buy poles in several sizes? Can a lamp be attached to the frame? How much physical space does the frame occupy? Can a quilt be folded and/or stored while still in the frame? Is it easy to get information, service, and help from the company that manufactured the frame? Use these questions as guidelines and consider your own quilting preferences as you search for a good floor frame.

Patchwork Basics

Most of the quilts in this book are pieced, though a few of them, such as the Dresden Plate and the Fancy Patch projects, are combinations of patchwork and appliqué. Read the following section to brush up on your piecing techniques.

Making Patchwork Templates

All of the patchwork templates in this book include ¼-inch seam allowances. To make a template, place a piece of template plastic, rough side down, over one of the pattern pieces in the book. With a permanent marker, such as an ultrafine-point Sharpie, trace the pattern piece, taking care to mark exactly on the cutting line. For pieces with straight edges, it may be helpful to use a ruler. For pieces with curved edges, mark slowly and carefully, creating a single line, rather than "sketching" a line by making frequent stops and starts.

Mark each template with any information you will want to remember about it in the future, such as the name of the quilt block, the letter of the pattern piece, how many of this piece to cut in which fabrics, and whether you'll need to reverse the position of the template for any of the pieces. The instructions, diagrams, and pattern pieces in each project are labeled with letters. If you will need to reverse a pattern piece, you will see a small "r" beside the letter of that piece (for example, pattern piece Cr). This means that you should turn the template over, which reverses it, and cut out the necessary number of pieces in this position.

Cut out each pattern piece consistently.

Whether you decide to cut on the outside or the inside of the line or directly on top of the drawn line, always follow the same practice for each pattern piece. Inconsistency in cutting can greatly affect the accuracy of your quilt, especially in block patterns that are made up of many small pieces.

To store templates for a quilt block, try keeping them together in plastic page protectors or in sandwich or freezer bags that you can seal. It's an easy way to organize your templates and you can see through the bags for quick pattern identification in the future.

Machine Piecing

It is extremely important to be accurate in sewing ¼-inch seams. A difference of as little as $\frac{1}{16}$ inch on several pattern pieces can alter the dimensions of your quilt by as much as an inch or more.

Some sewing machines have a presser foot that measures exactly ¼ inch from the point where the needle goes into the fabric to the edge of the presser foot. To determine whether this is true for your machine, insert your needle into a piece of paper and lower the presser foot. Mark a line at the edge of the presser foot. Remove the paper and measure the distance from the point where the needle was inserted to the line. If this distance is exactly ¼ inch, you can use your presser foot as a guide when you do machine piecing.

If this distance is *more* than ¼ inch, you won't be able to use your presser foot as a reliable seam guide. In this case, you may wish to mark an exact ¼-inch line on your machine by lowering the needle, lifting the presser foot and measuring over exactly ¼ inch from the needle. Place a piece of masking tape at that point and use that as a seam guide. If, however, it is *less* than ¼ inch on your machine from the needle to the edge of the presser foot, measure over ¼ inch from the needle and mark this point with a small piece of Dr. Scholl's Molefoam. The Molefoam is approximately ⅛ inch high, which creates a nice ridge for guiding fabric.

Straight Seams

To join two pattern pieces, place them right sides together. Begin sewing the seam without backstitching and sew from edge to edge. It is not necessary to backstitch at the end of the seam if another seam will cross it at this point.

Press patchwork seams to one side, toward the darker fabric whenever possible. With a dry iron on the cotton setting, press the pattern pieces while they are still right sides together, as shown in **Diagram 1A,** which will "set" each fabric in place. Then open up the seam and press from the right side of the fabric, with seam allowances facing the darker fabric, as shown in **Diagram 1B.**

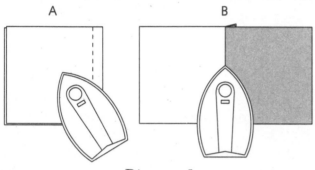

Diagram 1

Curved Seams

For sewing curved seams, such as in the Fancy Patch or Drunkard's Path quilts, place the pattern piece that has an outer curve on the bottom and the piece with the inner curve on top, as shown in **Diagram 2.** Place pins at the beginning, midpoint, and end of the pieces and sew the seam in the usual manner. Press the seam toward the piece with the outer curve.

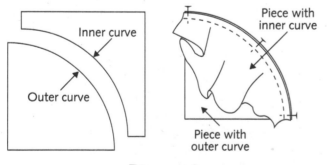

Diagram 2

Setting-In Pattern Pieces at an Angle

To set in a pattern piece at an angle, begin by backstitching and sewing the first seam in the usual manner, then stopping ¼ inch from the edge of the fabric and backstitching, as shown

in **Diagram 3A.** This is the point at which the third piece will be set in.

Open up these pattern pieces and place the pattern piece to be set in right sides together with one of the first two pieces, referring to

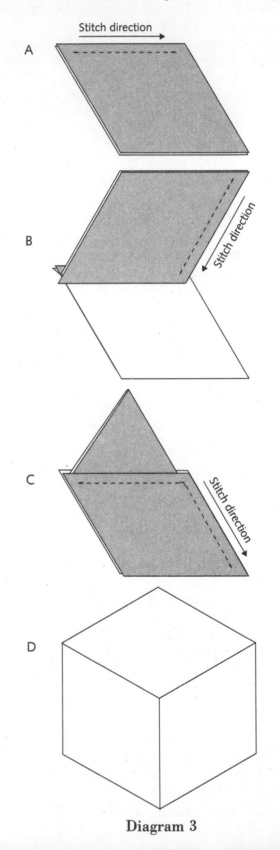

Diagram 3

Diagram 3B. Begin this seam by backstitching ¼ inch from the edge of the piece, sew to the exact point where the first seam ended, and backstitch again.

Rotate the pattern pieces so that you are ready to sew the final seam. Keeping the seam allowances free, sew from the point where the last seam began to ¼ inch from the edge of the piece, as shown in **Diagram 3C.** Press these seams so that as many of them as possible lie flat, referring to **Diagram 3D.**

Appliqué Basics

Appliqué designs are made up of curved shapes stitched onto a background square. The Rose of Sharon and Oak Leaf and Reel are classic appliqué patterns. A quilt like the Dresden Plate, while often thought of as an appliqué design, is really a combination of both piecing and appliqué. In this section you'll find lots of tips to help you master the art of flawless appliqué.

Making Templates and Preparing the Pieces

Because templates for appliqué are exactly the size of the finished pieces, there are no seam allowances included on the appliqué pattern pieces for most of the projects. To make an appliqué template, place a piece of template plastic over one of the pattern pieces in the book. Trace each piece exactly as it appears and cut it out directly on the lines.

With a quilter's silver pencil or another nonpermanent marker, trace around each template on the right side of the fabric. When you cut out each pattern piece, cut approximately ⅛ to ¼ inch *outside* these lines, as shown in **Diagram 4.** If you are appliquéing for the first time, start by using a ¼-inch seam allowance. With practice, you may like working with smaller seams (as small as ⅛ inch) that are easier to turn, and you may find that they give you more control over inner curves, outer curves, and points. The drawn line becomes the turning line when you appliqué each piece on the background fabric.

After you cut out the necessary pattern pieces, pin them in their correct positions on the background square, making sure to note where pieces must be layered or overlapped. If

you prefer, you may baste each piece in place using white thread.

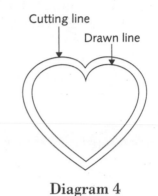

Cutting line

Drawn line

Diagram 4

Needleturn Appliqué

Needleturning is one of the oldest appliqué techniques, and it remains a favorite among quilters because of the minimal amount of time needed for preparation before stitching. Despite its name, needleturning can be accomplished easily by using a common household item as you stitch—a wooden toothpick! A toothpick will easily help you guide a seam allowance into the correct position for stitching. Its rough surface seems to "grab" the fabric better than the smooth surface of a needle. This will enable you to create sharp points and smooth inner and outer curves.

To begin stitching, place the first pattern piece in position on the background square. Thread a needle with thread that matches the fabric in the appliqué patch. Bring the needle up from underneath, on the drawn (turning) line, as shown in **Diagram 5A.**

Then fold under the seam allowance on the turning line. This will neatly encase the knot. Insert the tip of the needle into the background

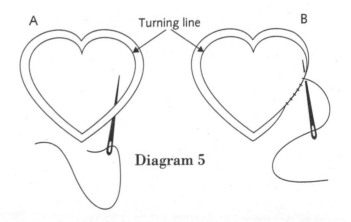

A

Turning line

B

Diagram 5

square, right next to where the thread comes out of the appliqué patch. The tip of the needle should enter the background square slightly underneath the fold. Bring the needle out of the background square approximately 1/16 inch away and up through the very edge of the fold, completing the first stitch, as shown in **Diagram 5B.**

Repeat this process for each stitch, using the toothpick to help you turn under fabric about 1/4 inch at a time. Stitch this far, then stop and use the toothpick to turn under the next 1/4 inch of fabric. With such small increments, it will be easy to stitch around any shape, whether it has deep inner curves, outer curves, or points.

To appliqué an outer point, stitch all the way up to the point, as shown in **Diagram 6A.**

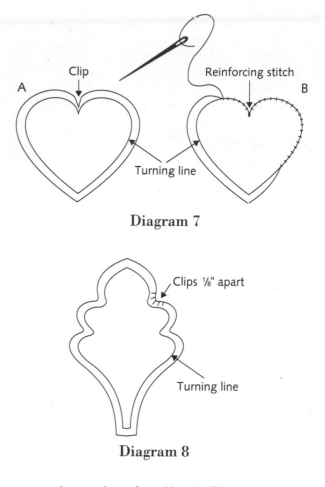

Diagram 7

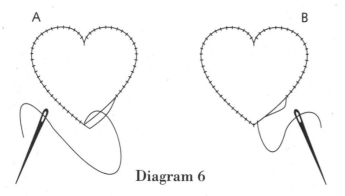

Diagram 6

Referring to **Diagram 6B,** tug gently on the thread to pull the point precisely into the correct position. Turn under the fabric on the other side of the point with the toothpick. Then insert the needle into the background fabric just a tiny bit beyond the point. Bring the needle up on the next side of the point. This stitch gives the optical illusion that the fabric comes to an extremely sharp point.

To appliqué an inner point, clip the seam allowance almost to the drawn line, as shown in **Diagram 7A.**

Stitch down to this point and take one small reinforcing stitch. Then turn under the fabric on the next side and continue stitching, as shown in **Diagram 7B.**

For an inner curve, make clips approximately 1/8 inch apart in the seam allowance, as shown in **Diagram 8.** Do not clip outer curves.

Diagram 8

Layering Appliqué Pieces

When you appliqué one piece over another, you may trim away some of the fabric from the lower piece so that you do not have to quilt through layers of fabric. If you do decide to trim out some of the lower fabric, cut approximately 1/4 inch inside the stitching line.

When one appliqué piece overlaps another piece, the underlying edge of fabric does not need to be turned under and stitched since it will be covered by the upper piece, as shown in **Diagram 9.**

After you finish each appliqué block, press it by placing the block right-side down on a terry towel. Spritz with water and press the block with a dry iron on the cotton setting.

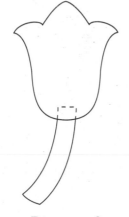

Diagram 9

Mitering Borders

Most of the quilts in this book have mitered borders. For each of these projects, the length of the border measurements is generous. This will allow you to sew the corner seams easily and trim away any extra fabric.

To make a mitered border, sew each of the borders to the quilt top, beginning and ending the seams ¼ inch from the edge of the quilt. Press the border seams flat from the right side of the quilt. Working at one corner of the quilt, place one border on top of the adjacent border. Fold the top border under so that it meets the edge of the other border and forms a 45 degree angle, as shown in **Diagram 10.**

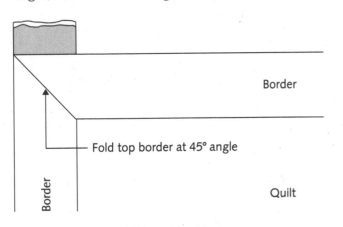

Diagram 10

If you are working with a striped border, check to make sure that the stripes match along this folded edge. Press the fold in place and bring the top border down so that the edges of

the border are aligned. With the pressed fold as the corner seamline and the body of the quilt out of the way, sew from the inner corner to the outer corner, as shown in **Diagram 11.**

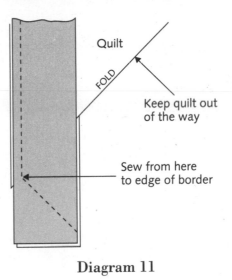

Diagram 11

After sewing this seam, open the border and check to make sure that all points match. Trim the border seam to ¼ inch and press this seam open.

Preparing the Backing

Most of the quilts in this book are large enough to need pieced backings. In the Cutting Chart for each project, you will find the dimensions and number of pieces of fabric that will need to be cut. Cut off all selvage edges from the fabric before sewing. Sew the pieces of backing fabric together with ¼-inch seam allowances and press these seams open. The backing will lie flatter, and it will be easier to quilt through the seam area if the seam is open, rather than pressed to one side, as you do for pieced blocks.

When it is sewn together, the backing should be comfortably larger than your completed quilt top so that there is ample space around the edges of your quilt. A 2-inch margin of backing and batting on each side of the quilt will accommodate the natural tendency of these layers to "shrink" or draw up during the quilting process. After you have finished all of the quilting, trim the batting and backing even with the sides of your quilt.

Which Batting Is Best?

There are many wonderful choices when it comes to the middle layer of your quilt. Some battings produce a flat, rather antique look, and others will give you a quilt that has a softly sculpted appearance. Some are perfect for creating fine hand stitching and some are especially wonderful for machine quilting. Decide on the type of quilting you want to do and the kind of loft (or puffiness) you wish to create, and select a batting that will best achieve it.

Cotton Batting: Cool in summer and warm in winter, cotton has long been a quilter's choice for batting. It has a thickness of approximately $\frac{1}{16}$ to $\frac{1}{8}$ inch, and it can be hand or machine quilted. Some 100 percent cotton battings will need to be quilted as closely as 1 to 2 inches apart to avoid shifting, but their big advantage is that they will not beard (fibers that migrate through your quilt fabric can create a fuzzy, "bearded" effect). They can be prewashed or used without pretreating; just be prepared for your finished quilt to shrink when you wash and dry it if you do not pretreat it.

Cotton/Polyester Blend Batting: These blends offer all the advantages of cotton without the need to quilt so closely. You can space your stitches as far apart as 3 to 4 inches. These batts are thin (perfect for the "antique" look), very durable, and suited to both hand and machine quilting. They can be prewashed or used without pretreating; just be aware of the shrinkage in a finished quilt.

Wool and Silk Battings: Wool and silk battings are special fibers that can offer certain benefits. Wool battings are very warm, without being heavy, while silk batting is very easy to needle and is drapable and lightweight. However, silk batts can be hard to handle since they resemble puffs of cotton candy!

Polyester Battings: These are by far the most popular batting today. They are generally higher in loft, or thickness, than cotton battings. Polyester batts are selected more often than any other kind, probably because of the wide range of thicknesses available, ease of stitching, durability, and simplicity of laundering. They do beard quite heavily, however.

Marking the Quilting Design

When you're ready to mark the quilting design, use a marker that will be visible on the fabric of your quilt and that will wear away or can be brushed out after the quilting is completed. Silver pencils, such as Quilter's Choice silver, Berol silver, or Berol Prismacolor white, work well on most fabrics, and there are other good choices, too. Chalk pencils and powdered chalk markers are now available in several colors at many quilt shops, and some markers, such as wax-base triangular markers, are economical because you use up virtually all of the marking substance in them. You may also like marking light fabrics with a hard lead .5 mm pencil, but make sure to avoid marking heavily with a pencil. It is a good idea to do some experimenting with several marking tools on scrap fabrics to decide which ones you like before you mark a large area of your quilt.

To mark a quilting design, use a commercially made stencil, make your own stencil by using a sheet of plastic (often available in quilt shops) and a double-bladed Exacto knife, or trace the design from a printed source. There are also helpful items, such as quilter's $\frac{1}{4}$-inch tape for stitching an even $\frac{1}{4}$ inch from seam allowances. Masking tape in many widths is available to help you space diagonal lines, straight lines, or crosshatching lines evenly without marking.

If you are using a marker that will stay visible for a long time, you can mark the entire quilt top before layering the quilt sandwich. If you decide to use a powdered chalk marker or a chalk pencil that will not remain visible for a long period of time, you will need to mark the quilting lines just before quilting them.

Make Your Own Light Box

With a quilt top that's black or some other dark color, it may be helpful to use a light box to mark the design. Tape the design you wish to mark on top of the light box and place the quilt top over that. The light will shine through both, making it easy to see and mark the lines. If you do not have access to a light box, you can make one of your own by placing a piece of Lucite or glass between two tables and setting a small lamp or other light source underneath its clear surface. Tape your quilting design to the top of the Lucite and place the quilt on top, being careful to keep the fabric away from the light source at all times.

Layering the Quilt Sandwich

To prepare the quilt "sandwich" for quilting, place the pressed backing right-side down and place the batting on top of it, smoothing out any wrinkled spots. Then place the quilt top over the batting, right-side up. Baste these three layers together with either thread or quilter's pins. If you decide to thread baste, use white thread so there won't be any residue of color left in your quilt when the thread is removed, and baste a grid of horizontal and vertical rows that are approximately 4 to 6 inches apart. Use long darning needles, or even 3-inch dollmaking needles, and thread a few needles with very long lengths of thread before you begin basting to save some time. If you pin baste, use rust-proof nickle-plated brass in size #0. This size pin has a narrow shank, which won't leave a large hole in your fabric. It is also a short pin, which will take only a small "bite" in the fabric, which helps prevent the fabric from slipping.

The Quilting Stitch

To achieve good results, try quilting a quilt of any size in a hoop or a frame of some kind. Keeping tension on the quilt as you stitch will produce an evenly sculpted look in your finished quilt. A round, 14-inch quilter's hoop is easy to turn in any direction, and it will allow you to quilt a fairly large area before you need to move the hoop. To insert a quilt into a hoop, place the quilt over the smaller, inner hoop and then place the larger, outer hoop over the quilt. Adjust the top hoop so that there is even tension on the quilt.

With a knotted thread, insert your needle through the quilt top only, about ½ inch away from the place you intend to make the first stitch, as shown in **Diagram 12.**

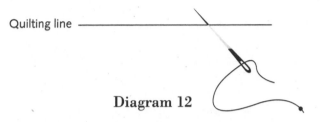

Quilting line

Diagram 12

Bring the thread out on the quilting line and tug gently, "popping" the knot through the quilt top, so that it lies inside, lodged in the batting, as shown in **Diagram 13A.** To take the first stitch, insert the needle through the three layers of the quilt, as shown in **Diagram 13B.**

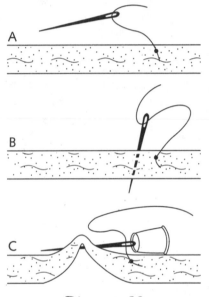

Diagram 13

When you feel the tip of the needle with your underneath finger, gently guide it back up through the quilt. When the needle comes through the top of quilt, use the thimble to guide it down again through the quilt to begin the next stitch, referring to **Diagram 13C.**

Continue to stitch in this manner, taking two or three stitches at a time. The smaller the distance between the exit and entry points of the needle, the smaller your stitches will be. As you begin to feel comfortable with this "rocking" technique of quilting, you may like taking more stitches at one time, but remember that the best quilting stitches are those that are even, not necessarily those that are tiniest. As you continue to quilt, you'll find that your stitches will tend to become smaller and smaller over time.

To end a thread, place your needle close to your last stitch, parallel to the quilt, and wind the thread around it two or three times. Insert the tip of the needle through the quilt top only, at the correct stitch length, and bring the needle out approximately ½ inch away from the quilting line. Gently tug the thread to "pop" the knot through the quilt top so that it lodges in the batting layer.

When you reach the end of a line of quilting but you still have a substantial length of thread, try this technique for moving to another quilting line without ending your thread. It's called "waddling" or "Tennessee Waltzing." Use it whenever you want to move to a quilting line that is farther away than the length of your needle would allow you to move. Insert the needle into the quilt top, creating the last stitch in this line of quilting. Bring the *tip* of the needle out about ¾ inch away, as shown in **Diagram 14A.**

Move the needle forward, as shown in **Diagram 14B,** so that the eye of the needle is encased in the batting layer. Then gently rotate the needle sideways, so that the eye of the needle moves toward the next line you want to quilt, as shown in **Diagram 14C.** When your needle is close enough to the new quilting line, bring the eye out at the point where you wish to take the first stitch on the new line. This rocking or waddling motion will allow you to move any distance from 1 inch to several inches without starting a new thread.

When you are finished quilting all of the areas showing in the hoop, release the tension and move the hoop to the next area. For quilting straight borders, you may like using a D-shaped hoop that has a fabric sleeve along the straight side. Place your quilt between the upper and lower halves of the hoop and pin the edge of your quilt to the fabric sleeve. Lower the top hoop over the quilt, creating even tension on the border of the quilt.

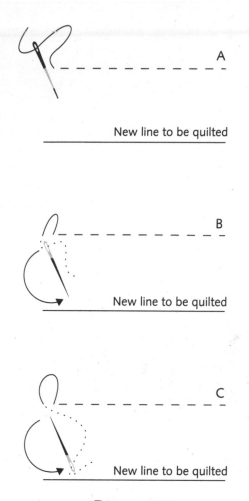

A

New line to be quilted

B

New line to be quilted

C

New line to be quilted

Diagram 14

Binding Basics

Binding gives the edges of a quilt strength and durability. You can cut binding strips from the lengthwise, cross-grain, or bias of the fabric. There is some stretch in cross-grain strips, but there is much greater stretch in bias strips. You can use bias strips for binding any quilt, but it becomes necessary on quilts that have curved edges or a lot of inner and outer corners to miter, such as the Double Wedding Ring and Grandmother's Flower Garden quilts.

Each of the quilts in this book lists separate instructions for the amount of fabric and the number of binding strips to cut in case you wish to bind your quilt in fabrics other than the ones shown. Cut all binding strips cross-grain, unless otherwise specified.

Double-Fold French Binding

Double-fold French binding is a durable and attractive edge finish. The yardages and cutting dimensions given in the book are based on double-fold binding. Both straight quilts and those with curved edges can be bound with this method, though curved edges require the use of bias, rather than straight, strips.

Binding Straight Edges

Begin by making a small fold at the short edge of the binding strip. Then place the cut edges of the binding even with the cut edges of the quilt. Leaving 2 to 3 inches of the binding free, sew the folded binding to the front of the quilt with a ½-inch seam allowance, beginning away from a corner point, as shown in **Diagram 15A.**

Sew to ½ inch from the next corner of the quilt, backstitch, and stop. Remove the quilt from the sewing machine and turn to miter the corner. Fold the binding strip up at a 45 degree angle, referring to **Diagram 15B.** Bring the binding strip down so that there is a fold at the upper edge, as shown in **Diagram 15C.** Insert the sewing machine needle exactly at the point where the previous seam ended. Continue sewing to the next corner point. Miter each corner in this manner.

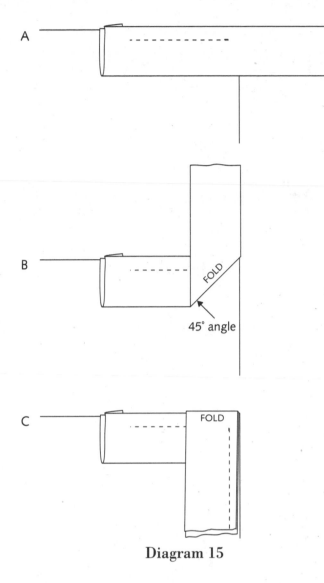

Diagram 15

To finish the binding seam, insert the end of the binding strip inside the folded edge at the beginning of the binding and then complete the binding seam by sewing over both strips, as shown in **Diagram 16A** on page 242. Then bring the binding around to the back side of the quilt and blindstitch it in place, folding the binding into a miter at each corner, as shown in **Diagram 16B.**

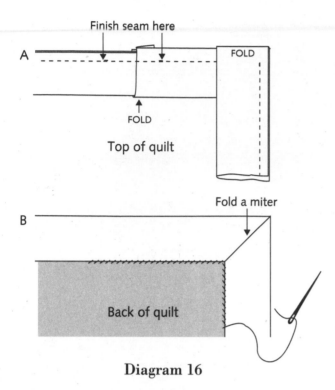

Diagram 16

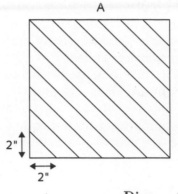

Diagram 17

Bias Binding

To bind a quilt with curved edges or a quilt that has a number of inner and outer corners to miter, you will need to make bias strips for the binding. Begin by cutting a square of fabric to the size indicated for bias strips (this will be clearly listed in the quilt project directions). Measure 2 inches over from each side of the lower left corner point and draw a line connecting these points, as shown in **Diagram 17A.**

This line establishes a true diagonal of 45 degrees. From this line, measure over the exact width you wish to cut your binding strips and draw a line parallel to the first line, as shown in **Diagram 17A.** Continue marking lines in this manner across the square of fabric and cut them apart to make the binding strips. If you wish to use a rotary cutter and ruler, it is not necessary to draw the cutting lines on the fabric. When all of the binding strips are cut, sew the short ends together with ¼-inch seam allowances, as shown in **Diagram 17B.** Press these diagonal seams open. This will help make the binding lie flatter when it is applied to the quilt.

Signing and Dating Your Quilt

One of the most important elements in the quiltmaking process is creating some kind of signature for your work. How many beautiful antique quilts have you seen and enjoyed, wishing you could know something about the quiltmakers and their lives and times? Written inscriptions, signatures, and dates can become meaningful legacies, not only to your own descendants and to anyone who has the opportunity to see and admire your quilts but to fellow quilters of future generations.

Signing a quilt can be a simple thing or an elaborate project in itself. You can quilt your initials and date into a corner of the quilt itself, or cross-stitch your name and date on a small piece of fabric and attach it to the back of the quilt. If you like, press the shiny side of a piece of freezer paper onto the wrong side of a piece of fabric to stabilize it and insert the fabric into a typewriter—and type your message. Or sign your name and write a personal dedication in permanent ink on a piece of fabric in whatever shape you like, edge it with delicate lace and stitch it to the back of your quilt. There are good permanent pens for fabric available in many colors. Be creative and have fun as you take this very last step in the creation of your quilts.

◆ RESOURCES ◆

To locate the tools and supplies mentioned in "Quiltmaking ABCs," visit your local quilt shop. If you live in an area where there are no quilt shops nearby, these mail-order sources may be able to meet your quilting needs:

Quilts and Other Comforts
Box 394-7
Wheatridge, CO 80034
(303) 420-4272

Notions and supplies for quilters, including coordinated fabric packets, see-through rulers, reusable self-adhesive quilting templates, quilting hoops and frames, quilting thread

Cabin Fever Calicoes
P.O. Box 550106
Atlanta, GA 30355
1-800-762-2246

Tools and supplies for quilters, including batting, 100 percent cotton fabrics, fabric marking tools, pins and needles, quilting hoops and frames, sewing and quilting thread, template plastic, thimbles

Keepsake Quilting
Dover Street
P.O. Box 1459
Meredith, NH 03253
(603) 279-3351

Appliqué film, white and dark batting, 100 percent cotton fabrics, extrafine-point permanent felt-tip pens, pins and needles, needle grabbers, quilting hoops and frames, rotary cutters, cutting mats, see-through rulers, thimbles

Osage County Quilt Factory
400 Walnut, Box 490
Overbrook, KS 66524
(913) 665-7500

Appliqué film, white and colored batting, 100 percent cotton fabrics, fabric marking tools, quilting thread, rotary cutters, cutting mats, see-through rulers, template plastic

Clotilde, Inc.
1909 S.W. First Avenue
Fort Lauderdale, FL 33315
(305) 761-8655

Sewing notions and quilting supplies, including Heat 'N Bond appliqué film, fabric marking tools, magnetic pin holders, scissors, seam rippers, quilter's ¼-inch masking tape, quilt soap

• *VINTAGE SEWING TOOLS* •

What are your very favorite quilting and sewing tools? The ones you can't do without—the ones you just "have to have" for each step of the quiltmaking process? Quilters of past generations had their personal favorite sewing tools, too. Julie Powell, one of the owners of **Vintage Textiles and Tools,** helps us take a glimpse into the past with the best-loved tools and equipment of our nineteenth-century sister quilters.

Triangles (page 1):

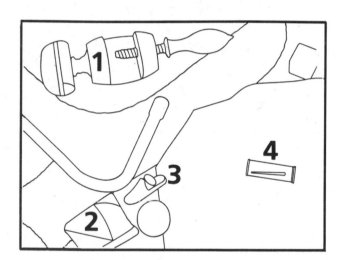

1. Wooden pincushions with screw clamps were easy to attach to any table in a nineteenth-century home and kept pins and needles conveniently within arm's reach.

2. Handmade pincushions and pin holders were common items in Victorian sewing boxes. Made of cotton fabric, hand-embroidered felt, or fine, delicately painted ivory, they held colorful, glass-head quilter's pins.

3. A tiny velvet slipper often held a needle-worker's "best" thimble. Embroidered with delicate designs, this one must have been a decorative addition to a quilter's sewing basket.

4. This marbleized tin needlecase has several wedge-shaped sections inside, each holding needles of different sizes. The top is a dial that

moves easily to each little compartment, and a needle pops out when the case is tilted.

Squares/Rectangles (page 53):

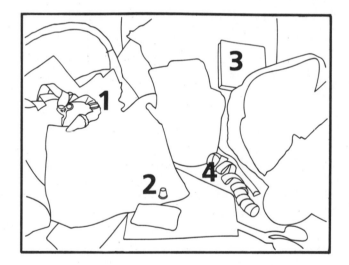

1. Chatelaines are as popular today as they were 100 years ago, providing easy access to much-used sewing tools. This one carries an emery-filled strawberry pincushion and a pair of classic stork embroidery scissors.

2. Thimbles became political campaign novelties after the Women's Suffragette law was passed on August 20, 1920. This aluminum thimble says "Coolidge and Dawes" on the blue band.

3. In the last century, young girls loved to receive gaily painted boxes, like this one, in the mail. This colorful lid indicates that there will be a tiny toy sewing machine inside the box.

4. Fabric tape measures were often used as advertising premiums in the latter part of the nineteenth century. Some were hand-numbered and lettered on cloth, and others were oil-coated fabric with a shiny, smooth finish for durability.

Curves (page 121):

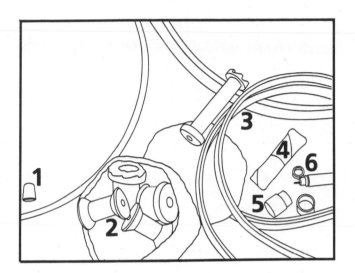

1. Silver thimbles with embossed gold scroll-work date from the early nineteenth century. In 1839, the Simon Brothers Company Silversmith thimble factory opened in Philadelphia, Pennsylvania, and is still producing thimbles like this one today.

2. Wooden spools were fairly common until 1975, when the last wooden spool factory, in the state of Maine, closed. The ones shown here with notches at each end were originally made to fit into the gears of commercial embroidery machines.

3. Wooden hoops used to be known as "tambours" and were used in sewing or lacemaking to keep laces and fabrics under tension.

4. Victorian women often made their own pincushions from scraps of fabric they had around the house. They liked to use emery as a filler because it kept pins and needles sharp.

5. Wooden thimble cases were used in the early days of this century to protect delicate silver or gold thimbles from damage when not in use.

6. A wooden needle case like this is common today, usually containing hand sewing or quilting needles. One hundred years ago, however, this type of wooden case was used to store sewing machine needles.

Starbursts (page 203):

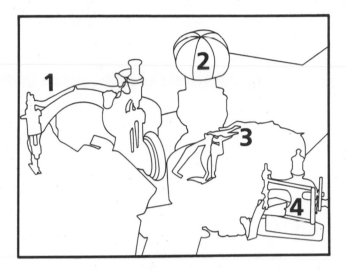

1. Willcox & Gibbs sewing machines were manufactured until the year 1894. This curved-arm machine is cast iron, with gold stenciling in a vine-and-berry trim. It sews a chain stitch rather than a straight stitch.

2. This unique crazy quilt pincushion has a walnut base with a rotating thread caddy and is signed and dated July 18, 1871.

3. Sewing birds provide a "third arm" for someone making braided rugs, handmade lace, or garments. This is a brass sewing bird from 1853 that still has the original pincushion.

4. The Gannett Press Printing Company used this toy sewing machine as a premium for sending in three subscriptions to their needle-craft magazine. It is only 5½ inches high and 4½ inches wide, but it makes a perfect little chain stitch.

For more information about antique sewing tools and equipment, contact:

Julie Powell, Kathy Sullivan, Helen Thompson
Vintage Textiles and Tools
Antique Quilts and Old Sewing Items
P.O. Box 265
Merion, PA 19066
(215) 668-8796

• ACKNOWLEDGMENTS •

We thank all of the people listed below for graciously allowing us to include their quilts in *Classic Country Quilts*.

Air Castles: *Bonnie Noland*, quiltmaker
Amish Baskets: *Marilyn Maurstad*, quiltmaker
Around the Stars: *Arleen Boyd*, quiltmaker
Bear's Paw: From the collection of
        The Great American Quilt Factory, Inc., Denver, Colorado
Beauty Everlasting: *Eleanor Kastner*, quiltmaker
Bow Tie: *Barbara Elwell*, quiltmaker
Crosses and Losses: *Marilyn Maurstad*, quiltmaker
Delectable Mountains: *Judy Knowles*, quiltmaker
Double Wedding Ring: *Esther Furst*, quiltmaker
Dresden Plate: From the collection of Bonnie Leman
Drunkard's Path: From the collection of JoAnne Ditmer;
        Alma Bausman Klepinger, quiltmaker
Fancy Patch: *Marilyn Fashbaugh*, quiltmaker
Flying Geese: From the collection of Suzanne Nelson
Galloping Star: *Kay Gallop*, quiltmaker
Grandmother's Flower Garden: *Barbara Atwater*, quiltmaker
Hearts Galore: *Suzanne Nelson*, quiltmaker
Irish Chain: From the collection of Bonnie Leman
Oak Leaf and Reel: From a private collection
Ocean Waves: *Kathleen McCrady*, quiltmaker
Pineapple Log Cabin: From the collection of Merry Silber
Rolling Stone: From the collection of Bonnie Leman
Rose of Sharon: *Dorothy Finley*, quiltmaker
Schoolhouse: Courtesy of *Quilter's Newsletter Magazine*
Sunshine and Shadows: *Marilyn Maurstad*, quiltmaker
Tea Box: *Betty Wolfe*, quiltmaker